BCM
Publishing

Soon To Be Released Titles From The *MIND UNDER PAR* series™

- •Routine: Guided Practice in Developing Consistent Performance in Golf
- •Stress Management for the Executive Golfer
- •The Mind Under Par series™ Scorecard
- •Setting Practice Goals for Golf
- •Lift, Clean and Place: Managing Yourself on and off the Golf Course
- •Swing Fix: Search for the Magic Bullet
- •Confidence, Chance or Choice?
- •Flow State Concentration=Peak Performance On and Off the Golf Course
- •Mind Under Par Audio Book
- •Mind Under Par CD ROM Book
- •Mind Under Par Series™ Questionnaire
- •The Wright Angle

Look for these products at our web site:

http://www.mind-under-par.com

COVER: Pat Burke and Mark Long,
Victoria Open, Australia 1994

MIND UNDER PAR

David F. Wright, Ph.D., PGA

BEHAVIOR CHANGE MEDIA

31441 Santa Margarita Parkway, Suite 283
Rancho Santa Margarita, California 92688

From the ***MIND UNDER PAR series™***

Toll Free 1-888-620-GOLF

MIND UNDER PAR

Behavior Change Media 1997

Illustrations by Michael Shelton
Photography by John Knight and Gil Nelsen
Cover design by Mika McMurray

For information contact:

Behavior Change Media
31441 Santa Margarita Pkwy., Suite 283
Rancho Santa Margarita, CA. 92688

Toll Free 1-888-620-GOLF

Library of Congress Cataloging-in-Publication Data
Wright, David F.
Mind Under Par / David F. Wright, Ph.D., PGA
Includes bibliographical references

ISBN 1-888787-00-7

1. Golf. 2. Golf and Psychology. 3. Golf and Mental Aspects 4. Cognitive Therapy

PRINTED IN THE UNITED STATES OF AMERICA

by Big Room Digital Press Irvine, Ca.

DEDICATION

To Lefty Wright. Thanks for showing me the importance of targets.

ACKNOWLEDGMENTS

I would like to thank the following individuals and publishers for their consent to reproduce player quotes and illustrations in the *Mind Under Par* series™

Golf Digest Copyright © (1996) NYT Sports Leisure Magazines

Golf World Copyright © (1996) NYT Sports Leisure Magazines

Golf Magazine Copyright © (1996)

Golf Tips Copyright © (1996)

The New York Times

The Putnam Publishing Group

Simon and Schuster

Peter Fox, M.D.

Johnny Miller

Byron Nelson

Jack Nicklaus

Gary Player

Sam Snead

Tom Watson

Mark Wiebe

Maggie Will

I would like to express my sincere thanks to Michael Shelton for his creativity and dedication in doing the illustrations for *MIND UNDER PAR*, to Mika McMurray for the cover design, to John Knight (Australia) and Gil Nelsen for the cover photography, and to Keith Bailly for contents design and creative publishing support.

I would also like to thank Jim Saxon and Montecito clothing company for their support over the last four years and the publishing staff at Behavior Change Media for their endless support.

Finally, and most importantly, the following people have contributed greatly through their friendship, support, encouragement, and teaching influence over the last fifteen years. I thank you from my heart: Derek Hardy, Tom Szwedzinski, John Hardy, Vince Lerma, Jeff Shaw, Dr. Jim Suttie, Mike Adams, Bill Moretti, Gregg McHatton, Jim Petralia, Glenn Deck, Ed Harrigfeld, Sandra Palmer and all my friends and fellow teaching professionals at Pelican Hill Golf Club and Coto de Caza Golf Club. Thanks also to all the PGA, LPGA, NIKE, and Mini Tour Players and amateurs from whom I learn daily about both golf and life.

CONTENTS

3

FINE TUNING YOUR NERVOUS SYSTEM

4

CONCENTRATION:

KEEPING YOUR HEAD IN PLAY

5

CONFIDENCE:

BUILDING MENTAL TOUGHNESS FROM THE GROUND UP

VISUALIZATION

PICTURES=PERFORMANCE

PAGE 153

HOW TO TALK TO YOURSELF ON AND OFF THE GOLF COURSE

PAGE 177

LIFT, CLEAN AND PLACE APPLYING WHAT YOU'VE LEARNED

PAGE 211

GREAT
BIG

INTRODUCTIONS

By Patrick Burke, PGA Tour

I began working with Dr. David Wright (David) in April of 1991. My career was going nowhere and I was completely stressed out. I was as close to wanting to quit as one could get.

I had played The PGA Tour the year prior, and I had a horrible year. I then proceeded to miss requalifying for the Tour by bogeying the last hole to miss by one shot. Beginning the 1991 season on the Hogan (now Nike) Tour, let's just say I wasn't very confident.

I had spent three years on a merry-go-round of swing "experts" in an effort to find the "perfect" swing. My obsession with mechanics had basically left me paralyzed on the golf course.

I had searched for a sports psychologist for quite some time. I read articles and books, and even listened to a few of the well known guys speak. Nothing I read or heard seemed to register, so I just kept digging deeper into the mechanics of my swing.

Luckily for me, a good friend of mine had a son who at the time was playing competitive golf. He had just begun working with David, and I had heard a lot of good things from them about David. I sat and watched one of my friends lessons on the range, and had the opportunity to meet and talk with David for awhile. It was one of the most fortunate things that ever happened to me.

It didn't take me long to realize that things just "clicked" with David. Like I mentioned before, I had researched many of the well known people in the field, but everything I read or heard seemed more confusing. Talking with David was very easy, and our first lesson was even better than I hoped for.

We went to the driving range for our first lesson. David was there with his clipboard and drills, and I was there with about five inswing thoughts and a life time's worth of negativity. David took me through a drill which consisted of hitting about six groups of ten balls and rating them on a 1 to 10 scale (10 being best). After each group of ten, we added another step in a preshot routine and also added more focus of visualizing the shot I was hitting.

The end result was in my last ten balls, I hit a series of nines and tens, with an additional five to six yards increase in distance with a seven iron. The first ten balls I hit weren't too bad, but I had three or four mechanical thoughts in each swing. I was completely focused on my swing, not the results. By the time I hit the last ten balls, all I was doing was picturing the shot I wanted to play and visualizing that shot through the swing. The results were incredible. David asked what swing thoughts I had on the last ten shots. I just stood there with a blank stare on my face and realization that I had just begun the process of relearning how to play golf instead of making golf swings.

Since that first day, my game has continued to improve. We expanded on drills, preswing, inswing and postwing routines and work both on and off the golf course. I won two tournaments in Australia, and requalified for the PGA Tour in 1994. David has been a major reason for this success.

You're probably asking yourself, what does this have to do with *MIND UNDER PAR*?

Well, back when I started working with David, the first thing he did was to give me a draft of the book to read. We've been working together for quite some time now, and I still use an updated draft as reference to keep me on track. It's not just a book of interesting content. It's a book you can use as a "how to" reference for years to come.

Most game improvement books seem to cover the same tired material over and over. *MIND UNDER PAR* is different. The book instructs the golfer on how to go about getting his/her mind working for instead of against him/her. More importantly, David explains why your thinking takes the path it does and how you can redirect your thoughts down the correct channel.

As I already noted, when I met David, I was completely stressed out and lost both on and off the golf course. I was ready to quit, had no confidence, and had an anxiety level high enough to make me sick. A very large portion of the time I had with David in the early part of our relationship was spent on dealing with these issues.

Once again, what does this have to do with *MIND UNDER PAR*? I believe that the most important thing I've learned during the years with David is that in order to change your mental approach to the game of golf, you're going to have to make changes in your mental approach to day to day life. *MIND UNDER PAR* addresses these issues and not only explains why you may need to work on these changes, but how to set out making these changes. *MIND UNDER PAR* provides the reader with a very effective, and believe me tested, complete mental approach to life both on and off the course.

David's unique golf, clinical, teaching, and competitive athletics background is the backbone to this book. I know of no one in the sports/golf psychology field with this complete and qualified background.

The heart of the book however is David's genuine care for his students. I've never worked with or seen a teacher who so thoroughly enjoys his students' successes. Anyone who has had the pleasure of working personally with David has probably gotten an update on one or more of his pupils. This does not come up because he is taking responsibility for any success (though he probably was responsible) but because he is truly excited for them.

I honestly feel that this is what makes David a great teacher (and writer!). Any success I've had or will have in the future is due largely to the help I've received from him over the years. He has helped me become a much improved golfer, but more importantly he has helped me become a much better person. I cannot begin to tell you how much he has helped me, but I can tell you how proud I am to have him for a friend.

If you read and practice the teachings in *Mind Under Par*, you too will soon be reaching your full potential on and off the golf course.

By Dennis Paulson, PGA and Nike Tour

When David asked me to write a little something about the *MIND UNDER PAR* series book and how it helped me, I told him he better be careful what he asks for because we might just have to start another book. To tell you how much he has helped me over the past three plus years in so few words is an injustice to David.

I had been a pro for about 7 years and I

had been successful at the mini-tour level but just hadn't made it on to the PGA tour. My instructor of about 4 years, Kip Puterbaugh, heard about David through the grapevine and advised me I should see someone about the mental side of the game. I was playing horrible, had a bad attitude and was about to give up golf entirely before I met David. I was so wrapped up in the mechanics of the golf swing I couldn't just play golf. All I wanted to do was make a perfect golf swing when all I really needed to do was hit a solid golf shot, two entirely different processes to get the same result.

Many who have come to know me and my golf ability over the years have said I should be on the PGA tour, "You've got the talent...if you only had a brain." David has helped me fine tune my golf mind.

When David and I first met we discussed the successes I've experienced in golf and the way I performed in those situations. The very first time David and I went out to the driving range the results were amazing. David got me to forget about the swing and I got back to picturing the shot I wanted to hit. You will never be able to hit the shot you want if you don't picture it first in your mind.

Many of my poor shots were off the tee and from the middle of the fairway. But from the trees and tough spots around the greens I would almost always hit a good shot. The main problem he found was that from the tee and the fairway it was like being on the practice tee. When I practiced all I ever thought about was mechanics and putting the club in perfect positions to hit the shots. But when I was in the trees and around the greens I had to be creative and see the shot I wanted to play. From the difficult places I would create and not force a swing. David taught me to focus on the target and not the swing.

From here is where David and I started. And now, two plus years later we have come a long way. I was just about to give up the game entirely just before I met him and now I'm completing my rookie year on the PGA tour with success.

Believe me, there is so much more to the game of golf than just having the perfect swing to hit shots. I'll take good mental preparation over a good swing any day. They said Jack Nicklaus and Ben Hogan were the greatest minds to ever play the game. This is what Tom Weiskopf said once of Jack Nicklaus on the 16th tee in the final round of the 1986 masters. Vern Lunquist asked Weiskopf: "What is Jack thinking right now?" and Tom came back with, "If I knew what Jack was thinking I might of won this tournament a couple of times." There isn't a player I know that wouldn't die to have Tom Weiskopf's golf swing and look at the respect Tom had for Jack's mental approach. Weiskopf knew what beat him. It wasn't Jack's ability to hit the ball. It was his ability to get the ball in the hole.

More importantly than hitting the good shots is how you deal with them once you've hit them. What good is a perfectly struck 5 iron to within 4 feet if you don't convert the putt; or to play the best round of golf in your life to finish double, double, double. Most of these things happen because you aren't thinking properly on the golf course. Every great player who plays this game has a great mental approach. Almost every great shot you have ever seen or hit has had good mental preparation before the shot was executed.

Likewise many of the famous chokes you have seen or even committed were caused by poor mental preparation..

Once David got me back on track hitting the shots I started messing up some great rounds with poor finishes. In one tournament I opened with a 31 on the front and birdied four of the next five on the back only to finish bogey, triple to finish with a 67. David and I talked about what I had done that night after the round. He asked what was going through my mind. I explained to him that I got ahead of myself by figuring out how many under par I would be if I could par this hole and birdie the easy par 5 instead of just picking a target and hitting a good shot period. That's all you can do. One shot at a time is such a cliche but it is the biggest truth in golf, believe me. In the same tournament two days later I started off bad but birdied 5 of my last 7 holes to lose by 1 shot. All I was thinking all day was, "Hit a good shot here." I wish I would have done that in the first round.

I took this theory to the extreme earlier this year. In the PGA Tour Freeport-McMoran Classic I shot a second round 10 under par 62 to lead the tournament after 36 holes. When I was in the press room after the round to describe the round all I could tell them were the scores I made on the specific holes. I honestly could not tell them I birdied this hole to go to so many under because I never thought about it once the entire round.

I'll bet the best rounds you have ever shot were when you didn't realize where you stood. The most common story I hear from amateurs is they are playing a little money game with a buddy and all they realize is where they stand in the match, one up, one down or even and they're on 18. On the way to the tee all they are thinking is, "Okay, let's birdie this last hole and beat this guy." And then you are reminded by your playing partner that if you par this last hole you'll break 80 for the first time. What happens? You double the last hole, end of story. Why? Because you lost your focus. You were thinking about your score all the way down the fairway instead of what was at hand. Just pick a target and make a good swing. Remember, good swings usually produce good scores.

The things you are about to learn in this book won't give you a great swing but it will teach the most important thing there is to learn in golf and that is to score. Remember, the second biggest cliche in golf: There's no room on the scorecard for pictures. An ugly par beats a solid bogey every damn time. You're not playing this game to win a beauty contest. You play this game for the enjoyment and the competition. There's no better joy or self satisfaction than reaching another plateau. Apply the things David is giving you and you will become a better player, even with the same old swing.

If it wasn't for David I doubt if I'd be playing golf competitively much less playing on the PGA tour. I owe an incredible amount to this man and you will to if you use this book to enjoy the game. No matter how hard you try you will never be able to make great strides in this game if you aren't having fun and learning not only from your successes but also from your mistakes.

You'll never be able to hit this shot if you're still thinking about the last one you just screwed up. Apply the methods David gives you. You won't regret it. I sure haven't! Enjoy!

By Marta Figueras-Dotti, LPGA Tour

I met Dr. David Wright through my dear friend Anne Marie Palli. He was working with Anne Marie on the range at one of our LPGA events. He looked extremely serious to me. Anne Marie had always spoken very highly of David, yet my personal experience with sport psychologists had not been very positive nor productive. So, I didn't think much of this serious guy.

I moved to San Diego and David lived just an hour north of me. I began spending time working with David. We started exchanging more and more ideas and experiences about golf and life. I was telling him how I wanted to have children in a the near future. The next time he came down to play, he stayed over for dinner and brought me a very "peculiar" (to say the least) present. I thought to myself: "This guy is cool, he is really cool!"

Between that time and today, I went through what I thought was the worst time of my life. Thoughts of quitting golf were very much in my mind. The best thing I did was to go back to see David.

I wanted to work not only on my career but also on my emotional state to gain peace of mind. We spent a long time together working hard. David set up a structured practice program for me. He helped me set specific goals. We reviewed all the content of this book, *MIND UNDER PAR*.

Three days later I flew to Hawaii and won my first LPGA tournament in 11 years on tour. *MIND UNDER PAR* was constantly in my mind. David's words were with me during the whole week, keeping me calm and focused during the most difficult moments on the golf course. His ideas and strategies and his practice programs helped me improve my mind faster than I ever imagined. *MIND UNDER PAR* has given me the awareness of knowing how good I can be when I put all these thoughts together. To top it off, I won again with PGA Tour player Brad Bryant in the December, 1994 JC Penny mixed team play.

You will find this book invaluable for use both on and off the golf course. As you will see, David's knowledge applies broadly to life and golf in *MIND UNDER PAR*. As he says, if you are going to change the way you think and behave on the golf course, you must change the way you think and behave off the course. This is not a book you will want to read casually. You will find yourself making notes in the margin and studying and referring back to the mental skills you will learn. Apply what you read and you will reap benefits both on and off the course.

By Anne Marie Palli, LPGA Tour

I have known David Wright for about eight years and besides being one of my best friends, he is a person filled with love, compassion, understanding and lots of patience, which when dealing with a french girl is a must.

I learned a tremendous amount from David and I know that the lucky people who will read this book will not only get an understanding about the psychology of golf but an insight into their own behavior on and off the golf course. Most of all you will get a positive plan of what to do when your mind starts going crazy.

I had the good fortune to win twice on the LPGA tour. During the last win in 1992, I had an opportunity to practice what I learned from David. For two days I was on the leader board and up to that point I had managed to stay in the present and to enjoy myself without too much expectation. But the last day I was in contention and with that I was starting to feel the consequence of it. My mind would start racing, feeling a mixture of anxiety and excitement and that's when I applied the tools I learned from David. On Sunday morning, I listened to some of my favorite music which put me in a relaxed state. I continuously moved slower.

Anytime I had a fearful thought I would tell myself to "shut up" and follow that comment with positive redirection and then I would become aware of the moment. By the time I got to the golf course, I was feeling calm, relaxed and in control. I managed to keep a quiet relaxed state of mind, enjoying the moment, focusing only on one shot at a time and doing my breathing exercises.

When I got to 18 I hit a good tee shot and 8 iron to the green which I managed to put about 12 feet from the pin. I was so focused on the moment, so focused on my routine, that it never crossed my mind that if I made the putt I would have a chance for a play off. So guess what? I made the putt and off I went back to the 18th tee with Laura Davies. At that point, I realized what I had done. I got really nervous on the way back to 18 which is probably one of the most challenging holes on the LPGA tour.

There again, I could hear David's voice in my mind saying, "Breathe, slow down, focus on your target. We are going to take this one shot at a time one moment at a time." I managed to hit a great drive and a great 7 iron that landed 2 feet from the pin while Laura hit her tee shot in the trees getting on the green in 3 and making a bogey 5. Again, I had another mental interference thinking, "Boy I will look really stupid if I miss that short putt," even though I could miss it, get down in 2 and still win. So I stepped off the ball took a deep breath, returned to my routine, focused on my target and made it for birdie. Yeah!!!

So believe me, I had a great opportunity to experience and practice some of the things you will learn in this book. And guess what!? It works. So enjoy it and use it!

By Kellee Booth, Arizona State University, 1995, 1996 All American, 1995, 1996, Ranked Number One US Women's Amateur

Listening to a recent telecast of a PGA tour event, I remember hearing an announcer criticize a young tour professional for consulting a sport psychologist. It's like the old saying, Golf is 10% physical and 90 % mental, the game is not entirely in how a golfer hits the ball. The game involves a preshot routine, the execution of the shot and the postshot routine. Two out of the three are strictly mental. The other involves the physical as well as the mental part of the game. Being young I have realized that I have a temper that is hard to control. Many other junior and amateur players have the same difficulties. This makes having a system of thought and routine on the course essential to a good round. I have lost my fair share of tournaments because I lost my temper, I let my opponent's play bother my thinking.

MIND UNDER PAR has helped me settle down and no longer become furious with myself. David Wright has worked with me for about three years and I owe a lot of my success as a junior golfer to him. I have learned patience (the essential aspect of golf), routine, focus, and visualization. These four aspects and many others are discussed in the following pages. Once you have achieved patience, very few things will distract you from your ultimate goal, hitting the next shot.

A constant routine will allow you to relax and get in a groove while playing. A routine should be perfected at the driving range or the practice green, not the course. Focus allows a golfer to concentrate on the next shot, whether it be a putt or a drive. Visualization instills a confidence in the execution of any shot. It erases doubt and the "I can't hit this shot," mentality.

The following pages are the words of a brilliant individual who has inspired many to be the best they can possibly be. I hope they will inspire you to work extremely hard at perfecting the mental side of the game. I once read a quote: "Golf is easy. It's people that make it difficult." *MIND UNDER PAR* will help you make golf easier and a lot less stressful.

By Ryan Donovan, Junior Golfer

I remember the first time I had a lesson with Dr. Wright. Listening to him speak to me about my game and my mental behaviors I was so interested in the explanation of the brain and how it works.

During my lesson I received a book called *MIND UNDER PAR* and I was excited to read it. Just by reading the title you know it's going to elevate your game. As I read a little every night I realized how important the mental game really is. It talks about routine, concentration, confidence, visualization, goals, etc.. This book talks about how to enjoy the game as well as conquer it. It gives great quotes and stories from all the great players and explains how their mental game helps them succeed the most.

Dr. Wright is a very positive person and that's what helps me the most. I learned that if you are always positive you will get the best out of life and your golf game. People that aren't positive tend to give up easier and don't enjoy life.

Whenever I talk to Dr. Wright about life and golf he always says something positive and it helps a lot. I feel that this book has helped my golf game tremendously and by applying what I've learned, I have gained a lot of confidence and my play has improved greatly.

Do you sometimes feel like you will never get out of that sand bunker?

Visit our web site
for bunker tips and much more.

www.mind-under-par.com

Mike Shelton

Mind Under Par
Mike Shelton

1

YOUR PERSONAL BEST

DID YOU KNOW?

- When Sam Snead played for the first time in a major match in 1936, he said he was shaking so much on the first tee he had to use both hands to tee up the ball. When he stood up, the ball was a total blur.[1]
- Byron Nelson taught Tom Watson to slow down his tempo by slowing down his movement in his routine.[2]
- PGA Tour player Vijay Singh never had any formal instruction. He learned to play golf by watching Tom Weiskopf's swing.[3]
- Gary Player did everything with a feeling of slow motion, from dining to grooming, the week he won the US Open in 1965.[4]
- Teaching great Harvey Penick said: "...If you can wash your mind clean each time while walking to your next shot, you have the makings of a champion."[5]
- Jack Nicklaus said: "Correct thinking plus a measure of self control will not only tame tension, but actually make it work for you."[6]
- Gary Player says: "The difference between an ordinary player and a champion is the way they think."[7]
- After winning the 1993 PGA Western Open, Nick Price said: "My concentration was unbelievable this week. For the 10 seconds leading into every shot, all I focused on was target."[8]
- Greg Norman says everybody likes to hear compliments when they hit good shots, but unless you play golf with your mother, you don't hear it very often. So, you have to learn to talk to yourself positively.[9]

- Johnny Miller says: "Everyone has his own choking level... As you get more experience your choking level rises."[10]

- Bobby Jones said the secret to every great golf shot he ever hit was a focus on the outcome of that shot to the exclusion of everything else.[11]

- Early in their careers, Bobby Jones,[12] Henry Cotton,[13] and Nancy Lopez[14] suffered from such severe bouts of nervousness they all had problems prior to a tournament with nausea and vomiting.

- Johnny Miller said: "If you have an ugly swing and hit good-looking shots, you can win major championships if you trust the rest of your game and work on the mental side. The swing is just part of playing golf.[15]

- Meg Mallon says: "When I'm playing my best, I know I'm focusing right down to the leaf on the tree I'm aiming at."[16]

- Chi Chi Rodriguez said: "...Putting is a state of mind. I have confidence that I can make the putts...I putted OK in the early 70's, then somebody gave me $50 to write an article on how I putt. When I tried to break it down, I couldn't figure it out and I didn't putt worth anything for a long time."[17]

- Fred Couples never hits a shot without thinking of that same shot he has hit well at sometime in the past.[18]

- Tom Watson said: "I know when I am playing my best I am not thinking of very many things, maybe not even a swing thought. Just whatever the shot requires."[19]

- Jack Nicklaus said: "If I could get inside the heads of most of the amateurs I've played with in Pro Ams, I'm certain the pictures I'd see would be mostly about club swing and ball striking. That's about as bad a mental mistake as you can make."[20]

- Johnny Miller said the following regarding advice to accomplished golfers: "Use your own darn swing and tell everybody else to shove it. Tell them to keep their swing thoughts to themselves."[21]

- Seve Ballesteros says he paints "positive pictures of smooth swings and successful results in my mind's eye."[22]

- Sam Snead says you should think back on your good shots and try to repeat them.[23]

- PGA Tour player Mark Wiebe says: "The guys who are champions are guys who are really good at clearing their minds and just playing the shots."[24]

- Jack Nicklaus and Ben Hogan expected to hit only a handful of shots a round exactly as planned.[25]

- Walter Hagen expected to hit seven bad shots a round.[26]

- Gary Player says: "There's absolutely no question that golf is a game of mind over matter...during every major championship I've won I concentrated so hard that I played rounds without knowing my score! I've often been in a don't-know-who-I-am sort of daze-total relaxation and complete control."[27]

In my opinion, the greatest golf psychologists are the tour players who have intuitively developed mental strategies and applied them during play. There's no theory, just application. Many of these players have been very articulate in describing their mental skills. Throughout this book, you will find quotes from the world's top golfers over the past ninety years regarding their mental and physical behaviors during peak and poor performances. You can learn from their experiences in the same way they learned from peers their first few years on tour. I have provided explanations for their descriptions and strategies which you can begin to incorporate both on and off the course. First, let's look at your personal best.

YOUR PERSONAL BEST

Let's start with a discussion of what your best "on-course" performance felt like and build from there. Consider the best round of golf you ever shot. Answer each question with a Yes or No.

_____ Did it require effort?

_____ Did you think about swing mechanics?

_____ Were you worried about what others were thinking during your round?

_____ Were you thinking about your score during and between shots?

_____ Did you feel tense and nervous?

_____ Did you lack confidence?

_____ Did most shots feel guided or steered?

_____ Did you have intrusive inswing thoughts?

_____ Did you change your preswing routine every few shots?

Now think about the worst round of golf you ever shot and ask yourself these same questions. Once again, please answer Yes or No for each.

_____ Did it require effort?

_____ Did you think about swing mechanics?

_____ Were you worried about what others were thinking during your round?

_____ Were you thinking about your score during and between shots?

_____ Did you feel tense and nervous?

_____ Did you lack confidence?

_____ Did most shots feel guided or steered?

_____ Did you have intrusive inswing thoughts?

_____ Did you change your preswing routine every few shots?

It is likely that you answered "No" to most of the questions about your best round of golf. Conversely, you likely answered "Yes" to most questions regarding your worst round of golf.

The best rounds of golf are described by tour players and amateurs alike as consisting of six basic characteristics:

1. A set **Routine** is followed: The routine is repeated in the same sequence on each shot. Preswing, inswing, and postswing routines are the same on each green, each tee box, each fairway, and for each trouble shot. Every top athlete, regardless of sport, follows a set pre-performance routine.

PGA Tour player Greg Norman has positive, supportive conversations with himself before and after shots as part of his mental preswing and postswing routines. [28]

LPGA Tour player Meg Mallon says she follows the same preswing routine whether she is hitting a shot on the range or during a tournament. [29]

2. They feel **Relaxed** and **Effortless**: The swing feels fluid and relaxed; movement around the course is relaxed. Some players report a feeling of moving at a slower than normal pace, while others purposely slow their pace.

Senior PGA Tour player Ray Floyd says when he is playing his best, he feels as if he is moving at half speed.[30]

Current and past PGA Tour players Davis Love, Gary Player, Johnny Miller, Byron Nelson, and Tom Watson all describe periods of purposely quieting their movement to calm their nerves.[31] 1995 British Open champion John Daly described slowing down his movement during his opening round 64.

3. They have a **Concentration** focus only on the shot they are playing: Thoughts are focused one hundred percent in the present and everything feels completely automatic. Each shot is played without consideration of anything but the present. Shots are played one at a time. The judgment of others, the last shot, score, or off-course concerns never enter the mind.

Jack Nicklaus describes a systematic process of going from a very broad to a very narrow focus until he hits his shot. Then he returns to a broad focus.[32]

Byron Nelson describes concentration as "standard equipment with all champions."[33] Similarly, Gary Player said: "...during every major championship I've won I've concentrated so hard that I played rounds without knowing my score!"[34] Player goes on to say: "Concentration takes years of practice to acquire. It's difficult to come by and easy to lose if you let up."[35]

4. Great players are **Nonmechanical**: There are no thoughts about swing mechanics during play. Many players slide from greatness and attribute their performance demise to becoming too mechanical. These players include Greg Norman, David Frost, Hal Sutton, Bob Tway, and Sandy Lyle. Greg Norman, David Frost, and Bob Tway resumed their previous swing styles and made major comebacks.

Other great players escaped the plunge by catching the mechanics focus before they slid too far. These players include Lee Trevino and Jack Nicklaus. The insights of each of these players and their mechanics struggles are discussed in the following chapters.

And then there is PGA Tour player Bruce Lietzke. He is a player who takes long summer breaks from the tour to be with his family and coach Little League baseball.

Reportedly, Lietzke seldom picks up a club to work on his mechanics. He always has, and likely always will, hit a big cut. His mechanics just don't change. And why should they? He has had great success with what he has playing a limited schedule with limited practice. An amusing story is told by one of his former caddies who didn't believe that Lietzke didn't practice during his winter layoff. So, he put a banana into Lietzke's driver head cover. Months later when he took out his clubs for a tournament, driver and banana were still together.[36]

Bruce Lietzke has the ability to compete and win. He won the May 1992 PGA Tour Colonial playing the last forty-two holes without a bogey through the weekend and without having touched a club for a month prior. He had won the same tournament in 1980. His plans after his win? Take another month off.[37] Again in 1994, Lietzke won the Las Vegas Invitational returning to the tour following an extended period off.

Nicklaus described his early years after turning professional and working on his golf swing. He said he grew up in the era of Ben Hogan and everything he saw, read, and heard indicated that Hogan had reached mechanical perfection. Nicklaus noted that he felt that all he needed was time to work to develop this perfection. Nicklaus commented on his perceptions of those early years:

"No matter how much work I did, one week I would have it and the next I couldn't hit my hat. This is still true today. I am a far better golfer than when I started out on the tour twelve years ago [written in 1974], and I feel that I have improved to some degree each year. But that is more the result of maturity and competitive experience than of improvement in the mechanics of my game."[38]

5. Great players have **Confidence** in every shot they play: If they don't have confidence in a shot, they don't play it. There is never a doubt before or during a shot about the ability to execute it. They focus on the success of each shot as they play. Their internal dialogue with themselves is positive. They are great coaches to themselves.

Great players like Sam Snead,[39] Greg Norman,[40] Johnny Miller,[41] Gary Player,[42] and Jay Sigel[43] describe the importance of focusing on your success rather than your failures if you are going to build confidence. In the following chapters, they each describe how they talk to themselves after a shot.

6. Top players describe **Visualization** as part of their preswing routine: Many of the top tour players describe seeing ball flight, their swing, the ball landing on a specific target, a similar shot they have hit well before, or any combination of these visual images. Most amateurs do not. Visualization is like every other mental strategy; it takes practice.

During an interview at the 1993 Hawaiian Open, PGA Tour player Paul Azinger says he started to play well when he began to visualize. Senior Tour player Dave Hill has won ten regular tour events, three Senior Tour events, a Vardon trophy, and played on three Ryder Cup teams. He says of visualization: "Imagination is very important in shot making. If you can't picture it, you can't do it."[44]

The most written and talked about visualization strategy is that of Jack Nicklaus. A variety of imagery strategies and player quotes are presented in the chapter titled

"Visualization: Pictures=Performance."

I have repeatedly heard how the top players watched the methods of other top players. Gary Player, Bobby Jones, Henry Cotton, Tom Watson, Tom Weiskopf, and Nancy Lopez are a few of many who acknowledge this as a strategy of their early days on tour. Each says they observed top players, modeled their behavior, and improved.

Tom Watson describes how he watched Nicklaus during his early days on tour: "I learned more playing with him than I did watching him hit balls. I really didn't try to copy his swing. But I learned the way he played shots."[45]

Johnny Miller advocates finding a pro model you like and imitating his swing. I refer to this as banking or storing the memory of a swing in your nervous system. Johnny Miller says he used images of different pros depending on whether he wanted to fade, draw or hit a straight shot.[46]

Similarly, PGA Tour player Vijay Singh watched Tom Weiskopf's swing on television as a child and modeled what he saw. His father taught him the basics. He had no formal instruction other than watching Weiskopf's swing.[47] Interestingly, Tom Weiskopf says he learned by watching Sam Snead and Tommy Bolt. He also noted that he learned by watching and competing with Jack Nicklaus.[48]

What can you do to increase consistent, effortless, focused, one-shot-at-a-time, confident play on the course? First, it requires an understanding of the six major characteristics of peak performance periods. Second, you must begin to practice the strategies presented in this book both on and off the golf course. These strategies include:

- *Developing a consistent repeating routine*
- *Controlling your nervous system*
- *Being nonmechanical with your swing*
- *Restructuring and focusing your thinking and behavior to the present*
- *Building confidence through positive internal dialogue*
- *Recalling images and feelings of past success, and creating positive images for future success*

If you practice these strategies, you will have more frequent periods of peak performance both on the course and in your day to day life.

Your behavior off the course dictates the way you will behave on the course. If you are going to change the way you mentally approach golf, you need to change the way you mentally approach your day to day life. Practicing the mental strategies off the course will provide you with well-rehearsed skills for play. This book will show you specific techniques for making changes both on the course and in your day to day life.

As you read, please remember what one of the greatest golfers of our time, Jack Nicklaus, said about attitude during play. He said that the more he approached golf as something to have fun doing, the better he played.[49]

Let's begin with the first characteristic of on-course peak performance, a consistent repeating **Routine**.

ENDNOTES

1. Sam Snead and Al Stump, *The Education of a Golfer* (New York: Simon and Schuster, 1961), pp. 10-11.

2. Peter McCleery, "How Nelson Helped Watson Become a Champion," *Golf Digest* (January, 1991): pp. 66-67.

3 Robinson Halloway, "Fiji's Finest," *Golf Magazine* (September, 1993): p. 51.

4. Gary Player, *Positive Golf* (New York: McGraw Hill, 1967), p. 82.

5. Harvey Penick and Bud Shrake, *And If You Play Golf, You're My Friend* (New York: Simon and Schuster, 1993), p. 107.

6. Jack Nicklaus and Ken Bowden, "How to Beat Tension," *Golf Magazine* (July, 1993): p. 90.

7. Player, *Positive Golf*, pp. 16-17

8. Geoff Russell, "The Dominator," *Golf World* (July 9, 1993): p. 43 and p. 46.

9. Greg Norman and George Peper, "Greg Norman's Instant Lessons," *Golf Magazine* (April, 1993): p. 52.

10. Johnny Miller, "Pressure on the Prowl," *Golf Illustrated* (May, 1989): p. 26.

11. Charles Price, "Bobby Jones Reveals His Inner Psychology," *Golf Digest* (August, 1989): p. 40.

12. Golf Digest Staff, "Paul Runyon," *Golf Digest* (August, 1994): p. 115.

13. Michael McDonnell, *Golf: The Great Ones* (New York: Drake Publishers, 1971), pp. 50-51.

14. Ed Weathers, "Nerves," *Golf Digest* (October, 1994): p. 71.

15. Johnny Miller, "Don't Go Changin'," *Golf World* (August 6, 1993): p. 24.

16. Andy Brumer, "Be A Thinking Golfer," *Golf Tips* (May, 1994): p. 38.

17. Jeff Williams, "The Golf Course," *Golf Magazine* (October, 1991): p. 73.

18. Golf Digest Staff, "Fred Couples," Golf Digest (July, 1992): p. 114.

19. Golf Digest Staff, "Tom Watson," *Golf Digest* (May, 1993): p. 186.

20. Jack Nicklaus and Ken Bowden, "My Strongest Weapon," *Golf Magazine* (December, 1993): pp. 44-45.

21. Miller, "Don't Go Changin'," p. 24.

22. Weathers, "Nerves," p. 75.

23. Snead and Stump, *The Education of a Golfer*, pp. 243-244.

24. Mark Wiebe, "When Want Gets in the Way," *Golf World* (August 20, 1993): p. 30.

25. Nicklaus and Bowden, "My Strongest Weapon," p. 45.

26. Price, "Bobby Jones Reveals His Inner Psychology," p. 40.

27. Player, *Positive Golf*, pp. 16-17.

28. Norman and Peper, "Greg Norman's Instant Lessons," p. 52.

29. Brumer, "Be A Thinking Golfer," p. 38.

30. Tom Callahan, "Stare Master," *Golf Digest* (September, 1992): p. 55.

31. Weathers, "Nerves," p. 75.

32. Nicklaus and Bowden, "My Strongest Weapon," p. 47.

33. Byron Nelson, *Winning Golf* (New York: A.S. Barnes and Company, 1946), p. 19.

34. Player, *Positive Golf*, pp. 16-17.

35. Player, *Positive Golf*, p. 16.

36. Gary Van Sickle, "Top Banana," *Golf World* (May 29, 1992): pp. 10-16.

37. Van Sickle, "Top Banana," pp. 10-16.

38. Jack Nicklaus and Ken Bowden, *Golf My Way* (New York: Simon and Schuster, 1974), p. 22.

39. Snead and Stump, *The Education of a Golfer*, pp. 243-244.

40. Norman and Peper, "Greg Norman's Instant Lessons," p. 52.

41. Johnny Miller, "Child's Play," *Golf Illustrated* (April, 1993): p. 47.

42. Player, *Positive Golf*, pp. 16-17.

43. Ken Blanchard, "Practice With A Purpose," *Golf Tips* (October, 1993): p. 49 and p. 79.

44. Golf Digest Staff, "The Hill Brothers," *Golf Digest* (May, 1992): p. 87.

45. Golf Digest Staff, "Tom Watson," p. 192.

46. Johnny Miller and T.J. Tomasi, "Shaping Your Shots," *Golf Illustrated* (September, 1992): pp. 22-25.

47. Halloway, "Fiji's Finest," p. 51.

48. Glenn Monday, "Tom Weiskopf: Still on Target," *Golf Tips* (August, 1994): p. 96.

49. Jack Nicklaus and Ken Bowden, "My Lessons of a Lifetime," *Golf Magazine* (March, 1993): pp. 58-59.

Notes

Mike Shelton

2

ROUTINE:

The Links to Success

After the second round of the PGA Westchester Classic in June 1992, David Frost said: "The more you can stick to a routine, the less chance of other things creeping in."[1] Frost went on to win that tournament.

June 14, 1992, LPGA Tour player Anne-Marie Palli won in Atlantic City to end a nine year drought. Her last win was in Phoenix in 1983. She described her mental style during her last round of the 1992 win: "Routine is what saved me." Anne-Marie went on to describe how slow and deliberate her routine was. She said she played the entire week "slowed down" and totally in the present.[2]

LPGA Tour player and former US Open Champion Meg Mallon says the following about routine: "The thing I've learned from Mike [McGetrick-her instructor] is that routine is such a big part of the shot. ...Every time I hit a shot on the range, I step back and line it up. I go through the same routine I go through on the golf course."[3]

Tiger Woods won the 1994, 1995 and 1996 United States Amateur titles. At the age of 20 in August 1996 he turned professional and won two events in eight starts. He finished twenty-fourth on the 1996 money list. Woods returned in 1997 to win the first event, The TPC.

A few years ago, at a tournament in Texas, Tiger was on a green during a round and his father, Earl Woods, was talking with Charlie Sifford, a former PGA Tour player, about Tiger's consistent repeating prestroke routine. Earl Woods reportedly turned his back to Tiger on the green and began to narrate Tiger's routine to Charlie Sifford as Sifford watched: "He takes one practice stroke, he takes another. He looks at the target, he looks at the ball. He takes another look at the target, he looks at the ball." Tiger's putter blade struck the ball at the exact instant Earl Woods said "impact."[4] A significant contributing factor to Tiger Woods' success is his consistent repeating routine. Consistent positive routines build consistent positive performance.

TYPES OF ON-COURSE ROUTINES

There are three distinct types of on-course routines: Preswing, Inswing, and Postswing. Your preswing routine consists of everything from checking wind direction and club selection, to your setup to the ball, what you say to yourself, and your mental images during each of these conditions.

Your inswing routine consists of your physical movements as you start the club back, impact and follow through, your discussion with yourself, and/or your mental images during the swing.

Your postswing routine begins as your follow-through ends. It consists of your physical responses and what you say to yourself or others about the shot. Your postswing routine continues on any particular shot as long as you sustain a mood, mental image of the shot, and/or carry on a discussion with yourself about the shot or related score. For example "If I just hadn't hit it out on Number 7, I would be ____ over/under." Or, "That shot on Number 6 has really saved my round. I salvaged two shots with that one save." Both of these thoughts take your focus out of the present, interfere with concentration, may create arousal, and so on.

Every top athlete, whether in tennis, football, basketball, baseball, or golf, follows a set pre-performance routine. Note that a basketball player bounces the ball the same number of times, inhales deeply, and exhales before each free throw. A tennis player bounces the ball the same number of times prior to each serve. Football players, baseball players, and golfers have similar pre-performance routines, as do athletes in all sports. When these athletes' routines abruptly change, a deterioration in performance follows. Therefore, your goal is to establish a consistent, repeating pre-performance routine. It is important to understand the role which your brain plays in building a successful routine.

Neuroscientists have explored the brain activity which precedes behavior. This research has demonstrated that the brain takes one and one-half seconds to develop a "motor program" for a simple voluntary movement, and one-tenth of a second to execute the behavior. This motor program is called a "readiness potential." During this "readiness potential" period, the brain is preparing the nervous system to act.[5] The quality of the information the brain receives is directly related to the quality of performance.

Other neuroscientists have found that the amount of brain activity prior to a behavior is less for previously used motor programs than for novel programs. We call these previously used programs habits. A well-practiced, positive pre-performance routine will consistently produce the best quality behavior.

Throughout this book you will read about the experiences of world class golfers who have learned the effects various thinking styles have on their performances. These thoughts are always a part of their routines. Please remember that the brain takes fifteen times longer to prepare the nervous system to behave than it does to execute the behavior. This extended period of preparation for performance is made up of thoughts and images.

ROUTINE AS HABIT

These pre-performance routines are part of everything we do. We are creatures of habit. We tend to follow a set daily routine. We get out of bed on the same side, we shower, dress, groom, and eat in the same sequence day after day. We put the same shoe on the same foot, and the same arm through our shirt sleeve in the same order each morning. These are automatic behaviors that we don't think about as we do them. They are part of our daily routine. These are examples of voluntary behaviors which rely on previously-used motor programs. Because the behaviors are so well practiced, less brain activity is required to initiate the behavior.

All behavior occurs as a habit. What happens when you get out of your routine? When you lose your place, so to speak, your concentration is disturbed. You become physically aroused. You become a bit disoriented, performance suffers, your irritability increases, and frustration tolerance is lowered. On the other hand, your performance will be enhanced when you follow a consistent, repeating routine.

THE PSYCHOLOGY OF LEARNING

Let's digress and examine the psychology of learning as it relates to routine. The concept of behavior chains is well known to psychologists who specialize in learning. All learned behavior occurs in a chain. Each link in the chain is an increment of behavior. Take the example of an infant learning to hold and drink from a bottle. The bottle is placed in the infant's mouth. The first independent step is the child supporting the bottle with both hands while drinking. In time, the child grasps the bottle with both hands as the bottle approaches his mouth. As an adult, the complex behavior of picking up a glass with one hand and taking a drink is initiated without thought.

Learning takes place in steps. I refer to these steps as links. The links form a chain and make a complete behavior in this example of taking a drink. If you remove or alter one link in the chain, the quality of the behavior (performance) deteriorates. If you remove one link in the behavior chain of taking a drink, you "break" the chain and spill or don't get the glass to your mouth (performance deteriorates). If you alter a link in this chain, you may spill the drink, or, at the very least, the behavior becomes less efficient.

This same chaining concept is true no matter what behavior you consider. Alter one link in the golf swing chain and what happens? Performance changes. The preswing, inswing, and postswing routines each occur as a series of chain links. Alter one of those links or change the order of the links and performance changes. The preswing chain and inswing chain are connected. The quality of performance is dependent upon consistently repeated, positive links in both chains. One weak link in either chain will alter performance outcome.

GOLF ROUTINES

In golf, we call pre-performance behaviors a preswing routine. Performance is improved when the exact same routine is followed, internally and externally, on every shot. These internal and external routines build a positive motor program. Positive, relaxed routines build good performance programs, while negative, tense routines build poor performance programs.

Your internal routine is what you say to yourself about the situation. The internal and external routines occur as distinctly separated chains of behavior. If one link in either the external or internal chain is disrupted, the other links in both chains will be affected and performance will suffer.

In his 1974 book, Jack Nicklaus said: "I feel that hitting specific shots-playing the ball to a certain place in a certain way-is 50 percent mental picture, 40 percent setup and 10 percent swing. That's why setting up takes me so long, why I have to be so deliberate...unless I can set up exactly right in relation to the shot I have pictured, I know I have no chance of executing it as planned." The internal and external behaviors that make up Nicklaus' mental picture and setup (90%) are his preswing routine.[6] In a 1995 article, he added ten percent to the importance of swing: "I believe golf is 80 percent preamble-strong visualization, correct gripping, aiming and aligning, sound ball positioning, proper posture-and twenty percent swing."[7]

A student I had in a school in Florida a few years ago asked me why I thought he played better in tournaments than in a casual round of golf with his friends. This came on the heels of a discussion of how competition produces arousal and how players tend to show a deterioration in performance when feeling the pressure of competition. I asked him to describe his routine during a round with friends versus a round in competition.

It became quickly apparent that during a round with friends, where he perceived himself most relaxed, he didn't step off his yardage or read putts as intently as he did during competition. In short, his routine changed.

You have a routine that you follow prior to each shot. It may not be a desirable routine, but one does exist. Your routine may change, depending upon the situation. Tournament play, frustration, good play, poor play, and many more situations will tend to "cue" changes in your routine. Your level of play will improve if you develop a consistent, positive preswing routine that doesn't change regardless of conditions.

PRESWING ROUTINE

MENTAL PRESWING ROUTINE

Your preswing, inswing, and postswing routines each occur as a chain. Each increment of behavior makes up a link in these chains. One weak link in any of these chains will impact upon your performance. Each of these three has mental and mechanical components that are integrated. I have separated the mental and mechanical in a discussion of each. Let's start with the mental side of the preswing routine (chain).

As I noted earlier, all behavior, whether it be internal or external, occurs as a habit. We tend to follow the same routine day after day, hole after hole. Your routine may change a bit on a particular hole. For example, if you frequently hit your tee shot into the trees on Number 6 on your home course, part of your preswing mental routine on the Number 6 tee might be "Don't hit it right." If you have another group or two watching on the first tee, you may have a mental routine of " Oh, God, just let me get it in the fairway."

Course Management

There are specific steps to follow to give yourself the opportunity to hit the best shot you are capable of hitting. As you approach your ball in the fairway, you must begin to mentally analyze the conditions and picture your pending shot in order to choose a club.

LPGA Tour player Meg Mallon says: "You have to visualize which way that golf ball is going and how you're going to play it. You have to be creative in looking at what the green is giving you or what the wind is doing for you, and allow those things to help you rather than hurt you in any given situation. It's taking in all the ingredients and in a positive way coming up with the shot that reflects the input."[8]

Let's look at the factors that make up this analysis to the point of club selection.

1. You approach your ball, survey your lie, and consider the natural trajectory that lie will produce.
2. You find a target.
3. You determine your distance from the target.
4. You check the wind.
5. You determine the type of shot you are confident you can hit (draw, fade, high, low).
6. You make your club selection, deliberately remove your club from the bag, and move quietly behind the ball.

These steps are called course management. The better your course management, the more likely you will choose the correct club and the more focused you will be on your shot. It is important that you know how far you can hit each club in your bag; then consider wind, weather, and course conditions. For example, if the conditions are damp, you will have less roll and need to carry the ball closer to your targets. Some elevated greens are not part of the natural terrain. These greens will tend to be harder and you won't be able to hold them as well with your approach shots. Choosing the right position to tee up your ball in the tee box and knowing what club you hit what distance in varying wind conditions are two examples of good course management.

Course management is a consideration of the broad information pertaining to your shot: weather, wind, lie, yardage, carry, history of success with this shot during practice and play, and so on. As you integrate this broad information and decide on the shot you are going to hit, your attention moves from a broad to a more narrow focus. The closer you get to hitting the shot, the more narrow your focus becomes. Your narrow focus is seeing the shot, and seeing and feeling the swing you want to make. Your total attention goes to a specific target, ball flight, and a feeling of the swing you want to make as you move into your setup. Your focus broadens again after the shot. Let's look at a few strategies for moving from a broad to a narrow focus.

Mental Preparation

Once you have finished your course management, there are several strategies you can use to get yourself relaxed, confident, and focused in the present. As you move behind the ball and look at the target, recall the same shot you have hit well in the past. Picture first the trajectory and then the swing you made. "Feel" the shot as you do.

Next, tell yourself with confident determination what you are going to do. You must believe in your ability to hit the shot. Images of similar successful shots from the past will reinforce this belief.

Your movement and "moment to moment" focus are important here. As you survey your target, you should be breathing deeply and moving at a pace that fits your desired swing pace. Your thoughts should be only on the present.

The concept of describing the shot you want to hit with confident determination is amplified in Tom Watson's description of his famous chip shot on Number 17 at the 1982 US Open at Pebble Beach. He was tied with Jack Nicklaus for the lead when he hit his tee shot over the back left side of the green. Watson had a sixteen foot chip to the hole from deep rough with a downhill lie and a downhill roll. Watson described his interaction with his caddie regarding that shot: "My caddie said, 'Get it close.' I said, 'Hell, I'm going to sink it.' I thought if I could get my shot on line it would hit the pin and go in. That's the way I envisioned it."[9] He made the shot for a birdie (two) on the hole.

If Watson had been trying to "get it close," his ball would have likely rolled five to six feet by the hole leaving him a testy putt back for par. He never considered anything but making the shot. He went on to birdie 18 and beat Nicklaus by two strokes for the 1982 US Open title. Watson focused on the target, described and felt the shot he wanted to hit, then made it. He only thought about what he wanted to do.

Patrick Burke, PGA and Australian Tour player, finished second in Bali one week and won the Victorian Open the following week. These finishes placed him at the top of the Australian Tour money list in November 1994. He said that describing the details of each shot he was going to hit out loud to his caddie kept him focused in the present and gave him confidence.[10]

Consider the same shot you have hit well in the past. See the trajectory of the ball, and see and feel the swing you made to hit that shot. This will build confidence and a positive motor program. Breathe deeply, describing the shot to yourself, and your mind will paint a picture. We call the picture visualization. The more aroused you become, the less accessible or fuzzier these visual images will be. The more confident you are, the more relaxed and focused you will be, the clearer these images will become, and the less likely you will be to add, delete, or change a link in your routine chain.

Take a practice swing. See and feel the swing you want to make. Settle into this image behind the ball and find an intermediate target in front of your ball with which you will align your club face. Begin to move back to the ball, slowly and deliberately, at a pace that you want to match your swing pace.

Move to your setup position. Your sensory input should be flooded with the feeling of the club in your hand, the weight, the texture of the grip, the feeling of the ground under your feet, your target, and the color of the landing area. This sensory flooding keeps your focus in the present and only on the shot you are playing. The links in your routine chain will remain unchanged with this "mindful" one-shot-at-a-time focus.

Once you are over the ball and have checked your setup, turn your focus back to the target. Look at least twice at your target and deliberately shuffle your feet into position, and slowly and comfortably waggle your club. Settle into this setup, take a final deep breath, and take another look at your target. Remember the following phrase: Stare at the target and glance at the ball.

You will read in a later chapter how Fred Couples never hits a shot without thinking of that same shot he has hit well in the past.[11] Sam Snead used a similar strategy for what he called "the first tee jitters" (discussed in the chapter "Fine Tuning Your Nervous System"). This strategy of thinking of a shot you hit well in the past has a similar neurophysiological effect to describing the shot you want to hit. This process is summarized in the chapter titled "Visualization."

I noted that your routine is like a chain and that each link in that chain makes up another step in your routine. Let's review the links in a preswing mental chain as it moves from a broad to narrow focus.

Broad Focus

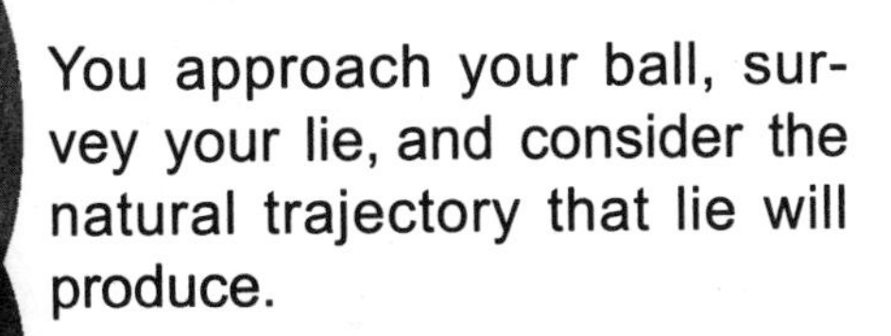

1. You approach your ball, survey your lie, and consider the natural trajectory that lie will produce.

2. You find a target.

3. You determine your distance from the target

4. You check the wind.
(Integration of Broad Focus Information)

5. You determine the type of shot you are confident you can hit (draw, fade, high, low).

Begin Narrow Focus

6. Make club selection, deliberately remove club from the bag, and move quietly behind the ball.

7. You recall (call up) a similar shot from the past you hit well.

8. You set up and take a practice swing. You see and feel the swing you want to make.

9. You find an intermediate target in front of your ball that is in line with your primary target.

10. You describe the shot you are going to hit to your primary target.

11. As you move back to the ball, you remain focused on your intermediate target. Your movement to the ball matches your desired swing tempo.

12. You feel the club in your hand and the ground under your feet as you return to the ball. Your entire visual focus is on your intermediate target.

You quietly set your club behind the ball and square your club face with your intermediate target.

Your eyes go to your primary target as you shuffle into your setup. Your eyes never leave your primary target until you are aligned.

You feel grounded and balanced. You stare at the target and glance at the ball.

Your waggle isquiet and deliberate, as you focus on your primary target and settle into your setup position in preparation to start your back swing. Again, you stare at your target and glance at the ball.

CHOOSING YOUR TARGETS

Notice the primary target focus in all phases of the preswing routine. The target is important in consideration of distance, type of shot, and club selection. Maintain ongoing visual contact with your target as you move back to the ball and during your setup. This will help you keep a target orientation and a one-shot-at-a-time focus.

LPGA Tour player Meg Mallon says: "A lot of people get locked into their golf ball and forget about where they're going to hit it."[12] PGA Tour player Doug Tewell describes a preswing routine where he doesn't take his eye off the target. He finds a target as he stands behind the ball and remains focused on that target until he sets up for the shot. Only then does he pay attention to his grip, stance, and posture. He says that feeling his way into the shot instinctively with this target focus produces more accurate shots.[13]

As a psychologist, I would say that the purpose of routine is to integrate broad focus information about the shot in a sequential progression that provides you with positive content in determining a club and target. As the routine chain progresses from one link to the next, your focus should narrow to a specific target, images of ball flight to that target, and a feeling of the swing to produce that shot.

This structured, repeated mental routine creates a one-hundred percent focus in the present, and ensures that you relax through movement and breathing while staying focused on your target. As you focus in the present, describe to yourself with confident determination the shot you are going to hit. This internal discussion will produce visual images of the shot and help you maintain a focus on your target. The net result of these behaviors is to provide the brain with information that produces the highest level of performance within your capability.

The positive, confident thoughts in your routine are incompatible with thoughts of hazards, your score, the last shot, what someone is going to think, tomorrow's meeting, and so on. In summary, this mental strategy ensures a one-shot-at-a-time focus. It blocks undesired, intrusive thoughts that are unrelated to the present or a focus on hazards looming in the distance.

Sam Snead, winner of eighty-one regular PGA and Senior Tour events, was playing against a young pro in Charleston, West Virginia on a course with which Snead was unfamiliar. As Sam stepped to the tee, the young pro said: "Now watch it Sam, over to the right, there's woods and a big drop off there and you can get into real trouble if you hit it there." Sam commented on the young pro's discussion of the hazard as follows: "This sort of strategy I cut my teeth on-warning a man of something so strongly that it'll prey on his mind to the point of creating an almost magnetic pull when you swing the club. Talk of trouble can draw you straight into trouble."[14]

If you have discussions on the tee with your playing partners regarding trouble, or you think about the hazards looming in the distance, the result is the same. The hazard will become your focus and target to hit or avoid. You will likely either hit into the hazard or to the extreme opposite direction of the hazard.

Ben Crenshaw won the 1990 PGA event The Colonial. During an interview after his win, he said he stood on the 17th tee with a four shot lead. He said on the tee all he was thinking about was not hooking into the trees on the left. He overcompensated and pushed his tee shot into the hazard on the right.

The focus on hazards becomes the target of your nervous system. The do's and don'ts of hazards don't matter when the sensory information is processed to the brain. The flood of sensory information of thoughts, images, and discussion regarding the hazards becomes the central focus or target in the nervous system. The chapter titled "Visualization: Pictures=Performance" provides a detailed discussion of how images are precursors to behavior through the "motor program" the brain constructs.

I would encourage you to ask the other members of your group not to discuss the hazards, just to describe and show you the targets. If you're on your home course, turn your focus to targets and off of hazards. When you walk onto a tee on a strange course, ask what your target is, not where the hazards are. Regardless of where you are, those hazards are stationary. If your ball is going to find them, it will. There's no reason to give your brain a head start!

Any time you approach a situation where you have had difficulty, your focus will likely go to the problem rather than your target. You may have difficulty hitting from sand or playing from the rough, or there may be a particular hole that you don't play well. If these thoughts intrude on your preswing routine, step off the ball and start your routine over from behind the ball.

A good saying to remember is: "What you feed attention grows." Feed attention to your targets and the fairways, greens, and cups will widen.

STARTING YOUR PRESWING ROUTINE

Technically speaking, your routine begins as you approach your ball and look at your lie. You find a target, step off the distance, check the wind, and determine the type of shot you want to hit and the club you want to use. This series of links in the preswing routine chain is referred to as course management. You have completed the analytical chain of your routine; now it's time to shut off the analysis and become creative.

Whatever triggers your preswing routine should always trigger it. Jack Nicklaus describes the beginning of his preswing routine as the point at which he steps off his yardage.[15]

I have heard sport psychologists say that your routine should be changed weekly or it will get "too learned." That's like saying you should change the triggers for dressing, grooming, eating, and so on. Why should you not change? You will feel uncomfortable and out of sync if you keep changing. Habits become ingrained and are easy to repeat once they are learned through repetition. Like Jack Nicklaus, keep the same trigger to start your routine.

The creative links of the preswing chain include: quieting the nervous system through movement, focus and breathing; removing a club from your bag; recalling a similar shot you have hit well in the past; describing to yourself the shot you are going to hit; and maintaining a present target focus. (The strategies for quieting the nervous system are covered in the chapter titled "Fine Tuning Your Nervous System.")

The analytical and creative are the two distinctly separate but connected chains of the mental preswing routine. It is important that you complete each link in the chains in sequence. Learning occurs in patterns. The completion of one link triggers the beginning of the next link. If you are going to pause between links in the two chains, the best time to pause is between the analytical and creative segments. Once you have considered your lie, the wind, and so on, and decided what club you are going to hit, this is a good "resting place" in your routine.

For example, let's assume you are playing in a group where you are waiting for others to hit after you arrive at your ball. You check your lie and the wind. You find a target, decide on the type of shot you want to hit, and choose a club.

Now, wait before you remove your club from the bag.

As you are waiting, stay focused on your target. The behavior of removing your club from your bag should trigger a movement and focus on sensations that are totally in the present, and related to your shot and target. Pulling a club from your bag should be the trigger to move from a broad to a narrow concentration focus. If you pull the club before it is time to hit your shot, you will introduce behavior links of thinking and action that are not part of the creative behavior chain of hitting the shot, and your performance will deteriorate accordingly.

Watch tour players as they walk onto a tee, or as they hit shots from the fairway or around the green. They pull the club from their bag only when it is their turn to play.

The only time you will see tour players take a club before it is their turn to play is when they hit a shot onto the green. They will almost always take their putter from their caddie once their ball is on the green and walk to the green, putter in hand.

The routine for the tour player begins several yards from the green. They look at the contour of the green before they walk onto it and survey their lie. They begin to read the green from both sides of the ball as they repair their ball mark and mark their ball.

The majority of you aren't tour players, and you don't have caddies. However, pulling your club at the right time will help you stay focused in the present and on your target. To build a solid routine, you will need to build discrete events that trigger your routine chain. Let's consider the conditions of the average course and discuss some good habits to establish starting points in the creative links of your routine.

If you are walking to an elevated tee from a riding cart and you know you are going to be using driver, leave the head cover on your driver. If you are hitting first, follow the movement, focus, and breathing strategies you will be learning as you remove the head cover. Drop the head cover between you and the cart on the path you will take back to the cart. Make this a habit and you won't have intrusive thoughts during your routine such as, "I have to remember my head cover."

If you walk onto that same tee and it isn't your turn to play, lean your club against a bench, a tree, or something else close to the tee ground. Pick up your club only when it is your turn to play. Taking your club in hand and removing the head cover initiates the beginning of your routine for that shot.

If you walk onto an elevated tee of a par 3, take three or four clubs with you. Again, rest your clubs against some object until it is your turn to play. Do your course management of checking the wind, yardage, and pin position, and decide on the type of shot you want to hit. When it is your turn to play, pick up all of your clubs, walk to an area just off the teeing ground on the path you will take back to your cart, and lay down the clubs you aren't going to use. Your routine starts as you take the club you are going to use and walk onto the tee.

How many times have you gotten to your ball, decided you didn't have the right club, and hit the shot anyway? If you are riding in a cart that must stay on the cart path, get in a habit of taking three or four clubs with you to your ball. If you hit a ball that you aren't sure is on the green, take every possible club you might use from the edge of the green. Your routine begins once you pick up the club you are going to use. Don't waste a stroke using the wrong club simply because you don't want to hold up play while you walk back to your bag.

I have one final note on the mental preswing routine. I was talking with a young mini tour player recently. He said he had read about the importance of a routine, but found that it disrupted his concentration. He said: " I think: 'Look at the target, waggle, look at the target and waggle again' and all that thinking messes me up." I laughed and said: "You're thinking instead of doing." You should not have to narrate your routine to yourself as you go through it. Practice your routine on the range with every shot you hit. With repeated practice on the range, it will soon become automatic. There is no single ideal routine. Your routine should include good course management steps, and it should be positive with a one hundred percent target focus.

The *MIND UNDER PAR* series™: *Routine Guided Practice in Developing Consistent Performance* has audio instructions of routines for tee and fairway shots, for shots one hundred yards in, and chipping and putting. Listening to this tape often and prior to each round prepares you for practice and play, and builds a consistent, repeating routine for each shot.

Mechanical Preswing Routine

As a golf instructor, I would say that the purpose of the preswing routine is to ensure good course management and proper setup. If you check your lie, wind direction, and distance, and you know how far you hit each club, you will likely choose the correct club for the shot.

I consider setup the most important mechanical link in the golf swing. If you don't have a good athletic position with good balance so that your arms swing freely, or if you don't have proper ball position at setup, your swing plane and the trajectory of your shot will be affected.

If you don't place your hands on the club correctly, so that your club head returns to a square position at impact, your shot will likely not go to your target regardless of how many mental strategies you employ.

If you aren't aligned square to your target line, your swing path will correct for alignment that will affect the ball flight of your shot, and again, you will miss your target.

These three areas, Posture, Grip and Aim (alignment) make up the final and most important links in the preswing chain. If one of these links is weak, altered, or incorrect, your performance will suffer.

There is no reason to work on any other part of your swing until your setup is correct. As I've said, if one of your preswing links is weak, mentally or mechanically, you'll likely hit a poor shot. Strengthen your setup and you will be pleasantly surprised with the rest of your swing. The source of swing problems can often be traced to setup problems.

When you practice or play, take yourself through a preswing mental checklist of Posture, Grip, and Aim before each shot. An easy way to remember setup is P.G.A.:

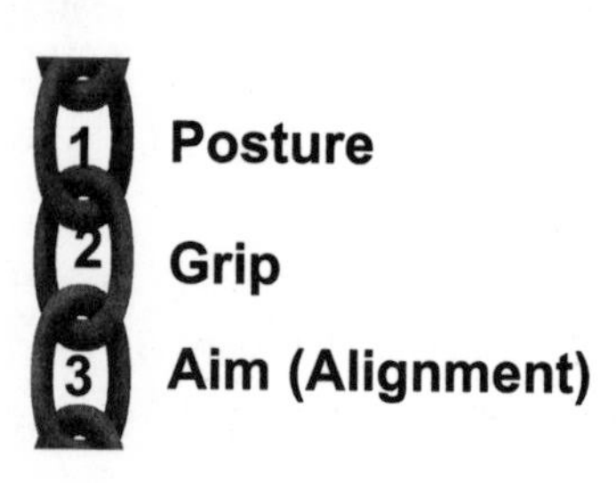

With repeated, focused practice, your setup will become automatic. During lessons and when you are hitting the ball well, focus your attention on the feeling of the proper setup.

Jack Nicklaus describes his thought focus when he sets up to a shot during play as being directed by "...plain willpower...you just have to force other thoughts aside. ...make yourself think exclusively about your aim and alignment and your ball position and your posture; make yourself do what you know is right in those areas, and make yourself keep on doing it time and time again, even though it doesn't seem to be working. ..if you have enough resolution-they will ultimately begin to work."[16]

There's a saying, "Don't miss the shot before you swing the club." This simply means, if you aren't set up correctly, you have a weak link in your preswing chain that will likely cause you to miss the shot.

I have often heard tour players describe how they have been setting up right or left of targets as they explain a swing problem they have been experiencing. I can't tell you how often I have watched top teachers make changes in a tour player's grip, posture, alignment, or ball position, and seen major changes occur in ball flight. The best way to check your setup is to consult your local PGA or LPGA teaching professional.

Al Geiberger set the record for the lowest PGA tournament round with a 59 on Friday, June 10, 1977. He attributed his low round to tempo, putting (twenty-three putts), and a setup change that he made a few weeks before which he says resulted in a swing change.[17]

Lee Trevino described his late spring 1992

swing changes as related to setup: "The last couple of weeks I had my feet too far apart at address. My stance is open anyway and I have a very bad habit of getting my left foot too far away from my body and not under my left shoulder. When that happens, I can't get over to my left side and I hit the ball a little left or a little right. So I fixed it. It's funny, but golfers tend to revert back to the same bad habits. When you're not playing well, you try to fix in your mind all the things you're doing right, but it's impossible to record every single aspect of it. It's like a big revolving door, and you just go through the cycle over and over again."[18]

Once a good setup is established and you are hitting the ball well, make a video and take still pictures of your setup. Post the pictures on a mirror where you can refer to them frequently. I have the tour players I work with use this as a check for their setup. Many of them talk about how playing in different conditions, especially strong wind, can affect their setup. The video and still pictures provide them with a setup reference.

Once you establish a setup routine, practice it daily off the course and with each shot you hit on the range.

Posture

Assuming the correct posture is relatively simple; however, static and dynamic balance must be part of the preswing and inswing chains. If balance is not part of the chain, if one of the links is weak, assuming your grip and alignment are correct, the best you can hope for is an "inswing save" or a decent miss.

Static balance is the stationary balance of the setup position. Dynamic balance is the balance maintained during the swing. One of the things all peak performers have is good balance. Look at the finish position of tour players. If you set up to the ball off balance, you will likely finish off balance. If you start with your weight on your heels or your toes, you will finish on your heels or toes off balance. Balance affects the club head path and the trajectory of the ball. When you go through your checklist as you practice setup, be sure you incorporate balance. Feel an athletic position.

Assume a setup position as though you are getting ready to hit a shot. Tense your thighs in this position. Notice how it feels as though your weight moves up your legs toward your thighs? One of the better players I work with describes a sensation of "skating on ice" when he is struggling with his swing. You get this sensation when you tense your thighs. During periods of stress and frustration, you will tend to accumulate more tension in your shoulders and thighs. Now relax your thighs and notice how your weight and balance change. You should feel more grounded. The sensation should be one of your weight leaving your thighs and melting into the ground or floor. Be sure you don't let your thighs get too relaxed. Firm, thighs, not tense, are important in establishing a good base from which to swing.

Senior PGA Tour player and former Ryder Cup captain Dave Stockton suggests that you pretend you are catching a medicine ball being dropped from above when you set up to the ball. He notes that you will most certainly flex your knees, your rear end will stick out, and your thighs will be firm, a good foundation for beginning and swinging in balance.[19]

You should feel well grounded at the ball. You should feel the same balance at setup you would feel as you prepare to field a ground ball, or the balance a defensive basketball player feels when guarding an opponent. You should feel an "athletic position" when you are balanced.

Square your clubface to an intermediate target, and then square your stance to the target line as you deliberately assume your grip, and then your posture. As you deliberately shuffle your feet into your stance, feel that static balance. Now you're ready to start your swing. Then begin to work on feeling that balance through your entire swing (dynamic balance) to your finish position.

Grip

You can consult any number of books or your local teaching professional about your grip and alignment. When you make a grip change as part of your instruction, it is going to feel awkward, uncomfortable, and unorthodox, as if you will never be able to make contact with the ball. It will take daily practice for the grip change to feel natural.

Ben Hogan advocates practicing your grip thirty minutes a day for a week when you make a change. Keep a club in your office or home where you can practice your setup often. Sam Snead, winner of one hundred and sixty tournaments, eighty-one recognized by the PGA of America, asserts that: "Eighty-five percent of all bad golfers have bad grips. I don't have any calluses. Tension is the worst thing in golf. Grip the club like you've got a bird in your hands."[20]

Some contemporary teachers advocate a firm grip to quiet the hands through the swing. Whatever your preference, stay with it.

Alignment (Aim)

Alignment begins as you stand behind the ball and pick out a target. The majority of the players I teach don't have specific targets the first time we get together. Their targets are flags or greens, not specific landing areas. Therefore, this concept may be foreign to you. I strongly encourage you to begin to pick out specific target landing areas, regardless of what club you have in your hands.

A good practice strategy for alignment is to set two clubs down at your feet when hitting balls. Align one club just outside the ball and your target line. Align a second club along your heels parallel to the first, your stance line. When you stand behind your ball, both clubs will have created a path that looks like a railroad track pointing directly to your target. As you stand behind the ball, the clubs are parallel. The club on the right points at your target. The club on the left, your stance line, is a couple of yards to the left of your target.

One of the most common problems players experience is in alignment. Practicing with clubs on the ground will help train your visual orientation to target. Another strategy to check your alignment is to set up to the ball, then take your club and lay it across both thighs. The club will be pointing to where you are aiming.

I had one of my better students miss the first stage of PGA Tour school. I met with him for a lesson and he said he had "hit everything right" the entire four rounds. To compound things, he said the course was set up to play a fade. On those shots where he set up to hit a fade, he hit the ball even further right. I watched him hit a few balls, and I put a club along his stance line at his heels and one along his target line. He was set up ten yards right of his target. He stepped back behind the ball and arrived at the same conclusion, shook his head, and said: "It was that simple, wasn't it?"

A few weeks prior to tour school, he had stopped using an intermediate target as a link in his routine during one of his rounds. As soon as he resumed using an intermediate target on the range, he began to set up at his targets and the ball started to fly right at the target with a nice draw. It was a tough learning experience, but one he won't forget.

The sequence of chain links is critical in alignment. Note that your eyes move from the intermediate target to the primary target before you assume your stance. As you stare at the primary target, you assume your stance.

14 *You quietly set your club behind the ball and square your club face with your intermediate target.*

15 *Your eyes go to your primary target as you shuffle into your setup. Your eyes never leave your primary target until you are aligned.*

16 *You feel grounded and balanced. You stare at your primary target and glance at the ball.*

No matter what mental strategies you use, if your setup has a weak link, it will show up in the shot. Don't miss the shot before you swing the club.

Remember, following a consistent routine will help you establish patterns that minimize distraction and ensure you are set up to the ball correctly and prepared to start your swing. Don't change your routine without guidance from your instructor.

Developing a good setup requires more than a single lesson on the teaching tee. Your old setup habits are well entrenched in your nervous system. New learning takes many repetitions of practice.

INTEGRATING THE MENTAL AND MECHANICAL PRESWING ROUTINES

In their 1978 book, The New Golf Mind,[21] Dr. Gary Wiren, and Larry Sheehan PGA teaching professionals, and Dr. Richard Coop, an educational psychologist, presented a theory of brain function that is quoted and used by many golf instructors to this day. The authors described brain function as "analyzer" (Left Brain) and "integrator" (Right Brain).

These authors presented the left brain "analyzer" as necessary in processing verbal information, while the right brain "integrator" is primarily responsible for the execution of the swing. They further note that too much left brain analyzer during the preswing interferes with successful shot execution.

Let's look at an integration of the mental and mechanical links of the preswing chain, and discuss the left and right brain functions and their places in the preswing routine.

PHYSICAL ROUTINE		MENTAL ROUTINE
Walk to ball.	1	Check lie (downhill, uphill, rough, up, down), and consider natural trajectory, and determine target.
Find distance marker and step off distance.	2	Calculate distance to landing area / target.
Toss grass into the air.	3	Determine strength of wind and club allowance (one club wind, etc.).
Look down fairway.	4	Find target and determine type of shot and club based upon lie, wind, distance, target and ability to hit shot (draw, fade, low, high).

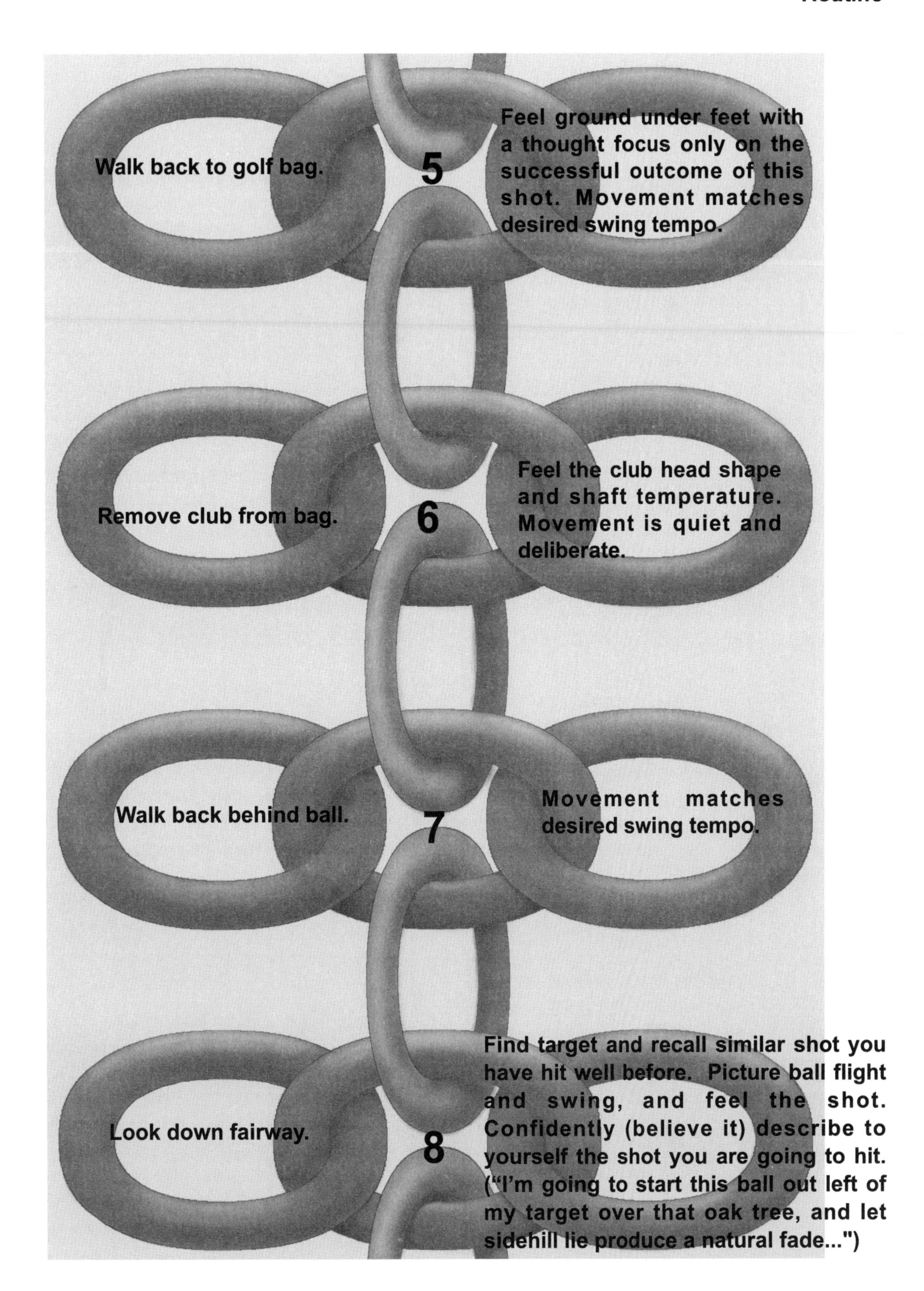
Walk back to golf bag.
5
Feel ground under feet with a thought focus only on the successful outcome of this shot. Movement matches desired swing tempo.
Remove club from bag.
6
Feel the club head shape and shaft temperature. Movement is quiet and deliberate.
Walk back behind ball.
7
Movement matches desired swing tempo.
Look down fairway.
8
Find target and recall similar shot you have hit well before. Picture ball flight and swing, and feel the shot. Confidently (believe it) describe to yourself the shot you are going to hit. ("I'm going to start this ball out left of my target over that oak tree, and let sidehill lie produce a natural fade...")

9

Take a practice swing.

Feel the swing you want to make to produce the shot as you hold a visual image of your primary target.

10

Walk to the ball.

Movement matches desired swing tempo. Eyes and thoughts never leave your intermediate target.

11

Square clubface to intermediate target.

Movement is gentle and relaxed as you continue to look at your intermediate target.

12

Your eyes go to the primary target. Then you shuffle into your setup and assume a balanced athletic position.

You stare at the target and glance at the ball. You hold a visual image of the primary target as you glance at the ball.

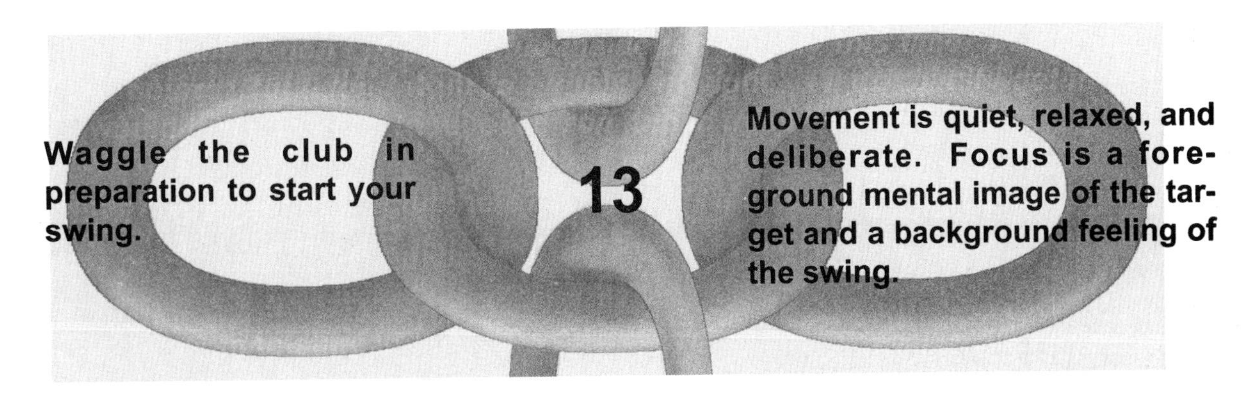

In the model presented by Drs. Wiren and Coop, and Larry Sheehan, the preswing routine has a left brain analyzer and right brain integrator. If you look at links one through four, you will find the verbal decision-making based upon an assessment of lie, wind, distance, obstacles, and so on. This is all a left brain function. Once you move to link five, the right brain (integrator) takes over and, for the best shot execution, remains in control. Let's review an example of this by looking at an intrusive thought between links twelve and thirteen.

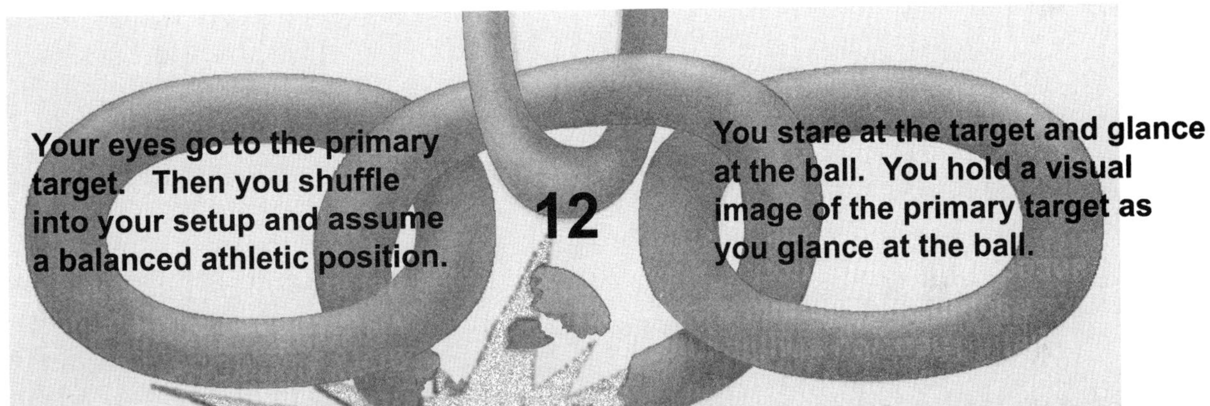

"I need to hit a good shot here. If I could birdie this hole, I can get back in the game and start to play better on the back side. Although the last time I had this lie, I hooked the ball.

"I need to be sure I don't pull the club inside too quickly this time. I think that's what I've been doing. But I don't want to hit this one right. I'll do that if I get the club outside. I would never be able to recover from those trees."

"I wonder if I have enough club here? Maybe it's a smooth 7 iron instead of a hard 8."

You begin to stare at the ball and glance at the trees to the right.

13

"If I get in those trees that's good for another double or maybe even a triple."

Anytime intrusive thoughts occur during the preswing routine performance deteriorates. According to the model of the The New Golf Mind, the intrusive thoughts take you from right brain back to left brain. From a learning perspective, these intrusive thoughts break a link in the behavior chains. This break in the links impacts upon the "readiness potential" by feeding undesired content to the brain mechanism that is developing the motor program. In this case, the motor program is being "rewritten" by thoughts and images of an undesired swing path and past poor performance with a similar lie. Regardless of what the explanation may be, the outcome is always the same: poor performance.

What should you do? Step off the ball and start your routine over. If, for example, your routine was like the twelve steps presented, you would walk quietly and deliberately behind the ball and start your routine over from step number seven. The same is true for putting.

There's a story that's told about Billy Casper's preswing routine. He approaches a fairway shot, stops at his bag, and pulls his yardage guide from his pocket. Then he steps off the yardage, puts the yardage guide back in his pocket, talks to his caddie about the shot, takes a club, and completes his routine behind the ball. He steps up to the ball, begins to waggle his club, and hears a camera shutter click. He steps back from his ball, glares at the photographer, walks back to his bag, drops his club in the bag, walks ten yards back down the fairway, turns around and starts his routine over. Here's a player who understands the importance of an uninterrupted routine.

THE MENTAL INSWING ROUTINE

Let's discuss the inswing chain. The swing is over so quickly that the primary mental goal is to relieve the nervous system of all the clutter so that an unguided swing can be made without distraction from the present.

The inswing chain is over in little more than a second. In their 1974 book, Jack Nicklaus and Ken Bowden presented an analysis of the swing speed of the top players of that era. Jack Nicklaus' swing was 1.96 seconds, Gary Player's 1.6 seconds, and Arnold Palmer's 1.36 seconds.[22]

Brain researchers have determined that the brain takes 1.5 seconds to establish a novel motor program for a simple behavior like raising your right index finger and .1 second to initiate the program. It takes the nervous system fifteen times longer (1.5 seconds) to prepare a novel motor program than it does to execute the behavior (.1 second). Considering that a motor program takes 1.5 seconds to prepare for a novel movement, there is not enough time for the brain to make an accurate correction once the swing has started. Behaviors that appear to be inswing corrections are often the result of a poor setup.

Target Focus

In discussing PGA Tour player John Cook's return to play and success after a long-term injury, Ken Venturi said: "He had to get back his tunnel vision. When you're a good player, you look at where you want to go. After playing poorly, all of a sudden you're looking at where you don't want to go."[23]

Nick Price lapped the field with his five

stroke win margin at the 1993 PGA Western Open. It was his third PGA Tour victory of 1993 and his second in two weeks. He had missed only one cut in his last thirty-five tournament starts, the 1993 Masters. His comments following his win show the intensity of his concentration and his target orientation: "My concentration was unbelievable this week. For the ten seconds leading into every shot, all I focused on was the target."[24]

I teach students to use one of three inswing visualization strategies: hold a mental picture of the target, ball flight, or ball landing through the entire swing. This is probably one of the most difficult mental exercises through which I take students. It is difficult because it is foreign to most players. If you have ever made a grip change, you can understand the difficulty. Holding a mental picture of the target is like trying to make a grip change. It doesn't feel right and you tend to attribute poor performance to the new grip since it feels so incongruent with your usual game. With practice, a visual image of target, ball flight, or ball landing during the swing becomes natural.

The target images change depending on the shot you are hitting. The target for putting is the spot over which you want to roll the ball. The spot on the green where you want to land your ball or the ball hitting the flag stick for a chip is your target. Make your targets precise and your play will improve.

PGA Tour player Nick Price says that targets should be distant and as small as you can see. He says if you are aiming at a house that you should pick out a shingle on the roof as your target. If you are aiming at a distant bunker, aim at a rake in the bunker. Be precise.[25]

LPGA Tour player Marta Figueras-Dotti says she has an image of the ball landing and bouncing as she swings.[26] LPGA Tour player Jennifer Wyatt has an image of the flight of the ball during her swing.[27] Nick Price says he holds an image of the target during his swing. He says the clearer his image of the target, the better his shot will be.[28]

If you have ever played basketball, football, soccer, baseball, or a similar sport, you know what a target focus is. Watch a basketball player at the free throw line. Not only does he follow the same routine, bouncing the ball the same number of times before shooting, but also he focuses on nothing but the target. A pitcher pays no attention to anything but the target: a spot in the center of the catcher's mitt. The outfielder's focus is to hit the cutoff man in the chest on a button or letter, his target. What would happen if the basketball player focused on the top edge of the back board, or the pitcher focused on the umpire's head or the top of the back stop and so on. This is equivalent to a golfer's focus on the out-of-bounds right or the hazard left. If you have a target focus, your focus is on your goal. Remember, your images become the targets of the nervous system.

When the basketball player sets up to shoot a free throw or a pitcher prepares to make a pitch, he is looking at his target. The golfer is looking at his ball and has to maintain an image of his target in his mind's eye. Can you imagine how a basketball or baseball player would perform if his focus was on the ball as he prepared to shoot or throw? He would likely become mechanical and steer the ball. Sound familiar? If so, I would suggest you begin to practice a target image through your entire swing.

One of the premiere teachers of the past ninety years, Harvey Penick, sums up target focus quite simply: "Once you address the golf ball, hitting it has got to be the most important thing in your life at that moment. Shut out all thoughts other than picking out a target and taking dead aim at it."[29]

PGA Tour player Billy Ray Brown says that many amateurs have trouble keeping their tee shots in the fairway because they aim at a large, generalized target. Their images are wide and so are their shots. Billy Ray suggests that players aim at a specific point in the fairway.[30] Once you determine that specific target point, keep a picture of it in your mind's eye through the swing.

I teach an inswing target focus beginning with putting and chipping. With the full swing, I have a player start with a wedge and rate both the shot and the clarity of the image on a one to ten scale. For a wedge, your target might be a bare spot on the range or discoloration of grass that is one or two feet in diameter. It's noteworthy that a direct relationship evolves between the rating of the clarity of the image and the rating of the quality of the shot. For example, shot ratings of ten will tend to have a clarity of image rating of nine or ten. Similarly, shot ratings of six or seven have image ratings of six or seven. This drill takes a good bit of practice to get the nine to ten clarity of image rating.

Learning good mental mechanics is not a lot different from learning good swing mechanics. Both require practice. The transition of mental mechanics from the range to the course is most easily accomplished through extensive practice. There are numerous variables that will affect both swing and mental mechanics. One such variable is arousal levels.

You will read about the effects of arousal on visualization in the chapter titled "Fine Tuning Your Nervous System." In summary, if you are under pressure, you will have difficulty visualizing targets during the swing.

Swing Keys

Many players use swing keys instead of target images through the swing. A swing key is something like: turn back, turn through, or A-B. Nick Faldo spent long hours daily rebuilding his swing under the tutelage of David Leadbetter. He uses swing keys to prompt his swing. He says he limits his swing key to one as he takes the club back and one on the downswing.[31]

Many players use swing keys to set their tempo or start their swing. Others use it as part of their preswing routine to set the stage for the type of shot they want to hit. Sam Snead used the word "oily" to create a relaxed, fluid feeling for his swing. Try using words that will "call up" the feeling you want to experience on a shot. For example, you may use the word "soft" for a chip shot you want to land gently. The word "leisurely" helps some players create their desired tempo. If you use a swing key, relate that key to a feeling in your swing. As you make the swing, feel the key.

Feeling Positions

If you must think of a swing position, think about and feel your finish position. This image and thought focus will get you aggressively through the ball, as will an inswing target image.

Whatever your thoughts, don't think about mechanics during your swing. Let me repeat that - Don't think about mechanics during your swing! If you do, disaster will follow.

For example, if you focus on the position of your hands at the top of your backswing, you will tend to stay on your right side for right handers and left side for left handers. If this is the case, the path of the club will create a push, cut, or slice as you swing through the ball. Or you may experience a deceleration of the club, causing you to hit the shot taking a very large divot. We call this a fat shot. Again, if you must think of a swing position, think about and feel your finish position.

If you play much golf, you have been faced with the same shot a number of times. For example, every time you play, you have a shot from the Number 1 tee. On many occasions, you have had the same shot from a greenside bunker, a short iron to the green, or a particular chip shot. At one time or another, you have hit every one of those shots well. Recall that situation. "Feel" and see yourself successfully executing the shot from the past. Whether you are able to recall the shot from the past or not, stand behind the ball and pick your target in the fairway or on the green. Picture the swing you want to make and ball flight in your mind's eye. Then, focus on nothing but your target. Swing to your target.

Fred Couples says he never hits a shot without "calling up" that same shot from the past. He says if he has an 8 iron to the green at the Masters, he recalls that same shot, for example, from the LA Open. He sees it, feels it, and then puts that same swing on the ball.[32] Sam Snead, Jack Nicklaus, Johnny Miller, and Bobby Jones all refer to this same technique in their writings.

MECHANICAL INSWING ROUTINE

There are thousands of PGA and LPGA instructors who teach inswing mechanics at clubs, ranges, and golf schools in this country. There are hundreds of books, magazines and videos which also provide instruction. I'm not going to add to this wealth of information with the exception of two considerations: grip pressure and tempo.

Both of these mechanical states are affected by the level of arousal in your nervous system. As you proceed through my instruction series, you will be presented with several strategies to fine tune this arousal.

Grip Pressure

A significant part of arousal is muscle tension. I believe tension is the single greatest offender of the golf swing. This tension is often expressed as increased grip pressure. Practice on the range feeling the same grip pressure throughout your swing. In reality, the centrifugal force produced in the downswing results in increased grip pressure. However, "feel" the same pressure throughout your entire swing from setup to follow-through. This technique will help eliminate "regripping," reduce tension, and reduce overuse of your hands in the swing like "flipping" at the ball with the club head.

Tempo

Tempo is another important part of the inswing chain and it filters through every link in the chain. A tempo that is too fast will throw off your timing and balance. A smooth tempo can help minimize the effects of swing flaws. During practice, try feeling the same tempo on both sides of the swing: backswing and downswing. In reality, your downswing is faster; however, "feel" the same tempo on both sides. Jack Nicklaus described this as one of his three best swing keys.[33] Once it's well practiced, take it to the course to play.

Nick Price is noted for a fast swing. He says that swinging fast is not wrong, as long as the arms and body work together. When a quick swing results in the arms and body working independently, that's when problems begin.[34]

Your tempo is a reflection of your personality, your level of on-course arousal, and associated movement around the course. Purposely slowing down physical movement around the ball, while walking the course and in your off-course day to day routine, is a relaxation procedure that is covered in the chapter titled "Fine Tuning Your Nervous System."

MENTAL POSTSWING ROUTINE

The mental part of the postswing routine takes place in the conversations you have with yourself following each shot. The content and timing of these conversations directly affect how you will play your next shot and, for that matter, your round. These conversations with self are often seen outwardly as a change of posture, especially following one or a series of bad shots: head down and shoulders forward.

Your postswing routine continues for any particular shot as long as you think about it or carry the feelings of anger, frustration, or excitement and the associated posture. If you are putting on Number 6 green, but are still thinking about the drive you pushed into the trees from Number 6 tee, your continued postswing focus on the tee shot will interfere with your focus on your putt. I'll address this more in the chapter titled "Concentration: Keeping Your Head in Play."

Your postswing routine should be positive and end before you approach your next shot. Your postswing thoughts should never be on mechanics, only on the "feeling" of the swing. Your postswing thoughts will either support you and build confidence, or tear down your confidence. I will reserve that discussion for the chapter on confidence.

Excitement and Arousal

There is a fine line between a positive postswing routine that is supportive and builds confidence, and becoming too excited. Too much excitement causes two problems:

1. *Your nervous system is flooded with an internal state of arousal that creates tension and hampers performance. (Tempo and movement quicken, and balance and sequential movement are compromised.)*

2. *This aroused state produces a flow of intrusive thoughts that interferes with concentration in the present.*

David Feherty, European and PGA Tour player, says that the younger, inexperienced players get too excited too early. He says: "The symptoms are a punch in the air and jumping up and down and getting excited very early [in the round]. Every player who has been around a long time has probably gone through that stage th selves. I know I did."[3]

Tom Kite's comments show insight into this process as he discussed his 1992 US Open win. He holed out a twenty yard pitch shot on the seventh hole of the final round at Pebble Beach. His comment regarding that shot: "I wanted to jump up and down, but the reality was I still had most of the golf course to play."[36]

This is not to suggest that your postswing conversations be limited; just keep a cover on the intensity. For example, "That was a great drive. That is perfect position for my approach shot. I drive the ball well. I am a good player."

Greg Norman says that everybody "...likes to hear words of encouragement as he faces a tough shot, and congratulations after he pulls it off. Unfortunately, unless you play golf with your mother you can't depend on hearing these things. That's why I talk to myself. Not aloud, but inside my head. The tougher the shot I'm facing, the more I talk. If I'm on the last hole of a tournament, facing a long iron shot to the green and needing a birdie to win, I'll say to myself, 'You know this shot cold, you've knocked it stiff a thousand times, and now you're going to do it again. I also talk after I hit shots. After a particularly long, straight drive I'll often say, 'Damn, Greg, I'm pretty impressed with that one.' These inner words can be more encouraging than the cheers of the gallery. You don't want to linger too long on your shots-good or bad-but you do want to stamp the good ones on your mind for future reference in pressure situations. Silent self-congratulations is one way to do that."[37] Note that Norman's quote includes both his preswing and postswing conversations with himself.

The preswing, inswing, and postswing conversations you have with yourself are called internal dialogue. You may have heard it referred to as "self talk." If you want your internal dialogue on the course to change, you will need to change your off-course conversations with yourself.

Anger

Let's talk about anger as part of your postswing routine. Is it good or bad? That's highly individual. Only you have the answer to that. If anger helps you improve your focus and you play better, great. If not, I would suggest that you look at making some changes. The physiology of anger produces extreme arousal. Extreme arousal promotes poor performance. I have worked with some players for whom a brief period of anger helps them get refocused and their play improves. I have never seen a player who stays angry for an extended period play well as long as he stays angry.

Sam Snead says he saw many promising amateurs and pros allow anger to ruin their game. He further states one might conclude that a calm quiet player should have the advantage; however, he disagrees with this. Snead says that you have to have fire. He cites great amateurs of his era, noting they could all fill the air with clubs at one time or another. He notes that in his prime "Byron Nelson could bend a club like a pretzel or beat a bush to death with the best of them."

As Snead says: "Show me the fellow who walks along calmly after topping a drive or missing a kick-in putt, showing the world he is in perfect control, yet burning up inside, and I'll show you one who is going to lose. This boy is a fake. His nervous system won't take what he's handing it. If you bottle up anger entirely, it poisons your control centers. But if you go all the way in the other direction, the practice of kicking tee markers, abusing shrubbery, and wrecking equipment can become such a habit that it spoils your muscular reflexes."

Sam concludes: "Good golfing temperament falls in between taking it with a grin or shrug and throwing a fit. I believe you should blow up at times, if it helps, but only if you can keep your wits about you. I couldn't beat any pro if I couldn't get my temper outbreak over with fast, then start thinking out the next shot. It's like opening a steam valve for a moment, then shutting it."[38] The problem for many is knowing how to shut off the steam valve. If the steam valve stays open, your play will suffer until the valve is closed.

Jack Nicklaus said he took an experience with anger as a young boy and realized that if he was going to play well, he would have to direct his anger constructively. "I began to use my anger to motivate me, first to recover as best I could from whatever mistake I'd just made, then to push me to improve my game more and more so I'd make fewer and fewer mistakes."[39]

PGA Tour player Fred Couples was commenting on his self management at the 1991 Ryder Cup. He notes he was playing a match against Christy O'Connor and was even going into Number 18. He says when he gets angry, he begins to pressure himself. He was upset with himself for chipping poorly on 15 and missing a four foot putt for birdie on 17. He felt he should be two up going to 18. (Notice that the postswing frustration for two shots on holes 15 and 17 was carried to the 18th tee. Fred was not mentally on the 18th hole.)

Christy O'Connor hit his shot to the green on 18 before Couples. Fred said he heard the gallery cheer and, from his vantage point, thought O'Connor's ball was one foot from the pin. Couples describes his thinking as follows: "I was pissed off ...now I'm pretty much thinking, 'I've lost to this guy.' I got the yardage and backed off. I tried to hit a hard 9 iron instead of an 8 iron... I just blocked it out to the right of the green and I chipped it to six feet." As it turned out, O'Connor's shot was more like three feet from the hole. "It was the only bogey I made."[40]

Sam Snead describes an experience in 1935 where he was playing at the Old Dominion Course in Newport News. He was on the 18th hole of the last round. If he birdied the hole, he would win the tournament. He said he was such an unknown that even the Village Idiot had more of a reputation than he. It was the first gallery of his life that he could call his own. He was making his second shot into the par 4 18th hole. The greens were hard, so he played a shot to hit the fringe and bounce onto the green. He hit his approach shot and said it looked so good he thought it might go in for an eagle two. Then, a spectator ran in front of the green and the ball hit his foot, bounced left, and settled behind a bunker in trampled rough. He said: "Everything went Red; I'll kill that S.O.B. I couldn't turn loose of the idea of murdering the fan-who'd wisely kept on running-even when I stood over the ball." Instead of hitting a nice, easy recovery shot, Sam hit the ball too shallow and nudged it into the bunker.

Sam concluded: "At some point in every outburst of anger, if it lasts long enough, you throw yourself into reverse gear. The minute you blow, a charge seems to go through your opponent and he begins to play better golf. ... by blowing, you bleed off your own energy from the job of making shots. Getting sore and staying that way is hard work."[41]

PGA Tour player and winner of the 1994 Australian Tournament Players Championship and the Victorian Open, Patrick Burke, played as much hockey as golf in his youth. His temperament both on and off the golf course used to resemble more that of a hockey player than a golfer. The net result for him was poor play.

He is able to recover and minimize the "melt down" on the course when he practices anger management. Interestingly, his first view of success with anger management came in the car where he often displayed his temper. He noted he was able to increase his self-control or let go of anger sooner by talking to himself rationally about the situation and discussing the potential consequences of loss of control while practicing deep breathing.

Patrick says he plays better when he briefly opens the valve for anger, talks rationally to himself as a "coach," and then uses that mental intensity to refocus on the next shot while breathing deeply and quieting his movement. Patrick says his anger used to get so intense it would take him into a self-destruct mode. He said it was almost as though he were saying to himself: "You think that was bad, watch this!"[42]

PGA Tour player Steve Pate was referred to as "the Volcano" his first few years on tour. By his report, he said he could spend six to seven hours fuming or ticked off. His instructor, Jim Petralia, recalls playing with Pate in the years past. He said: "All I had to do was get him mad and his performance would deteriorate." Now that his temper is under control, he has channeled these emotions into increasing his concentration.[43]

LPGA Tour player Anne-Marie Palli was playing in the 1993 LPGA Tucson tournament. She was five under on the day when she took a quadruple bogey on Number 15. She said she became very angry and determined to turn that bad break around. She proceeded to birdie 16 and 17, and lipped out a putt on 18 for birdie to finish with a 69 on the day.[44]

Sam Snead said: "In tournaments, I go by Mark Twain's advice, which was to count four when angry and when very angry to swear. Once in a while I'll step into the woods, out of sight, and beat the leaves off a bush. There's no club throwing though, nor abusing of officials, opponents or gallery. My practical side tells me that by slamming others or your sticks, you show yourself to be a damned fool to people who might be valuable friends."[45]

Patrick Burke was playing in a California mini-tour event with Tom Lehman. Upon missing a shot, Tom threw a club what Patrick described as a remarkable distance. Patrick turned to Tom and said: "Tom I think you'd better throw a provisional, I'm not sure we are going to find that one."

Remember, former President Lyndon Johnson used to say that it's always preferable to have someone inside the tent peeing out than outside the tent peeing in. If you are "outside your tent" peeing in, you are chipping away at confidence. The next time you hear yourself being critical of your behavior or play, tell yourself to get back inside the tent and pee out. Tour players have told me it is important to assume an internal playing posture that it is never your fault. It's a spike mark, not your stroke. I'll address this concept more in a later chapter.

There's an amusing story I've heard two or three times about a player who drove his cart past the 18th tee, by the players on the fairway and green. He was obviously coming from somewhere off the back nine. He stopped at the water hazard on 18, removed his bag, and threw bag and clubs into the water.

Five minutes later, the disgruntled player returned to the water hazard, took off his shoes and socks, rolled up his pants and waded into the water. He raised his bag out of the water, unzipped it, removed his car keys, and threw his bag back into the water. The moral of this story is: "Anticipate the consequences of your behavior before you act on your frustration."

What you tell yourself about a shot will ultimately determine your level of arousal, frustration, irritability, concentration, and confidence. If you are going to quiet your nervous system, increase your frustration tolerance, and lower your irritability level, what better place to start than in your day to day routine. Once practiced off the course, you can easily draw upon these strategies on the course.

Years ago we learned that it is important to deal with anger, to get it out. The advocates of this position were referred to as "ventilationists." Recent research shows that anger is magnified into increased arousal and anger when it is aggressively expressed. For the majority of players, this anger expression hampers performance. So, what do you do? Recognize that if you are angry, you will perform best by having a rational, quieting conversation with yourself. You breathe deeply, and you relax your aroused nervous system through thinking, movement, and breathing. [These strategies are presented in the *MIND UNDER PAR* series™: *Routine: Guided Practice in Developing Consistent Performance*.]

In these situations, it is important that your posture be as positive as your thinking. Assume an "as if" posture of confidence and contentment. Never allow your eyes to drop below the horizon either on or off the course. If your head is high, you will be reminded to stay focused on the present and to be positive. This posture is associated with good, confident temperament. Assume that posture and trigger these positive thinking styles.

MECHANICAL POSTSWING ROUTINE

As I stated earlier, after you hit a poor shot, set up again where your ball was and make the swing you wanted to make. Feel the correction. This will override the undesired short-term memory of the swing in your nervous system and help abate some of the anger and frustration. Don't rush through your swing correction. Other players in front of you will be hitting and you should have ample time. If you're on the tee, pause after everyone else has hit and take your practice swing correction. Have realistic expectancies and patience. Be sure to practice deep, diaphragmatic breathing and quieted movement to increase the recall of the corrected swing. Your inswing thought focus should be on your target, good tempo, and balance.

In summary, all behavior occurs as a chain, from your day to day routines to the way you set up to hit a golf shot. Some of these routines are positive and move you toward good performance. Other routines are negative and produce undesired performance. These routines are so insidious it takes concentrated, focused strategies to change the links of the ingrained old routines.

I'm sure everyone of you has a set routine in the way you drive from your home to work or school on a day to day basis. You have driven that route so many times you can picture it and probably feel you could almost do it "with your eyes closed." At other times you might use that same route to go to another destination. There have likely been days where you find yourself continuing on toward your work or school location instead of your intended destination. You have simply grooved the links of the chain of your day to day patterns. Once a chain of behavior starts, it will continue unless a thought or behavior interrupts it.

Golf routines are no different. You already have physical and thinking routines in your golf game. They may change depending on the conditions of your play, but they do exist. These routines may not be the most desirable, but they repeat out of habit.

You also have well established practice routines. That may be to rake and hit one ball after another or it may be to focus your attention only on mechanics. You may never consider posture, grip, alignment or targets during your practice sessions. No matter what these routines are, they will show up on the golf course. If they aren't routines that take you from a broad to narrow focus, get you relaxed and into your target, and that are nonmechanical, serious changes need to be made in both the way you practice and play.

The only way you are going to have success on the golf course is to practice these routines off the course on the practice range. Then, these same routines must be practiced under increasingly stressful conditions with the blind trust of knowing that if you follow your routine you can get the best possible outcome regardless of what your intrusive thoughts might be telling you.

Recall what Jack Nicklaus said when he described his approach to his routine. "...plain willpower...you just have to force other thoughts aside. ...make yourself think exclusively about your aim and alignment and your ball position and your posture; make yourself do what you know is right in those areas, and make yourself keep on doing it time and time again, even though it doesn't seem to be working. ..if you have enough resolution-they will ultimately begin to work."[46]

There are many factors, from tension to thinking, that can intrude on your routine and produce an undesired outcome. The following chapters explore many of these factors and teach you specific, corrective skills to get you back to a desired performance chain.

ENDNOTES

1. David Frost, Interview, June 1992.

2. Anne-Marie Palli, Personal Communication (October, 1992).

3. Andy Brumer, "Be A Thinking Golfer," *Golf Tips* (May, 1994): p. 38.

4. Peter de Jonge, "Tiger Woods," *New York Times Magazine* (February 5, 1995): p. 38.

5. Richard Restak, M.D., *The Brain* (New York: Bantam Books, 1984), pp. 83-84.

6. Jack Nicklaus and Ken Bowden, *Golf My Way* (New York:Simon and Schuster, 1974), pp. 77-78.

7. Jack Nicklaus and Ken Bowden, "My Strongest Weapon," *Golf Magazine* (March, 1995) p. 67.

8. Brumer, "Be A thinking Golfer," p. 86.

9. Bob Sommers, "Tom Watson: That's in the Hole," *Golf Magazine* (April, 1995): p. 129.

10. Patrick Burke, Personal Communication (November, 1994).

11. Golf Digest Staff, "Fred Couples," *Golf Digest* (July, 1992): p. 114.

12. Brumer, "Be A thinking Golfer," p. 86.

13. Doug Tewell, "Keep Target in Sight For Straight Drives," *Golf Digest* (March, 1989): p. 41.

14. Sam Snead and Al Stump, *The Education of a Golfer* (New York: Simon and Schuster, 1961), p. 233.

15. Jack Nicklaus and Ken Bowden, "My Strongest Weapon," *Golf Magazine* (December, 1993): p. 48.

16. Nicklaus and Bowden, *Golf My Way*, pp. 98-99.

17. Al Geiberger and Larry Dennis, *Tempo* (Connecticut: Golf Digest/Tennis Inc., 1980), p. 13 and p. 23.

18. Golf World Staff, "Talking Golf With Lee Trevino," *Golf World* (June, 1992): p. 96.

19. Tom Watson, "For Balance, Imagine Catching a Medicine Ball," *Golf Digest* (October, 1992): p. 24.

20. Michael Bamberger, "The Slammer Never Rests," *Golf Digest* (September, 1994): p. 76.

21. Gary Wiren, Richard Coop, and Larry Sheehan, *The New Golf Mind* (New York: Simon and Schuster, 1978), p. 40.

22. Nicklaus and Bowden, *Golf My Way*, p. 164.

23. Jim Moriarty, "The Downs and Up of John Cook," *Golf Digest* (May, 1992): p. 75.

24. Geoff Russell, "The Dominator," *Golf World* (July 9, 1993): p. 43 and p. 46.

25. Nick Price and Mike Stachura, "How to Hit it Miles Down the Middle," *Golf Digest* (July, 1995): p. 59.

26. Marta Figueras-Dotti, Personal Communication (January, 1994).

27. Jennifer Wyatt, Personal Communication (March, 1994).

28. Bob Rotella, Ph.D. and Bob Cullen, *Golf is Not A Game of Perfect* (New York: Simon and Schuster, 1995), p.58.

29. Harvey Penick and Bud Shrake, *Harvey Penick's Little Red Book* (New York: Simon and Schuster, 1992), p. 45.

30. Billy Ray Brown, "For Straighter Tee Shots, Aim at a Tiny Target," *Golf Digest* (October, 1990): p. 135.

31. John Hopkins, "Nick Faldo's Mystery Tour," *Golf World* (July 10, 1992): p. 27.

32. Golf Digest Staff, "Fred Couples," p. 114.

33. Nicklaus and Bowden, "My Strongest Weapon," p. 45.

34. David Leadbetter, "Don't Be So Quick to Judge Nick Price's Swing," *Golf World* (September 18, 1992): p. 64.

35. Golf Digest Staff, "David Feherty," *Golf Digest* (November, 1992): p. 114.

36. David Barrett, "Major Accomplishment," *Golf Magazine* (August, 1992): p. 92.

37. Greg Norman and George Peper, "Greg Norman's Instant Lessons," *Golf Magazine* (April, 1993): p. 52.

38. Snead and Stump, *The Education of a Golfer*, p. 82.

39. Jack Nicklaus and Ken Bowden, "My Lessons of a Lifetime," *Golf Magazine* (March, 1993): pp. 58-59.

40. Golf Digest Staff, "Fred Couples," p. 115.

41. Snead and Stump, *The Education of a Golfer*, p. 82.

42. Patrick Burke, Personal Communication (July, 1991).

43. Ivan Maisel, "Volcano Under Control," *Golf Magazine* (September, 1992): p. 44.

44. Anne-Marie Palli, Personal Communication (June, 1993).

45. Snead and Stump, *The Education of a Golfer*, p. 96.

46. Nicklaus and Bowden, *Golf My Way*, pp. 98-99.
:

HOMEWORK ***Routine***

The next time you play, observe your preswing, inswing and postswing routines and record these behaviors in the following exercise. When you finish your diary, ask yourself: Do these need to change? If so develop a written plan, practice the changes on the range with every shot you hit. Review your plan before every practice session and record your progress in a diary after each practice.

PRESWING ROUTINE

INSWING ROUTINE

HOMEWORK con't.

POSTSWING ROUTINE

NOTES

Mind Par
9
Mike Shelton

3

FINE TUNING YOUR NERVOUS SYSTEM:

Relaxation vs Arousal

AROUSAL ON THE TOUR

When Sam Snead was breaking into the golf business at the Greenbrier in West Virginia in 1936, the club pro organized a match to introduce Sam to some of the top players in the area. He paired Sam with two former National Amateur Champions, Lawson Little and Johnny Goodman and former US Open champion, Billy Burke. After the other three had teed off on the first hole, Sam describes the following scene:

"Bending over I had to take both hands to tee up my ball. The ball looked all blurred as I stood over it. My nerves were hopping right out of my skin. And then I stepped away and did something I had been practicing. I just let my mind take a rest by not thinking of anything in particular. If I thought of anything, it wasn't the crowd or the match, but sort of a mixture of all the good drives I'd ever made. Some people call it concentration, but to me it's more the trick of not thinking at all or letting the world go by. It's sort of daydreaming about a wonderful place you've been or something happy you've done, but with no details dragged in. In that frame of mind, the ball isn't anything fearful; it's just a thing you're going to hit well. This is something you can teach yourself to do, and I recommend it to all golfers who get the tee jitters. I swung and, upon looking up, heard the crowd gasp and saw my ball rolling down there 25-30 yards past anything else that had been hit. A good 280 yarder."[1]

I would encourage you to review Sam Snead's comment about thinking focused on "... a mixture of all the good drives I'd ever made" when he experienced "tee jitters." If Sam Snead's style during his early days of competition fits you, make a written note of his strategy and read it frequently between rounds and prior to play. Remember, Fred Couples never hits a shot without "calling up" that shot from another time.[2] "BANK" your good shots and call them up as you need them during play.

When you experience anxiety on the first tee, when you play so well you pass your comfort zone, or you look at the scoreboard and find yourself in the hunt, your nervous system begins the equivalent of an electrical storm. The overloaded circuitry of your nervous system has billions of neurons firing, so many that a flood of thoughts becomes part of this firing process and your ability to focus concentration diminishes. These are the times when you stand on the green trying to read a putt and can't stay focused long enough to visualize the line; or as you stand over the putt, you don't remember going through your routine or what you are doing; or as you set up to your tee shot, you just hit the ball without consideration of a target.

Bobby Jones said that many players make the mistake of overcoming their first tee apprehension by assuming indifference. He said: "When you try to keep your heart from pounding or hands from trembling you might get slack or lazy which can be worse than nervous."[3] Interestingly, Jones, like Henry Cotton, had trouble controlling his nervous system and this particular quotation likely reflects this difficulty. By one report, Jones would lose ten to fifteen pounds before a tournament, never ate breakfast or lunch, and only had dinner and a drink after 10 PM.[4]

In 1931 Jones described experiencing so much nausea on the days of competition that he was unable to button his shirt collar or wear a necktie. Similarly, LPGA Tour Player Nancy Lopez said that during her amateur days she would "...throw up in the morning, throw up on the way to the course and throw up at the golf club."[5]

EXCITEMENT AND AROUSAL

Bill Britton finished second in the Williamsburg, Virginia PGA Tour Anheuser-Busch Classic in July 1992. His comments regarding his play are interesting: "I try not to look at the scoreboard during a round, but I looked this time and saw that I was tied for the lead. Well, when I get excited I tend to hook the ball. I hit what was probably the worst shot of the tournament."[6]

The thoughts of the night before a round, the first tee of a big tournament, or seeing your name on the leader board may or may not lead to fear. The situation is "exciting." This excitement produces the same physiological arousal as fear, worry, anxious anticipation, and anger, and can disrupt anything from performance to sleep.

PGA Tour player Johnny Miller says one strategy that works for him and helps him get into a frame of mind to deal with pressure is to say to himself: "I can't wait to hit that shot, or play that round!"[7]

There is an important differentiation between the excitement of anticipation and the "can't wait to get to the tee" feeling of confidence. The arousal of "can't wait to get to the tee" produces a desired focus. Too much excitement can create a high arousal state. You have to learn to walk this fine line.

Tom Kite, winner of the 1992 US Open, and David Feherty, European and PGA Tour player, have both had experiences that taught them not to get too excited with good play, especially early in the round. Recall that Tom Kite holed out a twenty yard pitch shot on the 7th hole the last day of the 1992 US Open at Pebble Beach and kept himself from getting too excited. Tom Kite and David Feherty both say that too much excitement too soon can cause a good round to go south.

Miller Barber won at least one tournament a year while playing the regular PGA Tour from 1967 to 1974. This was matched only by Jack Nicklaus. Barber never won a major (PGA Championship, US OPEN, Masters or British Open) on the regular tour. He said: "I came close a couple of times, but it seems like I got too excited, too charged up mentally. I began to anticipate winning too soon."[8]

Similarly, PGA Tour player Davis Love III won nine times between 1986 and 1995, none of which was a major. He has never been a serious contender at a major. He says: "The secret is not to get too pumped. My game is good enough to win. I just have to go play my game. My problem has been that I don't go out and play golf."[9]

As soon as you put a value on a putt, shot, round, or tournament, you lose your present focus, your thoughts advance to the future, your nervous system accelerates, and concentration skills diminish as your physical movement and swing tempo quicken.

Regarding emotions, Jack Nicklaus said: "My experience is that the higher and lower you let your emotions range over particular golf shots you hit, the higher the total will be when they're all added up. Therefore, another of my mind game basics has been to stay as emotionally level as possible however I was at any given moment...every time I let myself get all juiced up about an approach landing close or a long putt dropping, or pretzled up about a miscue or bad bounce-whammo!-I'd end up getting nervous, and the more nervous I got the more trouble I'd run into. Eventually, with increasing maturity, I managed to find a way to look sufficiently happy about good shots and sad about bad ones without allowing my great internal peaks or valleys..."[10]

THE ORIGINS AND PHYSIOLOGY OF AROUSAL

My personal belief is that we inherit a nervous system style along a continuum of very relaxed to very aroused. This nervous system predisposition is amplified by direct learning experiences and vicarious learning through the adult and peer models we observe from infancy to adulthood.

The branch of our central nervous system that controls our breathing, heart rate, blood pressure, etc. is the autonomic nervous system, also known as the peripheral nervous system. There are two divisions of this part of our nervous system:

1. **Arousal** (Sympathetic Nervous System)

2. **Relaxation** (Parasympathetic Nervous System)

Physical changes occur in the peripheral nervous system as part of the total arousal picture. This part of the nervous system experiences the "fallout" from the brain when we sense danger, become angry, or there is some other threat to our social, emotional, or physical well being. Our brains process this information and produce neurochemicals in response. The following are a few of the physical changes these neurochemicals create:

Increased Heart Rate

Increased Blood Pressure

Slowing Toward Cessation of Digestion

Increased Muscle Tone (Tension)

Increased Breathing Rate

Constriction of Blood Vessels

Increased Blood Sugar Level

Pupil Dilation

Reduced Salivation (Dry Mouth)

Sensory Systems Become "More Alert"

Note that these physical events are produced as a result of our thoughts or perceptions of the environment. These events occur as a chain. If you alter one link, you will affect the other physical states of the chain. For example, if you are aroused and begin breathing slowly and deeply, you will "quiet" the physically aroused state. If your thinking doesn't also change to positive thoughts of calm and control, the aroused physical state will quickly resume.

It is not uncommon to find players who hold their breath during periods of stress. The oxygen starvation from breath holding has a similar effect to the shallow, rapid breathing style. Regardless of whether you are a breath holder or a rapid, shallow breather, the corrective strategy is the same: Breathe deeply and slowly making your exhalation last twice as long as inhalation.

CAUSES OF AROUSAL

What produces arousal? There are four primary producers of arousal:

1. ***Acceleration of thinking to the future***
2. ***Anger***
3. ***Fear***
4. ***Excitement***

1. A **future focus or anticipation** is an **acceleration of thinking to the future.** Both of these behavior styles are learned habits that produce arousal and distraction. When you got in the shower today, you were physically there. However, mentally your thoughts were likely on the events of the day, tomorrow, next week, and so on. Thoughts about the future accelerate the

activity of the nervous system. A sense of urgency, time focus, worry, anticipation, fear, or excitement are all possible characteristics of a future focus. This anticipation usually has mental images that accompany it. When you're late, you can "see" the disgusted look or "hear" the disapproval, and you begin planning your defense or worry about what "they will think."

A future focus on the course is something as simple as calculating score during play. Your thoughts and images take you to the clubhouse before you finish your round. This thinking style can create a loss of concentration and increased arousal.

2. **Anger** and frustration build when we are repeatedly blocked from a goal. A state of arousal accompanies this anger and frustration. A missed shot, performance less than we expect, slow play, a wait in traffic, or an inability to find something misplaced are all examples of situations that can produce frustration or anger.

3. **Fear** is a primary driving force in nervous system arousal. Anything that poses an emotional, social, or physical threat produces a future focus, anxious anticipation, or fear. Fear of judgment or disapproval from others, fear of failure, fear of success, or fear of the unknown are examples of fear driven arousal. Situations that produce fear or anxiety vary from one person to another. Standing on the first tee with three groups waiting to play and watching, playing your first tournament, playing with certain people, or attempting a shot out of or over a hazard, all can produce fear driven arousal.

4. Many players get **excited** when they are playing well, especially when they play through their comfort zone. Unless you control excitement, your nervous system will gradually evolve to an arousal state that will hinder performance. That's why tour players consciously avoid getting too excited too early in a round. PGA Tour players Tom Kite and David Feherty both describe the importance of controlling emotions during play. Recall that Tom Kite said he wanted to "jump in the air" after holing a pitch shot on the 7th hole of the 1992 US Open. He said he didn't because he still had eleven holes to play.

Arousal levels are very individual. Many of you take an aroused state to the golf course. Your arousal may be a personal style taken from our high stress, fast paced society. Deadlines, a constant focus and anticipation about future, concern with things that need to be done, or thoughts of what others are thinking about you are a few examples. Others of you have a frequent feeling of urgency and concern for time. You set your watch ahead, as well as your thoughts. You flush the toilet before you have finished urinating. You are in a hurry and on your way to the next life event, perhaps running your hands under the faucet as you pass the sink.

ON-COURSE

A state of physical arousal evolves on the course when you think about how others might judge your performance. Physical arousal is also produced by that three foot putt for the lowest score you have ever recorded, playing with people you perceive to be slow, or when you feel pushed by the group behind you. The out-of-bounds markers and hazards, especially when they are looming in front of your next shot, or noting you are well below your usual score after nine holes can also alter that balanced, internal physical state of comfort and relaxation.

Have you ever noticed how easy it is to practice on the range with people talking while you're hitting? What about the secluded 8th tee? When someone moves or makes a noise, why is that so distracting? You are aroused because of what you are telling yourself about the situation.

When you stand on the first tee of a tournament with a gallery of twenty people watching you hit, when you have a water hazard or large bunker to hit over, these conditions trigger or "cue" thought routines. You have a choice at this point, a choice most players don't know they have. If you are like Sam Snead or Fred Couples, you breathe deeply, relieve all the tension from your body, and begin to focus on a time when you hit the shot you are about to play successfully. You have confidence.

If you are like most players, the gallery of twenty produces a distraction from the shot you are hitting to thoughts of their judgment of your performance. If you have had recent problems out of bunkers or over hazards, a distraction of thoughts and images of those "failed shots" intrudes and your confidence deteriorates.

Jack Nicklaus says: "You can overcome the 'get-it-over-with, can't-stand-the-suspense' syndrome by consciously slowing down. Step back and take a deep breath or two or three while focusing your mind exclusively on the various practical factors-distance, lie, ground conditions, wind, hazards, etc.-that you must evaluate to decide your best course of action. Don't even take a club from your bag until you've done this clearly and conclusively."[11]

When you walk on the first tee, you carry the events of the day and the associated physiological state with you. Your physiology can affect your performance on the course, positively or negatively. When you relax, this state will positively affect performance. If you are tense or aroused, your performance will deteriorate in direct relationship to your level of arousal.

If you practice on the range by hitting one ball after another without stopping between shots to go through your routine, your swing tempo will gradually increase as you continue to practice. Your performance will deteriorate with this faster tempo. Go through your entire routine on each shot. Hit shorter clubs to get a feeling of the tempo. Slow and quiet your movement as you do. Leave the range and go to the putting green if this doesn't work.

What happens when you arrive at the practice range or course running late? Do you rush? If so, arousal will result. I have a playing partner who often is putting on his shoes on the first tee. He is always late, no matter where he goes, and his focus is in the future. It takes nine holes for him to mentally join us. Then he asks why he plays better on the back nine than on the front.

OFF-COURSE

Most of us stay mentally in the future when at home as we shower and dress, in our car, with our children, at work, and on the golf course. When our thoughts accelerate to the future, our nervous system accelerates. We become increasingly aroused. Thus, most of us undergo constant arousal as part of our daily routine.

An aroused state creates a condition of vigilance. This vigilance produces a continuous scanning of the environment. Concentration tends to be short. The internal agitation (arousal) of the nervous system results in a lowered frustration tolerance, irritability, distractibility, and quickened movement. If this state exists off the course, it will be with you on the course.

An off-course state of high arousal can disturb sleep. These difficulties usually are expressed as problems falling asleep or a restless night. Your awake periods are spent intermittently looking at the clock and mentally calculating how many hours of sleep you can get if you can "just fall asleep now." This mental calculation is as disruptive for sleep as mentally calculating your score during your round is for play.

Learning to slow down, developing a moment to moment focus, and applying the breathing and cognitive therapy procedures outlined in this book will not only benefit your performance on the course, but also your performance, health, and mood off of the course. I have successfully used these same strategies for years in treating a variety of physical disorders from migraine headaches and nausea associated with chemotherapy, to irritable bowel syndrome, panic and sleep disorders.

I also mentioned mood. How can this arousal state affect mood? When we are late for an appointment, we begin to rush. It is at these times, when concentration lapses, that we spill or break things or make mistakes on simple tasks or have close calls or accidents. Why? Arousal. We are future focused. We leave the moment. We don't concentrate. What happens at these times? Our IQ goes up. That doesn't mean you get smarter. Here, IQ means irritability quotient. Have you ever noticed how irritable you become at times like this? How short-tempered you can be? How your tolerance to frustration is lowered? How things you usually ignore become major irritants? All because of arousal? You bet. The irritability we experience internally as increased nervous system arousal is externalized as short-tempered irritability.

Thoughts can produce an internal state of tension. A phone call, a letter, a picture, or a song may serve as a "cue" to focus on a problem. The physiological changes these thoughts produce can cause your heart to race, your blood pressure to rise, muscles to tense, breathing rate to accelerate, and so on, as a generalized state of arousal. If this state goes uncorrected, it will be carried to the course or to bed. On the course, your golf performance will deteriorate. In bed, your sleep and sexual performance deteriorates. Practice the relaxation and thinking strategies in this book and you can improve everything from golf to sleep performance. And, oh yes, even sexual performance.

OTHER CAUSES

It isn't just the conditions of play, or pressures from work, or family or social situations that will produce this state of arousal. Diet and personality type may predispose you to excessive nervous system arousal that will impede your performance. The following is a list of some of these other factors that can affect arousal.

- ***Diet***
- ***Caffeine***
- ***Breathing Rate***
- ***Off-course stress: work, home, internally created.***
- ***Personality style***

As I already noted, the nervous system's electrical storm associated with arousal causes an acceleration of physiology and movement and swing tempo, all creating a deterioration in physical and mental performance.

Numerous physical problems like peptic ulcers, colitis, indigestion, migraine, and many other conditions are triggered by an internally aroused state over a prolonged period. Similarly, some people, even seasoned tour players, experience a restless sleep the night before a tournament due to an aroused state from anticipation. When anxiety is extreme, it is not uncommon for a person to experience nausea, constipation, diarrhea, or some other organ system involvement.

As mentioned, Bobby Jones reportedly lost between ten and fifteen pounds every time he played in a tournament. "He only had one meal a day and ate that one at 10 PM after he'd had a few drinks and had mellowed. He couldn't keep breakfast or lunch down."[12]

Henry Cotton and Nancy Lopez were also known for their stomach problems, and associated nausea and vomiting. Nancy experienced her difficulties during her amateur years.[13] Like Bobby Jones, Cotton's ability would place him in a dominating position only to slide in the final round. In the 1931 British Open at Carnoustie, Cotton was ahead after three rounds only to shoot a 79 on the last day. In the 1933 British Open at St. Andrews, he again shot a 79 in the final round to finish three strokes behind the winner, Denny Shute. Cotton's stomach problems would often accompany the final round decay. He would reportedly vomit just prior to the round.[14]

Future Focus

People who focus on the future tend to be anxious. Most of us live mentally in the future the majority of the time. What do you think about during your morning shower? Do you think about the soothing quality of the water or are you thinking about the afternoon, the next day, next month, and so on? This type of future focus is arousing. If your thoughts accelerate to the future off of the course, these mental habits will be with you on the course.

Remember, when top players play their best rounds, they report a one-shot-at-a-time, one hundred percent focus in the present, only on the shot they are playing. Your thoughts on the course that reflect a future focus may be on score and what you have to do to "get it back;" what you will have to shoot on the back side to improve your round; the difficult shot on the next hole; or something pending that doesn't even pertain to your round of golf.

AROUSAL AND CONTROL

So, what is arousal? We know the neurochemistry, the physiological changes that occur, and the impact it has on our health and performance. The signs of arousal and the stress response are the same. This high arousal state is stress. How do we recognize it?

One form of stress or high arousal is easy to recognize. Simply stated, it is a loss of control. Any situation in which you don't "perceive" yourself one hundred percent in control is a stressor and the physical changes described will occur. Consider the following examples:

1. You are playing with players better than you. You hit a shot out of one greenside bunker over the green into another bunker. Your next shot also flies the green. You notice your shoulders tighten as you hurry to your ball wondering what the others are thinking about your performance. Who is in control?

2. You realize that the group playing behind you is waiting on your group after every shot. You find yourself rushing and thinking about the group behind during your shots. Who is in control?

3. You enter a room with a group of people. You think about the judgment of others regarding your appearance, presentation, etc. Who is in control?

4. You are playing a tournament round and begin to wonder what the cut will be. Who or what is in control?

5. You are playing in a professional event. You begin to think about where you must finish to be eligible to play in the next event. Who or what is in control?

6. You are approaching the last couple of tournaments of the year. You find yourself thinking about how much you will need on the money list to retain your exempt status on tour. Who or what is in control?

7. You have a talk planned to a group and your thought focus is on what people will think of your presentation? Who is in control?

8. Someone asks you for assistance or your boss requests that you do extra work. You don't want to but you worry about what they might think or do if you decline. Who is in control?

9. Any situation you avoid for reasons of conflict, judgment, loss of love, etc. is not in your control. Who is in control?

In any situation in which your behavior occurs for others, out of fear, or concern for future consequences, you are not in control.

10. Habits of rushing, urgency, a focus on "time" and "living" mentally in the future or past are a loss of control.

11. Any situation in which you lack confidence, in which you don't believe in your ability to perform well, is a loss of control.

12. How many things can "go wrong" in the morning or how many red lights does it take when you are running late, or how many bad shots can you hit before you become frustrated, angry, and so on. How does this state affect your performance? Who or what is in control?

13. Many of us are taught during our childhood to be aware and concerned about "what the neighbors will think!" The concern for judgment of others is indoctrinated at an early age. Our clothing styles are a clear illustration of our level of social "self" consciousness. Who's in control?

RESULTS OF AROUSAL

PGA Tour player Johnny Miller says he enjoyed playing with a tournament leader and watching how he would handle the pressure. Miller describes two types of players. The first player he describes as the fear of failure type. He notes that this player "changes his playing routine, usually rushes more, takes fewer waggles, and starts blaming his equipment or the course." He describes the other player as just the opposite. He notes the other player anticipates success and you can tell: "He couldn't wait for the opportunity to succeed. People like him get a look in their eye. Raymond Floyd is one. When he's focused, he looks like he stuck his finger into a light socket."[15]

Tour player David Feherty further states that: "The guys who win all the money are the ones who control blind panic."[16] He describes coming down to the final holes of a tournament, "...in the lead by a shot with my backside the size of a shirt button."[17]

Nervous anticipation produces an arousal level in most people that creates a flood of undesired sensory information to the brain. This information processing is so rapid that concentration for more than a brief moment is difficult before intrusive thoughts override your thought focus with new content, usually unrelated to the moment.

Many people with this style of nervous anticipation have a fear of embarrassment and concern for what others will think or, at the very least, a period of anticipation of what's to come. Things begin to occur in your body related to your thought patterns. A mood state of irritability and nervousness, and a lowered frustration tolerance and anger are often part of this process. Other players get excited about how well they are playing, and thoughts of score and a great finish take them mentally to holes ahead or even to the end of the round.

When some players aren't putting well, there is pressure to hit it close to the hole.

We all become nervous at times. Each of us shows pressure differently. These telltale signs are followed by a change in tempo, a breakdown in the preswing routine, a lowered frustration tolerance or similar, quickened movement around the ball, or similar indications of an aroused nervous system.

The Performance Consequences of Arousal

Johnny Miller described the effects of arousal as he perceived them. He says the first step toward dealing with pressure is to admit you get tight under pressure, then recognize how it manifests itself. He states that the arousal produced by pressure "heightens your awareness; your brain gets knocked up a notch or two; it speeds up...and the way you process data is messed up. You've got all this information coming to you real fast, and you're not used to it, so you get confused. You have to take deep breaths to slow your heartbeat; or sing a slow song or walk more slowly. I've done all those things...I've likened pressure to tuning in a radio...Get too excited, tell yourself you want it badly, and it's static time. You can't let the moment overwhelm you and hold you captive."[18]

Let's look at a hypothetical situation of the first tee at a major tournament and the thoughts that could trigger the fight or flight mechanism, create a flood of intrusive thoughts, and take you out of your mental routine and the moment.

The sequence of events that evolves in this situation may be something like the following. First, the situation or "event" of the first tee "cues" or triggers one or more thoughts. Physical and emotional changes result from this thinking. The consequence of physical arousal is poor performance due to diminished concentration, muscle tension, quickened swing tempo, tremor, decreased confidence, mechanics focus, and so on.

EVENT  **INTERPRETATION**  **PHYSICAL/MOOD CHANGES**

[First tee

Gallery of 20

Tournament Play]

[Alarm Thought Chain]

[Fear/Nervousness/ Irritability/ Excitement]

1. *If I can just get this hole out of the way!*
2. *I was pushing my driver right on the range.*
3. *There's trouble right.*
4. *Just don't hit it right!*
5. *As long as I don't get my swing started outside, I'll be OK.*
6. *Maybe my stance has been open.*
7. *No, I feel a little discon-nected.*
8. *What are these people going to think.*
9. *It's embarrassing when I hit a bad shot.*

1. Increased Heart Rate
2. Increased Breathing Rate
3. Decreased Peripheral Blood Flow
4. Increased Muscle Tension
5. Slowing or Ceasesation of Digestion (increased gas and/or dry mouth)
6. Increased Blood Pressure
7. Hormonal/Neurochemical Changes
8. Flood of Intrusive, Negative Thoughts
9. Impaired Judgment

NET RESULT OF HIGH AROUSAL STATE

- ***BODY PHYSICALLY MOBILIZES FOR ACTION***
- ***SWING TEMPO AND OTHER PHYSICAL MOVE-MENT QUICKENS***
- ***ABILITY TO CONCENTRATE DIMINISHES***
- ***PERFORMANCE DETERIORATES***
- ***DECREASED CONFIDENCE***
- ***MECHANICS FOCUS***
- ***AND THE CYCLE REPEATS***

This example shows a chain of events that begins with the first tee of a tournament. These conditions produce a state of high arousal. This arousal state likely began one to several days before the tournament through anticipation and visual images associated with the day. At the very least, the arousal began on the practice range when problems hitting the driver occurred.

As a psychologist, teaching professional, and player, I believe that too much physical arousal and the associated tension are the greatest obstacles of the golf swing. Obviously, the exceptions are those few under-aroused players for whom arousal increases their focus and improves performance.

Johnny Miller intuitively recognized that excessive physical arousal creates increased muscle tension and changes in the nervous system that result in everything from a quickened swing pace to disrupted concentration.

Regardless of the cause, the vigilance and internal acceleration created by this aroused physical state cause changes in your nervous system that impede optimum performance. First, these changes produce an overload of sensory information as your brain gathers content from the environment in preparation for action. This flood of information interferes with concentration and the desired present focus, two mental states necessary for peak performance.

In turn, as your nervous system accelerates, physical movement quickens. Performance suffers with a faster than normal swing tempo, and timing and balance are compromised.

Let's review: Some event cues a thought pattern which results in an "alarm" that triggers emotional and physical changes. These physical changes include:

Increased heart rate.

Increased respiration or breath holding

Increased muscle tension.

When we experience negative anticipation, fear, alarm, or anger, our bodies mobilize for action. This mobilization is the "fight or flight mechanism." When primitive man saw danger on the horizon, an internal "alarm" went off and his body mobilized in preparation to either stand and fight, or flee the situation. This internal alarm is cued by thoughts of anger, pending danger or fear, resulting in both physiological and mood changes.

Much has changed since the days of primitive man. However, the physiological mechanism of fight or flight has not. Sam Snead experienced this physical mobilization on the first tee in 1936 when he had to use both hands to tee up his ball and he had trouble focusing his vision.

Obviously, when the alarm response occurs, the subsequent physical changes don't help performance. The muscle tension alone can create swing changes that result in poor performance. This sets off a cycle of tension, frustration, anger or anxiety, and repeat poor performance.

The most obvious change in your swing is tempo. The pace of your swing quickens as the pace of your internal physiology quickens. Your overall movement on the course quickens. The faster swing tempo magnifies swing errors, and your performance deteriorates as the entire process cycles.

When some off-course event sets off the alarm response, like a home or work situation, or being late for a tee time, performance is affected in the same way. For example, a pattern of rushing, a sense of urgency, or worry produces physical changes of muscle tension, breath holding, etc., which will result in an impaired swing when carried to the course.

Many people believe that the golf course is their place of relaxation. The course may help to refocus your attention away from troubling or distressing thoughts. However, your habitual physical patterns, once established as a daily routine, don't quiet during a four or five hour round of golf. Swing pace, speed of speech, and walking pace are good indicators of how internally "revved up" someone is.

UNDER AROUSAL AND PERFORMANCE

There is a population of people who are just the opposite. For these few players, their biggest problem is being under-aroused. These under-aroused players are usually the Tour players who need assistance with concentration skills to increase their ability to focus more on the present and shot at hand. These players need arousal induction, especially in the area of learning to focus concentration.

These under-aroused players perform best when their level of arousal increases. If you are unhurried, not focused on time, have few if any concerns of being late, or if you feel more focused and performance improves during periods of what you perceive as anxiety and high arousal, you may be one of the few fortunate under-aroused.

John Adams tied the Dubsdread course record in 1993 in the third round of the PGA Tour Western Open with a 63. He recorded seven birdies and an eagle. He described picking up his pace during putting as the turning point: "I hadn't made a putt for two days so today I decided to speed up my pace [on the greens]. I just kept rolling them in." The right pace is not always a slow pace, especially for the under-aroused.[19]

One of the first professionals I worked with years ago played on the United States LPGA and Japanese LPGA Tours. She described an inability to perform well when she had a routine 6 or 7 iron to the green. "But," she quickly added, "put me behind a tree and watch me play!" She was what we call "laid back." She appeared very relaxed and unshakable.

You could see it in her deliberate pace and hear it in her voice. She was "laid back;" however, she wasn't focused. That routine 6 or 7 iron was just that: it was routine. The difficult shots from behind a tree required creative thoughts, and a discussion with herself and her caddie about what she was going to do with the shot.

She used the same procedures for the routine shots that she used for the more difficult shots around and over obstacles. She would stand behind the routine fairway shots, describe to herself and her caddie the shot she was going to hit, go through her routine with that focus, and hit it. For example, she would check the wind, her lie, the terrain, and her target. Then she would identify the landing area on the green, taking several deep breaths during this process, and say something to the effect of: "I'm going to start this ball out at the right edge of the top branch on that large oak tree and draw it into my target, watch it bounce twice, and roll in the hole."

Whether you are relaxed and under-aroused or fast moving and over-aroused, the same principles apply. The under-aroused player is definitely in the minority. I recently did a playing workshop for the PGA of America where there were fifty club professionals and former PGA Tour players in attendance. After an extensive introduction regarding the physiology and characteristics of over and under-aroused players, I asked for a show of hands of those individuals who would categorize themselves as under-aroused or perceived themselves as needing to "get up" to play well. Not one person raised his hand.

The majority of players are over-aroused both on and off the course. These over-aroused players have to tone down their nervous system to reach an optimum level of arousal so they can focus.

As already discussed, a cascade of events occurs with nervous system arousal. If the nervous system is naturally under-aroused, this cascade of events moves the person closer to optimum arousal for performance. If our normal level of arousal is moderate to high, minor increases in arousal or anxiety cause a flood of thoughts to begin. Movement quickens, breathing and heart rate accelerate, frustration tolerance is lowered, and the ability to focus a singular thought on one event diminishes.

I was working with a player on the putting green one day after several prior discussions regarding his low arousal. We were discussing conditions under which he experienced increased focus and improved imagery, especially during putting. He said when he experienced more anxiety, he got more focused. My first thought was: "That makes no sense," especially with what I know about the way the nervous system works. I know that anxiety tends to impair singular, concentrated focus and produces a "hair trigger" for distraction. Then I began to wonder if he was talking about the same anxiety I was. After continued discussion, I realized we weren't. This is a guy who calls and doesn't seem to ever be in a hurry to get off the phone. When he has a plane to catch, no worry; if he misses the flight there is always another one.

These same players can be pushed to the point of too much arousal under conditions of extreme pressure. Place them in contention to win a tournament, let them know where they are on the leader board, and arousal kicks in. This is the time they need to quiet their nervous system and work toward an internal balance as they walk the tight rope of arousal while sustaining peak performance.

PERFORMANCE MODEL OF AROUSAL

The stress response creates an internal state of arousal. This aroused state relates directly to performance. Research shows too much or too little arousal affects performance. Optimum arousal levels produce optimum performance levels, so researchers say.

Earlier in this chapter, I addressed the irritable mood often associated with arousal. This same arousal state can impede performance. What happens to your performance when you are running late or thinking about things other than what you are doing? What happens to your thinking when you are rushing? Do you feel physically aroused? Is this the time you spill or break something, or injure yourself, or almost have an accident in your car? Is your thinking in the present or in the future? What happens to your social or physical performance when you worry about what others are thinking?

These questions imply that there are a number of different kinds of arousal: the mental states of concentration, images and thoughts, and the physical signs I've reviewed. The role each of these plays in performance is highly individual, although related in a chain of internal events.

High Arousal Characteristics

How do you know whether you have a high arousal or low arousal personality style? The following are a few of the indicators of the "highly aroused" person. These indicators are not an all or none situation. They occur along a continuum, depending on the degree of arousal.

1. ***Acceleration in thought (short concentration span).***
2. ***Quickened movement and tendency to rush.***
3. ***Breathing rate that exceeds five complete breaths in a thirty second period (unless you hold your breath at times of stress).***
4. ***Fist clenched.***
5. ***Neck and shoulder tension.***
6. ***Tendency to spill, break, or forget things.***
7. **Easily startled.**
8. **Easily frustrated and a tendency to be irritable.**
9. ***Time oriented, purposely sets watch ahead and frequently checks clock or watch.***
10. ***Rapid speech.***
11. ***Easily distracted.***
12. ***Impatient.***
13. ***Thoughts are future focused.***
14. **Sense of urgency.**
15. ***Difficulty falling asleep.***
16. ***Concerned regarding the judgment of others.***
17. ***When experiencing high arousal, judgment is impaired and performance deteriorates.***

In older years:

18. ***Tendency to have minor accidents.***
19. ***Physical complaints: headaches, nausea, shoulder and neck tension, and bouts with minor illnesses within one or more "target organ" systems.***

Low Arousal Characteristics

The characteristics of the low aroused person are just the opposite of the highly aroused. A few of the low arousal characteristics are listed as follows:

1. ***"Easy going." Don't just look "easy going" as some of us do; seldom aroused internally.***
2. ***Not worriers.***
3. ***No urgency in life; always have time to talk.***
4. ***Not governed by the clock: "So I miss my flight;there will be another one."***
5. ***Great tolerance to frustration; more patience than the average person.***
6. ***Slower, deliberate movement and speech reflect an under-aroused nervous system.***
7. ***The under-aroused player must get mentally aroused to focus clearly in order to perform at his peak.***
8. ***Breathing rate in thirty seconds is five or less.***
9. ***Relaxed, "laid back" posture.***
10. ***They enjoy life in the present.***
11. ***No difficulty falling asleep.***
12. ***They talk and move more slowly than others.***
13. ***Noise and distractions will have little impact on the low aroused players.***
14. ***They are not easily startled.***

The under-aroused player can fall victim to the negative effects of too much arousal, especially in times of close competition in the final round or last few holes. At these times, they can use arousal reduction and focus techniques to end a tournament.

PERFORMANCE AND HIGH AROUSAL

Just because players have a tendency to be over-aroused doesn't mean they can't play well. It's a matter of diagnosing nervous system style, then teaching strategies to control arousal for improved performance. Remember, all peak performers report the same internal state when they perform their best. They don't all use the same strategies to get to that state. Some need to increase arousal to get more focused, while some need to quiet their nervous system to reduce arousal.

PGA and Australian Tours player Patrick Burke is a good example of the over-aroused player. According to Patrick, the majority of the tour players fit his nervous system style. Patrick has one of the nicest golf swings I have ever seen. I've heard other PGA Tour players and television analysts make similar comments. Swinging and playing are two different things. Patrick and I have spent a good bit of time working on strategies for him to think and move that would quiet his nervous system while remaining mentally focused.

Both the under-aroused and highly aroused personality styles are part of the nervous system's anatomical neuronal network and neurochemical makeup. Therefore, to change your nervous system's "programmed responses," you will need to practice the prescribed daily changes over several weeks, and in a variety of low to high stress conditions. Repeated exposure to a variety of situations is necessary before learning "encodes" anatomically and neurochemically. This encoding process evolves as behavior occurs across many levels of low and high arousal situations. These experiences will bring gradual success in arousal management and performance. It's like climbing a ladder one rung at a time.

Johnny Miller describes this process as follows: "Everyone has his own choking level, a level at which he fails to play his normal golf. As you get more experienced, your choking level rises."[20]

You will experience changes in your performance dependent upon the conditions in which you play. Your level of arousal will change from a casual round to a tournament round to playing partners. For example, how would playing with an LPGA or PGA Tour player affect your arousal levels?

Rookie tour players tend to struggle to make the cut and experience arousal. Once they have a little success, their first major is the cue for arousal. The final rung, for those who make it that far, is qualifying for and playing as a member of the Ryder Cup team.

PGA Tour player Steve Pate needed a top ten finish in the 1991 PGA Championship at Crooked Stick to qualify for the Ryder Cup team. Pate needed a par on the last hole to finish in the top ten. He made the par and the team. Mark Wiebe described the conversation he had with Pate after that round: "I was so happy for him because we hang out together. He [Pate] said, 'Man, I was choking my butt off.' It wasn't because it was the PGA Championship. It could've been Hattiesburg [A PGA Tour event formerly played the same week as the Masters]. It's because the Ryder Cup is just about the ultimate in golf."[21]

European and PGA Tour player David Feherty says everyone who has success has choked. "Absolutely everyone has done it..." He further states: "It's not what happens to you that matters in the long run. It's your attitude. That's what determines how you cope with the next experience that comes along...Quite often it's how you deal with failure that determines how you achieve success...The mental process is like building a muscle. It's not letting your whole framework of thinking fall down around you. It's having the resolve and mental toughness to take it on the chin, keep your head up, and feel good about yourself for having done that. You can either feel bad because you failed or good because of your positive reactions to it. That will give you the armor to cope with it the next time."[22]

AROUSAL REDUCTION FOR IMPROVED PERFORMANCE

As already noted, during a physically aroused state, your brain increases the sensory information it processes in the event of crisis. This overload blocks the ability to focus for any period on a singular event. Nervous system activities, like visualization, are hard to capture during an aroused state.

To overcome this aroused state, apply the relaxation techniques you are going to learn. Your concentration will improve, you will feel more relaxed, confident, and in control. Producing a state of relaxation assists in quieting the sensory overload to the brain and sets the stage for selective information processing for a focus in the present. On the golf course, this is a one-shot-at-a-time focus. There is no consideration of score, what others are thinking, the hazards of the course, home, work, or anything else other than the shot at hand and your target. Eastern practitioners of meditation call this present focus "mindfulness."

Have you ever stood behind your ball on the putting green reading a putt, trying to find the line or path your ball is going to take to the hole, or attempting to get a sense of the feeling of the stroke without success? The next time this happens, begin breathing deeply, step away from the ball, quiet your movement, resume your routine, and become mindful as you continue breathing deeply. You will find that this strategy will clear your focus, increase your ability to visualize, and relax you.

Have you ever stood over a putt distracted and suddenly realized where you are as you are ready to make your stroke? You find yourself wondering where the line is because you lost your concentration, and you were just going through the motions behind the ball. The difference between the tour player and the amateur in this situation is that the tour player describes stepping away from the ball as he gathers his concentration and reads the putt again. The amateur says: "I just go ahead and stroke it, and hope it gets close." I'm sure you can relate to this in the full swing as well. The correction of this is obvious. Step off the ball, become mindful, and start your routine over.

AROUSAL REDUCTION STRATEGIES

Some sport psychologists refer to low arousal training as a "band-aid approach." I agree, if the singular goal is to teach someone to quiet his nervous system without consideration of focused concentration, visualization, movement, confidence, routine, and a plan for management of emotions as well.

I have presented nine strategies for arousal reduction on the following pages, and I have provided the mechanism and rationale for each. These strategies are:

1. Breathing
2. Movement
3. Focused Thought: Mindfulness
4. Visualization
5. Routine
6. Stretching
7. Posture
8. Biofeedback
9. Confidence

BREATHING

Our breathing style and frequency directly affect our performance and quality of life. A relaxed person breathes deeply and slowly. A person who is tense, anxious, and aroused breathes in a rapid, shallow fashion or he has periods of breath holding.

PGA Tour player and former US Open

champion Curtis Strange says: "Under pressure, one of the most important things I have to remember to do is breathe."[23]

Tour players who use deep breathing during pressure situations include Tom Watson, Paul Azinger, Mike Reid, Helen Alfredson,[24] Johnny Miller,[25] Dennis Paulson[26], Patrick Burke[27], Jan Stephenson[28], Marta Figueras-Dotti[29], Jennifer Wyatt[30], Laurie Rinker[31], and Anne Marie Palli,[32] to mention a few.

Some players, like Fuzzy Zoeller and Jerry Heard, are well known for whistling during a round.[33] Have you ever tried to whistle without taking a deep breath? Whistling perpetuates deep breathing, and thus, helps sustain relaxation. Let's look at why breathing produces relaxation.

The physiological events that make up the aroused state occur as a chain, as all internal and external behaviors do. You can learn to quiet this chain of arousal by controlling one of the links, breathing. Learning deep diaphragmatic breathing is essential to relaxation and improved performance. This breathing instruction is provided in an audio tape from the *MIND UNDER PAR* series™ *Routine: Guided Practice in Developing Consistent Performance.*

If you alter or remove a link in any chain, the rest of the chain changes in some way. When you experience arousal and the associated signs of increases in heart rate, blood pressure and so on, diaphragmatic breathing will quiet these and the other links in the arousal chain. When you use this deep breathing procedure, it is important to remember that your exhalation should last twice as long as your inhalation.

Place one hand on your chest and one hand on your stomach. Now take a deep breath. What expanded most, your stomach or your chest? Your stomach will expand most with proper deep diaphragmatic breathing. The abdominal contents push downward on the diaphragm, causing the stomach to expand. Chest expansion alone with breathing points to shallow breathing.

As you exhale, find areas of tension throughout your body and relax them. Start with your forehead and scan your body in your mind looking for tension. Scan from your forehead, to neck, shoulders, chest, back, arms, buttocks, legs, and feet. This procedure is called a "Body Scan." Scan your body for tension and relax through deep breathing during any work, play, or social activity.

As you use these breathing and body scan procedures, your nervous system will calm, and you will be able to maintain clearer mental images of target and produce greater total body relaxation.

The physical changes associated with acceleration of your nervous system reverse when you practice relaxation strategies like diaphragmatic breathing. Blood flow resumes in the periphery, your hands warm, muscles relax, breathing returns to a "normal" rate, digestion resumes, and so on. However, unless thinking remains calm, confident, and positive, the arousal state of the accelerated nervous system will return, resulting in a resumption of the physical signs of "fight or flight." Strategies for restructuring intrusive thoughts and staying focused in the present appear in later chapters.

How can you tell if you are relaxed or aroused? Once you get used to an aroused state, it becomes your reference for relaxation. You can determine just how aroused you are by counting your breaths for a thirty second period. One full breath (inhalation and exhalation) is a count of "one." Try not to alter your breathing rate or the quality of your breathing as you count. A relaxed breath count is three to five in a thirty second period. Anything above five suggests an aroused nervous system. If you are aroused, your breath count will be high. The greater the level of your arousal, the higher your breath count will be.

If you are going to impact upon your level of arousal, you will need to practice deep diaphragmatic breathing and body scans sixty to seventy times per day. Every time you hear a phone ring, walk through doorways, and apply the brakes in your car, take a deep diaphragmatic breath. Use deep diaphragmatic breathing in your practice and play. As you walk between shots, when you walk on and off greens, when you mark your ball, when you are behind the ball as part of your preswing routine, just before you stroke your putt, as you walk on and off the tee, and when you pull a club from your bag, take a deep diaphragmatic breath.

Take a deep breath and hold it. Notice the tension in your chest, shoulders and neck. Can you imagine trying to putt or swing a club while holding your breath? Many players unknowingly do. For putting, you should be starting your stroke as you complete your exhalation. Your shoulders drop with relaxation as you exhale. In your full swing, you should be approaching the end of exhalation of a deep diaphragmatic breath as you begin to move the club away in your backswing. You should feel a relaxed heaviness in your upper body as you do.

If, however, you focus on your breathing during a putting stroke or swing, poor performance will follow. Thoughts of breathing or related mental strategies are as bad as a mechanics focus during your swing. Just think of the mental strategies as mental mechanics. As noted, you need to practice these skills off the course and on the range, until they become automatic and occur in all settings without conscious thought.

Breath holding is common in conditions such as high winds and extreme tension. Try breathing as you hold your head out the window of a car going thirty miles per hour. Your breathing will be shallow or you will hold your breath. Breath holding reduces the supply of oxygen to muscles, causing increased tension and quickness in movement. The first place the quickness will likely show up is in your putting stroke, then the full swing. Tour players will tell you that playing in the wind will result in a shorter, faster swing. When playing in the wind, turn your back to the breeze, breathe deeply, and stay relaxed.

PGA Tour player Dennis Paulson experienced this breath holding phenomenon while playing in thirty to forty mile per hour winds at the 1994 AT&T at Pebble Beach. He had ingrained a deep breath in his routine. This was especially important in his putting. In the high winds at Pebble Beach on Saturday, he began to unknowingly hold his breath. He struggled with his putting the entire round. After the round, he corrected his breathing and on Sunday began to putt with deep breathing and relaxation, and once again he began to roll the ball well on the greens.[34]

As I noted, the audio tapes in the *MIND UNDER PAR* series™ *Routine: Guided Practice in Developing Consistent*

Performance provide instruction in various relaxation and focus strategies, including preplay and on-course strategies.

There are a number of other strategies you can do with breathing that will quiet arousal and promote improved performance. Diaphragmatic breathing is one of the oldest used in both clinical and performance conditions. Slowing down your movement, while focusing on the activity you are doing, is another one of these strategies.

MOVEMENT

Advice to a Tour Player: Quiet Your Movement

In June of 1974, the US Open was at Winged Foot Country Club in New York. Tom Watson was leading after three rounds. On Sunday in the final round, he shot a 79. Byron Nelson, in analyzing Watson's Sunday performance, told him his swing was too fast and jerky-indicating that's why his performance deteriorated and he shot the high score.

I'm sure you can imagine what the level of arousal must be for a PGA player who is leading a major after three rounds, looking for his first tournament win, as Watson was, while still trying to remain focused and relaxed.

Byron Nelson went on to explain that he felt Watson had one fault: he was too smart and his mind was too active. Tom Watson does everything quickly. Nelson continued that, due to this quickness in his off-course personality, he would always swing fast. He needed to learn to control the increased quickness produced by the arousal of competition, especially under pressure.

"To help him slow down his swing, Byron Nelson taught Tom Watson to move more deliberately as he set up to his shots. By shuffling his feet into his stance at a slower speed, and feeling the slow waggle of the club before his take away, he ingrained a more fluid feeling into his swing." Tom Watson said the most important lesson he learned from Byron Nelson was tempo.[35]

Watson says: "My rhythm is better now than it has ever been. I've learned that rhythm is the basic factor why people play well or badly. Under pressure, your rhythm gets faster. It is hard not to swing a little bit faster or think a little bit faster when you are under pressure."[36]

How many tournaments are won on the last nine holes where the leader is overtaken? I would suggest that a good percentage of these wins result from the leader losing a moment to moment, one-stroke-at-a-time focus, and quickened swing pace and movement as he comes down the stretch due to arousal produced by the thoughts of score or position.

Your golf game is no different. If you know how you and top athletes feel and behave when experiencing peak performance, you can strive to facilitate this state. You can correct a high arousal state by practicing the relaxation and concentration strategies you will learn in this book.

The faster paced swing produced under pressure is usually self-diagnosed as a swing flaw. Faster than your "ideal tempo" will produce swing flaws. That is not to suggest, however, that all swing flaws result from poor tempo.

Jack Nicklaus says: "The more you hurry in golf, the worse you probably will play, which leads to even heavier pressure and greater tension."[37] The other side of this discussion is Nick Price who is known to have a fast swing. Price says: "Being really slow under pressure can be just as bad as being really quick. Just don't go against what you normally do."[38] The key is to recognize that pressure results in quickened movement and tempo. That's a difficult thing to feel during play. A feeling of slowing down will bring you back to your best performance zone. Some of you naturally swing too quickly. Slow down for improved performance.

Jack Nicklaus notes that "first tee nerves" have the potential to ruin an entire round, especially if these nerves spill into the first swing and you play the first hole poorly. He doesn't describe it as such, but Nicklaus recognizes that an aroused nervous system produces a faster tempo. His strategy is to see the swing he is about to make on the first tee in his mind's eye "almost as if it's happening in slow motion...with no effort to force the shot in any way." He further notes that this strategy will often produce the best drive of the round.[39]

Some tour players have intuitively developed their own relaxation strategies, while others have incorporated deliberate movement into their routines. Ray Floyd describes his periods of peak performance: "I feel like I'm going half speed. I'm not hitting the ground very hard when I walk. I'm aware there are people around, but I don't see them. I might talk to a player I'm walking with but I don't know it. I'm alone and I'm at ease."[40] Tom Weiskopf described a similar feeling of "slow motion" when he won the US Senior Open in July 1995.[41]

Sam Snead described removing all the tension from his body, making his first swing with that tension removed, and then trying to keep that up for eighteen holes.

When Jack Nicklaus wants to hit it long, he says he builds up to it while walking from the last green to the tee. His primary objective is to get good and relaxed. Then, once he is loose, he hits before any muscular or mental tension evolves.[42] Nicklaus also says that starting the club back too quickly is a common fault, especially under pressure. Again, he says he gains a visual image of shoulders, arms, hands, shaft, and clubhead moving back together in one piece with a picture of slow movement.[43]

John Jacobs, a well-known teacher and former European Tour player, describes preparing for a tournament day. Upon arriving at the course, he took ten minutes to put his shoes on.[44] Johnny Miller says he would often take up to twenty minutes to shave on Sunday, the morning of the fourth round of a tournament.

Gary Player prepared for the 1965 US Open by slowing down his pace in life weeks before the event. Shaving and dining became prolonged rituals. Additionally, Player says he saw his name next to the number one spot every time he passed the leader board the week of the Open.[45] Davis Love III and Byron Nelson described slowing down movement as pressure increased during play. Love said he would: "Walk slower, play slower, swing slower."[46]

John Jacobs, Johnny Miller, Jack Nicklaus, Gary Player, Byron Nelson and Davis Love III intuitively quiet their nervous system by slowing down movement. Ray Floyd noticed that his times of peak performance were associated with a feeling of moving at half speed.[47] As discussed, you will recognize that slowing down your movement will give you a feeling of control. When your nervous system is aroused, your physical movement quickens and your mental focus goes to the future. There is also a feeling of loss of control that builds with increased arousal.

HIT IT LONG BY QUIETING YOUR MOVEMENT

PGA Tour player Mark Calcavecchia's advice to hit it long is to slow down the club going back. "Low and slow" is common advice from tour players as a preswing thought. Calcavecchia notes that amateurs tend to move the club away too quickly. Again, we visit "tempo."

Tom Weiskopf describes slowing the pace of his swing to counter anxiety: "Pressure speeds you up. I tell myself to swing a little bit slower and let the anxiety pick up the pace of my swing. Remember, everybody gets a little nervous, so when you have that feeling or sensation, swing a little bit easier..."[48]

When the club moves quickly away from address in the backswing, the player tends to lift the club rather than turn his body. Often, there is also a "regripping" that, when paired with lifting, increases tension. This increased tempo and tension produce a rushed transition from the backswing to downswing, resulting in an errant shot.

Simply stated, start the club back from address with a smooth, even tempo. Practice on the range with a feeling that your grip pressure never changes in the swing and that your downswing is at the same speed as your backswing. In reality, neither of these is the case. Notice how much more in balance you feel with these drills.

Applying Movement and Breathing in a Pressurized Situation

PGA Tour player Patrick Burke finished in the top ten of the 1992 and 1994 PGA tour qualifying school. To qualify for the PGA Tour, you have to complete three stages. The first two stages have anywhere from 90 to 120 players attempting to qualify. About one-third of the players in each of the first two stages qualify to move to the next stage. If you don't finish in the top one-third of any stage, you don't advance to the next stage. The first two stages consist of four rounds each, and the last stage is six rounds. Imagine, you are thirty years old and your life's goal is to play the PGA Tour. To do so you need to play fourteen consecutive rounds of golf, the majority of which must be sub-par rounds. On top of that, you must pay a $3,000 entry fee.

Johnny Miller describes the stress level of PGA Tour qualifying school: "As pressurized atmospheres go, the qualifying school ranks with the US Open and the Ryder Cup."[49]

Patrick's primary goals at the 1992 Tour school were to stay away from mechanics analysis and slow down his movement. He not only slowed down his movement during the various rounds, but also he began to slow down his movement as soon as his eyes opened in the morning and he rolled over to get out of bed. He continued to quiet his movement and stay focused in the present as he got ready to leave for the course and in preparation for play.

He admits that the arousal got to him a bit

the morning of the last round of tour school. He realized he already had his shoes on when he remembered he was to have taken five minutes to do so. He simply stepped back into his slowed, deliberate routine as he hit balls and putted. He shot a 68 the last day with one out-of-bounds and one unplayable lie. Most importantly, he reported that the out-of-bounds and unplayable lie didn't phase him.

Patrick describes using the same breathing and movement strategies on his way to winning the 1994 Tournament Players Championship on the Australian Tour. He noted that his anxiety was high, especially the last two rounds.[50] He led the tournament from the second through fourth rounds, and won by a shot. Tour players will also tell you that overtaking the leader in the final round is much less pressure than holding a lead over three or four rounds.

As noted by Byron Nelson, your faster paced individuals off the course will speed up under pressure on the course. It is only natural. I'm not suggesting that all players should swing with the same tempo. I am suggesting that each of you should have the same tempo in every swing and that you should employ specific strategies to keep a consistent tempo. It isn't necessarily that players swing too fast; it's just that increased arousal increases their swing pace, no matter how fast they normally swing. This quickened swing pace often results in a separation of arms and body, and this produces an errant shot.

Remember, if you move quickly off the course, you will move quickly on the course. If you are going to learn to quiet your nervous system, it requires off-course movement, breathing, and focused concentration practice.

FOCUSED THOUGHT: Be Mindful

After winning the 1992 Kaanapali Classic in Hawaii, Tommy Aaron said: "It feels great to win; I was so wrapped up in playing each shot that it hasn't sunk in."[51]

July 11, 1993, Nancy Lopez recorded her forty-seventh win at the Youngstown-Warren LPGA Classic. Lopez played a 3 iron 198 yards to the green that came to a stop twenty-five feet from the cup on the par 5 18th hole. She rolled in the putt for an eagle to tie Deb Richard, and won on the first playoff hole with a birdie. Lopez and her caddie had talked before the final round about the importance of her staying calm. This is something she had not done well when she got in contention earlier in 1993: "I told my caddie that I had to be patient today. I knew I was hitting the ball well, but in the past I've been putting too much pressure on myself in the last round."[52]

Why do you have problems concentrating on one shot at a time on the golf course? Why is it that your mental focus is on your last shot, score, or "getting it back" on the back side? That's simply because this focus on things other than what you are doing is a well-practiced habit off the course.

When you took a shower this morning, what did you think about? Did you think about the water as it hit your body or the texture of your washcloth? As you left your home, did you feel the front door knob in your hand, or see the colors in the trees, grass, or flowers? As you drove in your car, did you notice what the steering wheel felt like? Most of us have a constant future focus of concentration. When we take a shower, leave home, or drive, mentally we are some place else. This focus can produce a constant state of arousal.

As I said earlier, peak performers describe a one hundred percent mentally present focus of concentration. How can you expect yourself to be one hundred percent mentally present on the golf course if you are seldom one hundred percent mentally present off the course? When your thoughts go to score, what others are going to think if you don't do well, or if you begin to think about something off the course, it's because it is a well-practiced habit pattern off the course.

Practitioners of Eastern meditation techniques call a one hundred percent concentrated focus in the present mindfulness. You will find increased control and improved performance in both your life and golf game if you will only learn to channel your attention one hundred percent into the present while practicing slowed, deliberate movement, diaphragmatic breathing, and self-supporting conversations with yourself.

The practice of mindfulness began with Buddhists 2500 years ago. In addition to being one hundred percent mentally present, mindfulness calls for an "eavesdropping" on your thinking with a dispassionate response to intruding thoughts. Assume a nonemotional indifference to the content of your thinking while you observe the themes of your thoughts. This will give you insight into the themes of thoughts that drive your moods and nervous system.

As events occur, listen to your thinking and be dispassionate. You simply practice accepting things, void of any emotion. Then, after a brief period of listening to your thoughts, remind yourself to return your thinking to a one-hundred percent present focus. Experience the physical feelings, the colors, the sounds, and smells of your surroundings. Be one hundred percent mentally in the present.

Narrate your behavior. Describe the intent of every move you make and the sensations associated with each movement. Do this with everything from eating, bathing, and dressing to opening doors, driving and answering the telephone. Notice the sensations of peacefulness, calm, and relaxation that come with this exercise. Start your day with mindfulness, and plan to build it into your day to day life and routines off the course. When you feel a need to rush, don't. When you experience an internal feeling of urgency, remind yourself to slow down, breathe deeply, and be mindful.

Once you become proficient at mindfulness off the course, you can apply these same strategies on the course. Be dispassionate in response to your performance. Without emotionally responding, accept the outcome of each swing, the conditions of the course, and situations that arise with other players. Remain mindful and calm. Practice deep diaphragmatic breathing and supportive, reinforcing dialogue.

While Patrick Burke was quieting his off-course pace during tour school, he focused his thoughts in the present. He focused his thoughts on every move he made. He felt the floor under his feet and heard the air conditioning, as he moved to the bathroom, and then slowly to the shower. He focused his attention and concentration on the water as it hit his body. He felt the faucet knobs in his hand, and experienced the sensation of the soap as he washed. His thoughts were one hundred percent in the present.

Deliberate movement and mindfulness are strategies you can use in times of distress, as a thought restructuring procedure, or as a life style you incorporate into your day from the time you open your eyes in the morning until you close them at night. Let's assume you have left your office upset over some event. You find yourself holding tension in your arms and shoulders. You have a strangle hold on the steering wheel. Practice a nonemotional, dispassionate response to the upsetting event. Accept the situation fully and consume it before it consumes you.

Quieting your movement and focusing your thoughts in the present will bring you into the moment and quiet your nervous system. If some action is necessary, for example a meeting or phone call, schedule it; then return to your mindful focus. Feel the relaxation move from your forehead to your feet like a wave. Notice the sounds and smells and other cars as your hands relax gently around the steering wheel.

While using mindfulness, you will have a feeling of control in the slowed movement, and a demonstrable, positive change in your mood as you begin to disrupt the chain of distressful thinking through a dispassionate, nonemotional, accepting response.

Mechanically slowing down activity, with an "awareness" of each movement you make, produces a slowing down of internal physiology and promotes relaxation. Mindful activity creates a "here and now" present focus. It directs all of your attention to the events of the moment. You can use this attention focus as a thought changing strategy. It takes you away from excited or negative thoughts of the future or past, and places you totally in the present moment, here and now. Use the relaxation strategies during this procedure. World class athletes experience a number of mental characteristics in common during their best performances. One of these characteristics is a one hundred percent focus in the present.

On the course, feel the back of your golf shoes as you slip them on one at a time. Look at the colors, hear the sounds, and experience the smells of your environment. Feel the texture of your golf balls and tees as you remove them from your golf bag. Note what your golf glove feels like as you slip it slowly and deliberately on your hand. Experience the feeling of your clubhead as you remove the club from your bag. Be in the present. Be mindful.

As you move from course management to club selection, your concentration should become more and more narrow. It's like walking through a funnel of concentration where you start with a broad focus and move progressively to a narrow focus. As you approach your setup to the ball, the more narrow your focus becomes. After you hit the shot, you return to a broad focus of positive, casual conversation or thoughts about the landscape. As you approach your ball on the next shot, your focus should begin to narrow again as you start your course management.

Some degree of mental arousal is important for concentration. Fine tuning your level of desired arousal is a goal. The window for success is relatively small. It's a matter of knowing how to quiet thought and physiology while at the same time directing all of your senses into the present.

PRACTICE OFF-COURSE CONCENTRATION

How often is your body in the present, but your mind is on the events of the last hour, week, or year, or your thoughts are anticipating the events of tomorrow, next week, or next month? At these times, you put your body and mind on full automatic, and go about your day as a robot. Mindfulness will take you out of this automatic behavior pattern and place you in the present.

How often have you heard people talk about requiring two or three days of vacation before they can really relax? That's like sending your body on vacation to the countryside with your mind still in the city. Repeated practice of mindfulness with vacation activity will put your mind with your body, and you will experience increased relaxation and a feeling of control.

You don't have to wait for a vacation to practice being mindful. Try starting in the morning when you awaken, and use it on your way to work, as you do errands, or as you work. You will note a positive impact in whatever you do, work or play.

Consistent and persistent practice is necessary for success. Remember, you have taken a lifetime to arrive at your present habits; change will be gradual and in small steps. It is upon these small steps that you will build major gains. If you are someone who demands immediate results or is looking for a quick cure, you won't find it here. These strategies require planned, hard work to impact upon the neuroanatomical and neurochemical structure of your nervous system.

The neural circuitry of your brain will continue to fire in the same sequence unless you change the network through daily practice over several days. How long is several days? There is no set number. No, it doesn't take twenty-one days; it takes as long as necessary to change the neuroanatomical and neurochemical structure of the brain. The time to change is dependent on a number of variables: how long, how frequently, and in what conditions did the old habit occur, and how frequently and under what conditions will you practice the new habit?

Building quieted movement and mindfulness into a daily routine will provide you practice with this strategy. This practice will start your day in a more relaxed fashion and give you well-practiced thought changing and relaxation strategies you can draw upon as needed.

Remember, your present thinking habits are encoded in the neural circuitry of your brain and are triggered by environmental events. If you choose to change these habits either on or off the course, set goals and times to practice the alternative habits. Neuroanatomical changes will occur only with extended, repeated practice in a variety of situations. The chapter, "Lift Clean and Place," provides hypothetical situations and a recommended structure to begin change.

VISUALIZATION

A recent research study had a group of people perform physical movement while the parts of their brain involved in the movement were mapped. These same people visualized the physical movement they had performed. Interestingly, the same parts of the brain showed activity with both physical and visualized movement with the exception of the motor cortex, that part of the brain responsible for initiating physical movement. This study shows that visualized movement creates a firing in the neural circuitry of the brain that prepares the nervous system to perform the visualized behavior.[53] The visualization process is an integral part of constructing the motor program. The brain scans from this study appear in the chapter titled Visualization.

Recall that neuroscientists have found that it takes 1.5 seconds for the brain to construct a "motor program" and just 0.1 seconds to initiate movement. This 1.5 second period is called the "readiness potential." The brain takes fifteen times longer to plan movement, than it does to initiate it. Visualization helps formulate the motor plan and establish a target for the behavior.

Thus far, we have discussed quieting the nervous system through breathing, movement, and focusing attention through mindfulness. Practicing positive visualization can produce a present focus, increase relaxation and confidence, and prepare the nervous system for peak performance. Conversely, negative visualization (hazards, out-of-bounds, conflict, and so on) will create arousal, decrease confidence, and prepare the nervous system for poor performance. The chapter, "Visualization," details the use of this important strategy for improving performance by drawing upon images of past success, increasing confidence, increasing relaxation, developing a present focus, and "lighting up" the appropriate areas of the brain for success.

ROUTINE

The first chapter of this book covered routine in great detail. I am not going to elaborate, except to note that a set routine will establish a structure of links in a mental and physical chain that provides a barrier for distraction and associated lapses in physical and mental routines. This mental focus blocks intrusive tension-producing thoughts and facilitates relaxation.

STRETCHING

When Ray Floyd turned fifty years of age, he was asked what kind of exercise program he used. He said he had done nothing but a stretching program for twenty to twenty-five minutes a day.[54]

When the body is in an aroused state, muscle tension is one characteristic of the chain of physical events. Stretching exercises produce an elongation and relaxation of these tense muscles.

Arousal is not the only cause of tense muscles. A prolonged posture of sitting, standing, or reclining can also cause tension. As we age and are less physically active, muscle tension accumulates much more readily.

The golf swing requires a flexible muscular system. Without flexibility your joints can't reach their full range of motion, and you won't experience your maximum performance capabilities. Older players will notice that they play better and hit longer shots as a round progresses, especially in warm weather. This is often due to the increased muscular flexibility and relaxation that comes with the heat and continuous play.

I am not going to fill the pages of this book with pictures and instructions for a stretching program. There are some excellent resources available. Please look in the reference section for the following:

Bob Anderson: *Stretching* [55]

Frank Jobe: *30 Exercises for Better Golf* [56]

Pete Egoscue: *The Egoscue Method of Health Through Motion* [57]

POSTURE

When you are happy, positive, and relaxed, you walk with your shoulders back, your head erect, and a smile on your face. When you are down and depressed, your shoulders are forward, your head is down, and you are not smiling (perhaps frowning). You can affect your mood and attitude by changing your posture. Assume an "as if" posture. Behave "as if" you just hit the shot of your life and you are on your way to more success. Put your shoulders back with your head high. Never let your eyes drop below the horizon. Practice deep diaphragmatic breathing and body scans as you move around the course and your ball. Your internal mood and physical state will begin to assume the same style as your external posture.

This "as if" style of behaving was first used as a clinical treatment by Alfred Adler, a Viennese Psychiatrist, in the late 1800's and early 1900's. Adler had his patients act "as if" they were the person they wanted to be. It is an extremely effective therapeutic style. Try it. You won't be disappointed. Note both the mood and performance changes that occur. Research shows that there is a change in physiology that matches postural changes. An anxious or angry posture produces an acceleration in nervous system activity. A relaxed calm posture produces a deceleration of nervous system activity.

BIOFEEDBACK

Biofeedback is a clinical procedure that was first used by psychologists in the late 1960's and early 1970's. A good bit of the early research centered on yoga and meditation practitioners who could alter their physiological state.

Biofeedback is a procedure where biological information is "picked up" through surface electrodes and converted to information that is "fed back" to a person through audio or video signals. This knowledge of results enables a person to voluntarily induce a more relaxed state.

Two types of biofeedback commonly used are Electromyography (EMG) and Temperature. The EMG measures the amount of electrical discharge in the muscle fibers. A tense muscle has a greater electrical discharge than a relaxed muscle. Electrical discharge from the muscles is measured in a unit called a microvolt. The higher the microvolt reading, the greater the muscular tension.

Circular discs called electrodes are placed on the muscle group being measured. Knowledge of the levels of tension and relaxation facilitates learning to voluntarily relax those muscles.

Temperature training is another common procedure used to increase levels of relaxation. The blood flow to your skin surface is what produces your skin temperature. When you become aroused, blood leaves the periphery (skin) and goes to the deeper musculature. Simply stated, your hands become cold. Electrodes that sense temperature are attached to the skin surface of the fingers. You can learn to voluntarily increase the blood flow to your hands or feet through biofeedback training. These same physical changes will occur simply by practicing deep diaphragmatic breathing, focused thinking, and quieting movement.

Biofeedback is useful clinically in treating a variety of psychophysiological problems like pain, headache, anxiety disorders, and phobias. Some therapists use biofeedback as an adjunct to psychotherapy. Unless you are suffering from some stress-related disorder or you are unusually highly aroused, biofeedback is overkill for you. However, biofeedback is useful as a measure of the effectiveness of other arousal reduction strategies.

A comprehensive biofeedback evaluation will establish your baseline levels of arousal. The other strategies listed here are practiced for four or five weeks. At the end of this practice period, the biofeedback evaluation is repeated. A comparison of the two evaluations shows the effects of practice of the other strategies on your generalized arousal level.

Anyone can learn to relax in a darkened room seated in a recliner while being provided with feedback regarding muscle tension or skin temperature. The real test is staying relaxed throughout the day at home, at work, on the course, or out socially.

CONFIDENCE

The feeling of control is at the heart of both arousal and relaxation. Control brings us full circle back to the word "confidence." When we are confident, we are in control and relaxed. When we are tentative, apprehensive, second guessing, or fearful, we are not in control and we become tense. Jack Nicklaus describes the number one tension reliever for anyone in golf as confidence. If you know you can hit a shot, you will have a relaxed swing. He says the second biggest tension reliever is concentrating.[58] Focusing on your routine, describing your shot, quieting your thinking and movement, and images of success are examples of this.

Many great players are different from the rest of the field in their belief that, "...nobody is better and nearly all inferior."[59] This style of thinking will definitely quiet the nervous system of the over-aroused player. Anything you attempt with that kind of confidence, you do relaxed. I am not going to elaborate further on confidence here. It is the topic of a later chapter.

The nervous system consists of billions of neurons. Our day to day experiences cause these neurons to communicate at lightning speed. The pathways of these neurons fall into a patterned circuitry and they are triggered by conditions in the environment. We call these patterns learning. Your level of arousal across a variety of conditions tends to follow a predictable set style. If you are going to change the neural circuitry that leads to arousal, you will have to practice the corrective strategies both on and off the course, and in both low and high arousal states.

For example, you should be practicing deep diaphragmatic breathing, quieted movement, positive visualization, focused thinking (mindfulness), and confident internal dialogue throughout your day.

These strategies require some form of guided practice instruction. Guided practice is instruction that provides step by step guidance for learning. Repeated practice produces neuroanatomical and behavioral changes that result in improved performance. The *MIND UNDER PAR* series™ *Routine: Guided Practice in Developing Consistent Performance* provides instruction in all the areas listed except biofeedback and stretching.

ENDNOTES

1. Sam Snead and Al Stump, *The Education of a Golfer* (New York: Simon and Schuster, 1961), pp. 10-11.

2. Golf Digest Staff, "Fred Couples," *Golf Digest* (July, 1992): p. 114.

3. Charles Price, "Bobby Jones Reveals His Inner Psychology," *Golf Digest* (August, 1989): p. 40.

4. Golf Digest Staff, "Paul Runyon," *Golf Digest* (August, 1994): p. 115.

5. Ed Weathers, "Nerves," *Golf Digest* (October, 1994): p. 71.

6. J.P. May, "Some Like It Hot," *Golf World* (July 17, 1992): p. 21.

7. Johnny Miller, "Pressure on the Prowl," *Golf Illustrated* (May, 1989): p. 26.

8. Chris Millard, "Barber's Still X-tra Hard to Beat," *Golf World* (April 1992, Masters Edition): p. 30 and p. 34.

9. Steve Hershey, "Low Key Approach Latest Move by Love in Bid for a Major Title," *USA Today* (August 9, 1994): p. C-10.

10. Jack Nicklaus and Ken Bowden, "My Lessons of a Lifetime," *Golf Magazine* (March, 1993): pp. 58-59.

11. Jack Nicklaus and Ken Bowden, "How to Beat Tension," *Golf Magazine* (July, 1993): p. 90.

12. Golf Digest Staff, "Paul Runyon," p. 115.

13. Weathers, "Nerves," p. 71.

14. Michael McDonnell, *Golf: The Great Ones* (New York: Drake Publishers, 1971), pp. 50-51.

15. Miller, "Pressure on the Prowl," p. 26.

16. Tim Rosaforte, "Running to the Horizon With His Arse on Fire," *Golf Illustrated* (July, 1992): pp. 36-37.

17. Golf Digest Staff, "David Feherty," *Golf Digest* (November, 1992): p. 111.

18. Miller, "Pressure on the Prowl," p. 26.

19. Golf World Staff, "Tour Talk," *Golf World* (July 9, 1993): p. 60.

20. Miller, "Pressure on the Prowl," p. 26.

21. Mark Wiebe, "When Want Gets in the Way," *Golf World* (August 20, 1993): p. 30.

22. Golf Digest Staff, "David Feherty," p. 111.

23. Weathers, "Nerves," p. 71.

24. Weathers, "Nerves," p. 75.

25. Miller, "Pressure on the Prowl," p. 26.

26.Dennis Paulson,Personal Communication (January, 1994).

27. Patrick Burke, Personal Communication (June, 1993).

28. Jan Stephenson,Personal Communication (March, 1994).

29. Marta Figueras-Dotti, Personal Communication (January, 1994).

30. Jennifer Wyatt, Personal Communication (June, 1994).

31. Laurie Rinker, Personal Communication (October, 1994).

32. Anne Marie Palli, Personal Communication (March, 1992).

33. Weathers, "Nerves," p. 75.

34. Dennis Paulson, Personal Communication (January, 1994).

35. Peter McCleery, "How Nelson Helped Watson Become a Champion," *Golf Digest* (January, 1991): pp. 66-67.

36. Golf Digest Staff, "Tom Watson," *Golf Digest* (May, 1993): p. 186.

37. Weathers, "Nerves," p. 74.

38. Weathers, "Nerves," p. 74.

39. Jack Nicklaus and Ken Bowden, "Nicklaus' Bear

Images: See S-L-O-W to Beat First Tee Nerves," *Golf Digest* (April, 1990): p. 58.

40. Tom Callahan, "Stare Master," *Golf Digest* (September, 1992): p. 55.

41. Jaime Diaz, "Free at Last," *Sports Illustrated* (July 10, 1995): p. 40.

42. Jack Nicklaus and Ken Bowden, *Golf My Way* (New York: Simon and Schuster, 1974), p. 78.

43. Jack Nicklaus and Ken Bowden, "Bear Images: Start Back 'Ridiculously' Slowly," *Golf Digest* (September, 1992): p. 29.

44. John Jacobs and Ken Bowden, *Practical Golf* (New York: Macmillan, 1972), p. 160.

45. Gary Player, *Positive Golf* (New York: McGraw Hill, 1967), p. 15 and p. 82.

46. Weathers, "Nerves," p. 75.

47. Callahan, "Stare Master," p. 55.

48. Glenn Monday, "Tom Weiskopf: Still on Target," *Golf Tips* (August, 1994): p. 63.

49. Johnny Miller, "Paul Harney or Bust," *Golf World* (February 11, 1994): p. 21.

50 Patrick Burke, Personal Communication (December, 1992).

51. Norm Guenther, "Tommy Guns Them Down in Hawaii," *Golf World* (November 6, 1992): p. 40.

52. Peter Mollica, "Lopez Knows a Good Finisher," *Golf World* (July 16, 1993): p. 20 and p. 22.

53. Peter Fox, M.D., Personal Communication (June 7, 1993).

54. John Hopkins, "Floyd Looks at 50," *Golf Illustrated* (October, 1992): p. 40.

55. Bob Anderson, *Stretching* (Bolinas, California: Shelter Publications, 1980).

56. Frank Jobe and Diane Moynes, *30 Exercises For Better Golf* (Inglewood, California: Champion Press, 1986).

57. Pete Egoscue, *The Egoscue Method of Health Through Motion* (New York: Harper Collins).

58. Nicklaus and Bowden, *Golf My Way*, p. 94.

59. McDonnell, Golf: *The Great Ones*, p. 133.

Mind Par
Mike Shelton

4

CONCENTRATION:

Keeping Your Head In Play

Jack Nicklaus describes going from a broad focus prior to shots to a narrow focus as he approaches a shot. Then, he returns to a broad focus after he hits a shot: "I still can't concentrate on nothing but golf shots for the time it takes to play 18 holes. Even if I could, I suspect the drain of mental energy would make me pretty fuzzy-headed long before the last putt went down. ...I've developed a regimen that allows me to move from peaks of concentration into valleys of relaxation and back again as necessary.

"My focus begins to sharpen as I walk onto the tee, then steadily intensifies as I complete the process of analysis and evaluation that produces a clear cut strategy for every shot I play. It then peaks as I set up to the ball and execute the swing, when, ideally my mind picture of what I'm trying to do is both totally exclusionary and totally positive.

"Unless the shot finds serious trouble, when I might seriously start processing possible recoveries, I descend into a valley as I leave the tee, either through casual conversation with a fellow competitor or by letting my mind dwell on whatever happens into it. The next build up of concentration begins as I reach the marker from which I'll pace the distance to my ball and start figuring yardage. [Note that this is where Nicklaus' routine begins on each shot.] My focus then gradually tightens as my caddie and I complete the math and I again finalize a clear cut play strategy, until it again peaks at address and during the swing."[1]

Nicklaus describes his third phase of concentration on approach shots to the green: "As I walk toward the green I return to the valley although rarely quite as deeply as after the tee shot. Then I gradually begin to emerge again at whatever point I can begin to assess my next shot, be it a putt, chip, pitch, sand shot or whatever. The peak occurs during the setup and swing or stroke after which my focus remains fixed and sharp until the ball is finally in the hole."[2]

Larry Bird led the Boston Celtics to three world titles and was the NBA Most Valuable Player three times. He said: "My biggest fault as a golfer was my strong point as a basketball player-concentration. ...On the court, I could never have told you who was sitting in the front row. Everything but the game was invisible to me."[3]

Paul Azinger had a bout with cancer during the 1994 season. He made his return to the PGA Tour at the Hawaii Tour stop in 1995. In June, 1995 Azinger said: "For the six-or seven-year stretch I felt like I out-concentrated 90 percent of the field 90 percent of the time. I don't feel anywhere near that right now. I recognize that as a problem. I'm trying to get back into that level of concentration and committed focus that I was on when I left the game."[4]

THOUGHTS ABOUT CONCENTRATION FROM TWO OF THE GREATS

Byron Nelson finished in the money in 109 tournaments in a row. He won eleven consecutive PGA tournaments and a total of nineteen tournaments in 1945. He was voted athlete of the year by the Associated Press Poll in both 1944 and 1945.

Nelson says that good concentration is "...standard equipment with all champions." He further states: "Success has eluded many golfers of mechanical excellence simply because they either did not realize the importance of concentration, or had been unable to develop this power. Concentration is this decisive-a player who has 'all the shots' and fails to fully concentrate each time he plays one, will often lose to an opponent of inferior mechanical ability who exercises to its fullest his faculty for close mental application."[5] Nelson said that a loss of concentration due to mental fatigue was a primary factor in his 1945 win streak ending.[6]

Gary Player, winner of all four majors (The Masters, The British Open, The US Open, and the PGA Championship) and numerous other tour events, has similar comments about concentration: "The difference between an ordinary player and a champion is the way they think. It's as simple as this: If you don't concentrate, you're not playing your best. There's absolutely no question that golf is a game of mind over matter. A golfer has to discipline his mind to keep absolute attention on what's happening that very moment-not on the bogey he made on the last hole or on the tough par 5 coming up next, but on the particular shot at hand to the exclusion of everything else. ...during every major championship I've won I concentrated so hard that I played rounds without knowing my score! I've often been in a don't-know-who-I-am sort of daze - total relaxation with complete control."[7]

Player goes on to say: "Concentration takes years of practice to acquire. It's difficult to come by and easy to lose if you let up. An integral part of developing concentration, of course, is self discipline-the kind of self-control that teaches your mind to do what you want it to do."[8]

THE NEURO-MECHANISM OF CONCENTRATION

There is a system located in the brain stem that neuroscientists refer to as waking brain. This system processes the sensory information to the brain and selects out content that makes up conscious thought. We refer to this filtered focus as concentration. The desired concentration level on the golf course is similar to that which many people achieve when they are reading a book they like. No matter what is going on around you, you don't hear or see it because you are so focused on the content of the book. Your mental filter is working so that no content outside the book comes to a level of conscious awareness.

The average golfer plays the way many of us used to study a school subject we found uninteresting. We could read a chapter or several pages and not be able to recall any of the content. Our mental filter was letting all the extraneous content into our conscious awareness while filtering out the content of the book we were attempting to study. Many golfers just aren't mentally present during a shot.

I believe the "zone" or "flow state" so many great players describe when they play their best is mostly a function of concentration. However, your ability to concentrate is dependent on many different interacting variables. Most of these variables interface in and around the neuro-mechanism of concentration in the brain stem that ultimately affects the higher brain and vice versa.

When we become aroused, the body mobilizes for action and there is an acceleration of activity in the part of the brain stem that serves as the filtering center for concentration. The body mobilization or alarm is a "danger signal" produced by the higher brain. The process begins with information entering the nervous system through the filter in the brain stem.

At these times of arousal, this filter system selects out information for conscious thought, and opens and sensitizes us to each area of sensory information by scanning the environment for impending danger. This scanning produces an overload of sensory information. Hearing and vision become more acute, the senses of touch, taste, and smell heighten, and it is difficult to think about one thing for very long.

The overloaded circuitry of your nervous system has billions of neurons firing like an electrical storm. There are so many that a flood of thoughts becomes part of this firing process and one's ability to focus concentration diminishes. This wreaks havoc when we are faced with life's three footers.

CONCENTRATION STRATEGIES OF TOP PLAYERS

When you played your best round of golf, what were you thinking about? What did you think about before you got to the golf course? What did you think about before each shot? What were you thinking about during the shot? Were you patient with poor performance and bad breaks? Let's look at how some of the top players think when they perform their best and see if they are similar to you. Most of you will see that their thinking is not much different from yours when you perform your best.

During an interview after the third round of the 1992 Honda Classic, where he had a two stroke lead, Fred Couples said he did not like to get too far ahead. He said he used to think about winning when he would be ahead and then not win. Now he thinks about playing a hole at a time. If your thought focus is on anything other than the shot you are playing, your performance will suffer.

LPGA Tour player Sherri Steinhauer won

the du Maurier Classic in August 1992. Since the beginning of the 1989 season, she had started the final round of seven tournaments in first, second, or third place only to falter. She summed up the change in her thinking during the final round as follows: "I just tried to play one shot at a time and not think too much about where I was or what I was trying to do."[9]

LPGA Tour player Carolyn Hill was a college All-American, a 1979 Curtis Cup Team member, and winless on the tour fourteen plus years after turning pro. She won her first event August 1994 at the McCall's LPGA Classic at Stratton Mountain, Vermont. She described years of work with a variety of professionals from sport psychologists to martial arts experts. Regarding her win she said: "I really did a good job of playing one shot at a time. I stuck right with it moving the ball from point A to point B. I wasn't thinking about the last shot or the next shot."[10]

Similarly, Gilberto Morales won the Junior World Championship in July, 1992. The Venezuelan shot an eleven under 279 for the week. Morales credited his victory to a focus on hitting good shots one hole at a time.[11]

Upon winning the Paine Webber Invitational in May, 1993 senior PGA Tour player Mike Hill said: "I practiced being more alert. Sometimes I just go through the motions on Friday, almost like I'm shadow boxing. This week I thought I should concentrate harder on Friday."[12]

Patty Sheehan won the Standard Register Ping to place herself in the LPGA Hall of Fame. She said of her final round: "I didn't start off very well so I kept telling myself, one shot at a time; don't think about anything else."[13]

Jack Nicklaus says: "The more tense I am, the more I try to think of just one shot at a time, one situation at a time."[14]

It's not only when you're playing poorly that your concentration diminishes; it can also occur when you are playing well. Sam Snead was playing a 1953 Ryder Cup Match against Harry Weetman. He recalls that after 30 of 36 holes he had Weetman four down. He was so sure his record of never having lost a Ryder Cup match was safe, he said: "In my mind I was ordering a nice thick steak dinner when we walked up to Number 31." Sam lost five of the next six holes to lose to Weetman by one. Sam Snead concluded from this experience: "A good rule: Never collect any trophies in your head until you have them in your hand."[15]

Similarly, in the 1966 US Open at the Olympic Club, Arnold Palmer held a seven stroke lead going into the final nine holes. It appeared he clearly had the title won. Palmer said he lost track [focus] and began to think about trying to break Ben Hogan's US Open scoring record. Palmer dropped his seven stroke lead and lost the Open title to Billy Casper in a playoff.[16]

PATIENCE

Patience is a process of combining focused concentration and redirecting thinking that is unrelated to the present. Patience is a big part of mental toughness. Mental toughness is a trait all peak performers have. When you lose patience, you lose focused concentration. Simply stated, patience is the ability to stay focused, and resist emotional and physical decay in the face of frustration.

Sam Snead described a practice round at his first PGA tournament in Hershey

Pennsylvania in late 1936. He played with George Fazio and two other tour professionals. He discussed his first four shots. The first two were big slices out-of-bounds into a chocolate factory. His third tee shot went into the water just off the front of the tee. He had hit three shots and none of them were in play. The other three professionals had hit 260 yard drives down the middle of the 345 yard hole. Two of the professionals grumbled about Sam's level of play, but George Fazio calmly and patiently told Sam to hit another ball. Sam's fourth tee shot landed on the green twenty feet from the pin. Sam shot a 67 in that practice round. His point to this story is: "Never give up."[17]

Many players hit a bad tee shot and immediately conclude they have bogeyed, doubled, or tripled the hole; they give up; they have no patience; they lose their focused concentration. Sam Snead summarizes the process of giving up: "In tossing in your cards after a bad beginning you also undermine your whole game, because to quit between tee and green is more habit forming than drinking a highball before breakfast."[18]

Players not only learn the bad habit of giving up on a hole, they give up on nine or the entire round once they lose concentration. How many times after six or seven holes of marginal or poor play have you thought: "I'll get it back on the back side." As soon as you lose your focus, your play will deteriorate further.

Sam Snead cites another example of having patience and staying focused at PGA Tour stop Westchester Open. He said he hit "3 straight drives so far out-of-bounds on the third hole that the Eagle Scouts couldn't have brought one of those balls back." He further adds that he had patience, continued to play a shot at a time, and was carried off the 18th green on the shoulders of the crowd when he won the tournament.[19]

When you hit a ball out of bounds, into a hazard, or you have a big lead going into the final holes, stay focused, don't quit, don't guard your lead, and play every shot as though it's the only shot you're going to hit that day.

When tour players describe the reasons for their wins, it is not uncommon for them to cite patience as a reason. Craig Stadler attributed his 1991 PGA Tour Championship to being patient.[20] Jack Nicklaus reportedly attributed his 1972 US Open win to patience. Everybody was three putting due to the conditions of the greens. He reflects that he just had enough patience to finish and win.

Patience for the weekend golfer is hitting several bad shots without analyzing his swing and attempting corrections. Don't try to create the shot or analyze why. That belongs on the range with an instructor. Recognize this is the time to practice patience and be mentally tough.

PERFORMANCE EXPECTANCIES

What happens when you drop your last bit of change into a soda machine and nothing comes out? Well, you probably try the coin return or another selection. If that doesn't work, you might hit or kick the machine as you walk away. Why? Because you have a one-to-one expectancy. That is, you expect to deposit a set amount of money into the machine and receive a soda. Many golfers have this same one-to-one expectancy on the golf course. They expect to hit a good to great shot every time they swing the club.

The frustration and anger produced by "failure" to produce positive results (a soda or a good to great golf shot) in these situations stays on your mind and disrupts your concentration until you are able to set it aside.

DECAY

Psychologists call this process of a gradual decline of behavior, due to an inability to produce positive change, extinction. The inability to produce positive change relates to anything from hitting a golf shot to waiting in heavy traffic. The resulting behavior is frustration, irritability, and an inability to focus your thoughts on what you are doing for any length of time.

Mental toughness is the ability to persevere, avoiding frustration and anger, or to express "PATIENCE." Instead of extinction, I refer to this process of frustration, anger, and loss of concentration as decay.

When we behave in ways we believe should result in some change and nothing follows, we try again, and again, finally giving up with anger, loss of concentration, and frustration. Muscles tense and physical arousal follows as part of this decay. We lose PATIENCE.

The person who lasts the longest at the soda machine or who can hit several bad shots or experience repeated "bad breaks" without aroused aggression, loss of concentration and performance deterioration has low arousal, high frustration tolerance and PATIENCE. How long would you last at the soda machine? How many bad shots or bad breaks does it take before you experience a deterioration in performance? Do you have a high resistance to decay?

How many three footers do you need to miss before you lose your concentration during putting, or you consider changing putters or making some mechanical change? Most of us expect perfection in performance. We expect to make most putts from five feet. We expect to hit most fairways off the tee. We expect to hit most greens in regulation and so on. The reality is that the best players in the world don't meet the expectancies you have for yourself.

Nicklaus says that when he and Hogan were playing their best game, they expected to hit only a handful of shots in a round exactly the way they wanted to. He further says that even at the highest levels of golf, perfect shots are mostly accidental and extremely rare.[21]

Walter Hagen reportedly expected to hit seven bad shots in a round.[22] When Walter Hagen hit a bad shot, he just "chalked it up" to one of the seven bad shots he was going to hit that day. What a nice way to fend off the emotional and physical consequences of decay.

Expect to hit every shot perfectly, but when you don't, talk to yourself about realistic expectancies. Consider Hagen's, Nicklaus' and Hogan's strategies for yourself. These will help you be patient and maintain your focused concentration.

Jack Nicklaus said that he "took the little bit of patience that came with the blessing of having a disciplined disposition, and worked it up into a lot of patience through conscious and hard-willed self-control."[23]

If you are striking the ball well on the range,

expect to strike the ball well on the course, one shot at a time. If you expect to score well just because you are striking the ball well, or you expect to hit every shot perfectly, one of two things will likely occur:

1. When you hit a shot sideways, your tolerance to frustration will be lowered. You will become more easily frustrated and your concentration will begin to diminish. This will likely lead to a swing analysis of "why?"! The increased frustration and associated arousal state will spill into a faster tempo.

2. Your concentration focus will be on score during the round. Your thoughts will be predominantly on the future as you calculate score and not on the shot you are playing.

LPGA Tour player and former US Open Champion Meg Mallon says: "You're just going to have those days when it isn't there. But more often than not, if I'm practicing before I play and I'm comfortable with how I'm hitting it, I'll go out on the course and spray it all over the place because I've lost my focus and concentration and have relaxed too much."[24]

THE DISTANCE DISEASE

Let's discuss distance as an expectancy. Men, in particular, are fixated on distance. When they find themselves in a group with a long hitter, they tend to compete. There must be some unwritten guideline of level of masculinity being equated with distance off the tee. These pairings with long hitters tend to create effort and tension in the swing of the shorter hitters in the group that spills into a deterioration in performance. This results because of a change from focused concentration on hitting targets to another player's performance.

Kenny Knox earned $423,025 in 1991 on the PGA Tour. Then at the 1992 PGA Championship he was paired in the final round with John Daly, who eventually won. Knox acknowledges that Daly's distance got to him. Not long after that tournament, Knox pursued instruction to learn to hit the ball further. With his swing changes went the rest of his game. Kenny Knox said it best: "The feel that you have, that's how you play the game. I really have lost that ability to play the game. That's what I'm looking for. I'm tired of swinging like somebody else wants me to. When you're thinking mechanics, you're always changing your thoughts on the golf course. You make a good swing and say, 'That reminds me of a swing I made at the 1986 Honda Classic-now I'll try this...'"[25]

There is also the matter of attention. Remember, what you feed attention grows. PGA Tour player Tom Watson estimates that between fifty and seventy percent of golf fans want to watch John Daly, the 1990's PGA Tour long driver, first and foremost.[26]

I find it amusing to watch amateurs, usually men, try to compete with the distance of a long hitter in their group. I also find it interesting to listen to the "awe" expressed over a long drive. "Did you see that? He hit it off the planet!" Or, "He nearly drove the green on number 7!" Shots close to the pin or long putts are admired, but nothing like the long drive.

Advertisers are aware of the distance disease: "Hit it further," or "The longest Ball in Golf." They must sell balls; these slogans have been around for a while.

When Senior Tour driving distance leader Jim Dent was asked how he has changed over the years, he says: "Chipping and putting, which I worked on a lot before I came out on the Senior Tour. [Years ago] I almost never worked on them. I used to practice hitting the ball long because I thought that's all I had to do. I found out that wasn't true. You have to get the ball into the hole to [score well]."[27]

Ben Crenshaw finished twenty-third on the 1995 PGA Tour with $737,475 in official money. His average driving distance was 253.1 yards. He was one hundred seventy-second on tour in driving distance and forty-ninth in putting.

Corey Pavin finished number one on the PGA Tour money list in 1991. He was named PGA Player of the Year. His average distance off the tee was 252 yards in both the 1991 and 1992 seasons. He says: "I lost concern for distance long ago. I can hit it 270 when I want to and that's far enough. I made eight eagles last season..." Pavin finished eighteenth and eighth on the 1993 and 1994 money list respectively with similar driving statistics.[29] He won the 1995 US Open, finishing sixty-six out of seventy-three players in driving distance with an average of 257.3 yards.

Tom Kite, winner of the 1992 US Open, ranked fifty-first in hitting fairways, twenty-ninth in hitting greens, and fifth in putting among the sixty-six players who played the final two rounds. Kite had twenty-five putts both Saturday and Sunday. During the last round he made putts of fifteen, eighteen, twenty, and thirty-five feet, and shot an even par 72 to win by one shot. Similarly, Jeff Sluman hit only six greens on Sunday while making only one bogey and shot a one under par 71 to finish second in the tournament.[30]

Annika Sorenstam and Laura Davies finished first and fourth respectively on the 1995 LPGA Tour money list. Sorenstam ranked fourth in putting and Davies tenth for the 1995 season.

Monte Scheinblum was the 1992 National and World Long Drive Champion and finished second in that event in 1991 and 1993. Monte's goal is to one day play on the PGA Tour. He's a good player. Two weeks before winning the Long Drive Championship in October 1992, he shot a 63 at Southern Links in Illinois to tie Ray Floyd's course record. Monte will be the first to tell you that he didn't tie the course record by hitting the ball long; he did it with his short game. The better he hits his short irons, putts, and chips, the lower his score. Due to his distance and course management, Monte uses his driver much less than the average tour player.[31]

PGA Tour player Dennis Paulson finished the 1994 season second in driving distance. His longest drive of the year was 385 yards. Jose Maria Olazabal shot a course record 63 on Thursday, the first round of the PGA Freeport-McMoran Classic. Dennis broke the course record the next day with a ten under 62. He followed on Saturday with a 74 and finished fourth in the tournament. Dennis said he didn't hit the ball much better the day he shot 62 over the day he shot 74. The difference was his putting.[32]

When Jack Nicklaus won the 1992 Senior US Open, he reportedly used his driver seventeen times in 72 holes. Gary player won the 1962 PGA Championship at Aronimink without ever using his driver.[33]

So, what should you do when everybody is hitting it past you and you find yourself swinging for the fences trying to keep up? Peter Thompson won five British Opens and some one hundred other tournaments around the world. He relates advice he received from Sam Snead: "Sam once gave me a wonderful tip. He told me on the downswing, the longer you take to hit the ball, the farther you will hit it. It's just a feeling. You wouldn't vary one 10/100ths of a second-but it's the feeling of not rushing that's the trick."[34] Recall that one of Nicklaus' three swing keys was to feel the same pace on the downswing as on the backswing.[35]

I would also encourage you to practice with a focus on grip pressure. Feel a very light grip pressure and hold that same pressure feeling for the entire swing. If you go after a ball on the tee, you will likely increase your grip pressure at the top of the swing and hit an errant shot.

Research shows:

1. ***Twenty-five percent of the game is wood play.***
2. ***Forty-three percent is putting.***
3. ***Approximately seventy-two per cent of the game is played from 150 yards in.***

When you are on the tee, focus your concentration on your fairway target and repeat the feeling of your practice swing. A distance focus will tend to create effort, tension, and errant shots. Your best distance and accuracy will come naturally, not forced.

REALISTIC PERFORMANCE GOALS

The 1995 PGA Tour statistics show the top players hit an average of between ten and thirteen greens in regulation. More specifically, the top Tour player in greens in regulation was Lennie Clements with 72.3 percent.

The top putter in 1996, Brad Faxon, averaged 1.709 putts per green in regulation. Mark O'Mera wasn't far behind at 1.737. What are realistic expectancies for you if the top players on tour hit ten to thirteen greens and average just under 1.75 putts per green in regulation?

Other statistics show that the average tour players make:

1. ***Forty-five to fifty-five percent of 6 foot putts.***
2. ***Fifteen to thirty percent of 10 foot putts.***
3. ***Ten to twenty-two percent of 15 foot putts.***
4. ***Six to sixteen percent of 20 foot putts.***
5. ***Less than ten percent of 25 foot putts.***[36]

The best players in the world make about one-half of their putts from six feet. What would you think if you missed two in a row from that distance?

Do you have realistic expectancies? As I said, I want you to expect to make every putt-be determined and confident. However, when you miss, place that miss within a realistic expectancy. Resist decay! Stay focused in the present and your next shot.

Once again, if you hit what you perceive is a bad shot, stay where you are. Set up and make another swing. Your nervous system will store your last swing for a brief period.

You want to groove memories of good swings, not bad swings. Secondly, taking another swing will help you deal with the emotional discharge of frustration.

PLAY THE COURSE, NOT YOUR COMPETITOR

Ben Hogan had an interesting approach for tournament play. He never concerned himself with competitors or leader boards. His focus was the course. The contest was between his playing ability and the course. He would walk the course during a practice round, assess the conditions, and decide what score he had to shoot to win. As part of his tournament preparation, Hogan would walk the course backwards starting on the 18th green. He would determine the best landing areas for approaches to the greens. Then he would place his skills in a contest with the course, not his competitors.[37]

When Hogan won the U S Open at Oakland Hills in 1951, he shot a 76, a 73, and a 71 the first three rounds. Upon recording a 67 his last round he said: "I vowed I would bring this monster to its knees."[38]

Similarly, girls junior champion Kellee Booth won twenty-four of fifty-seven national junior tournaments she entered. She finished out of the top ten only twice. She claimed her eighth national title of the year with a victory at the 1992 Edgewood Tahoe Junior Classic. Following this victory she said: "Everything has come together for me this year. Before when I had the lead, I would play the other players. Now, I'm more set on playing the course, and I am able to focus better on the last round."[39]

Once Hogan started a tournament round, he would often not acknowledge a great shot hit by another player. A story is told about Hogan being paired with Claude Harmon in a PGA Tour event. Harmon made a hole in one. Hogan made no comment. When they got to the next tee, Hogan asked who was hitting first.

In summary, play the course as your challenge, not your playing partner. When you focus on the judgment of others, or when in competition you become occupied with another player's play, your score, or anything that takes you mentally out of the present, your performance will suffer. Playing the course will keep you focused on the task at hand.

Also, treat yourself as you would a good friend. Be a good friend when you talk to yourself. Have realistic expectancies and accept poor shots, while at the same time, expect peak performance. Have patience; be mentally focused and tough! The chapters titled "How to Talk To Yourself On and Off the Golf Course" and "Lift Clean and Place" will teach you strategies to stay focused.

ONE SHOT AT A TIME

Nancy Lopez had forty-three career LPGA victories going into the Rail Charity Classic in Springfield in late August 1992, not having won in over a year. She said of her recent history: "I hadn't won in a year and my nerves weren't good. I'd look at a leader board and make a bogey on the next hole." She took some time off at home with her family. Upon her return, she won in Springfield and again in Portland the following week. Regarding these two wins she stated: "That winning concentration that I hadn't felt for a while crept back in last week and it was with me again here. With that concentration, the putts started dropping for me again. That had been my problem. I had been striking the ball well but not making many putts."[40]

Greg Norman describes the intensity of his focus during the rounds where he recorded some of his lowest scores. "Doral and Turnberry stand out. The 62 at Bay Hill and the 62 at the 1986 Canadian Open come to mind. All it is, you get so focused on what you're doing that you don't even know what score you're shooting."[41]

Nick Faldo was leading the 1992 French Open by two strokes on the 14th tee. He then lost five strokes over the last five holes and shot three over on that round, finishing tied for third. He described his thinking during this five hole struggle: "I'm a nerd. I screwed up 14 and 15, but even at 15 I hit a really good shot. At 17 I was brain dead. OK, I thought to myself, I've had enough. My mind was on the 18th green. I hit it as though I was mentally drained."[42]

In the 1990 Masters, Wayne Grady approached the 18th hole of his last round. He thought that all he needed to finish in the top twenty-four, which would get him an invitation back to the Masters in 1991, was to par 18. He was on the front of the green in two. He ran his first putt by the hole six feet. His second putt for par missed again running by two and one-half feet. He was certain he had missed the top twenty-four and said: "I was in sort of a daze and I walked around and missed the next one!" As it turned out, a bogey would have made the top twenty-four. Regardless, Grady won the 1990 PGA championship. That win earned him a return trip to the Masters.[43]

Remember, it's never over until your ball rolls in the hole on 18. If the Fat Lady starts to sing before your final stroke on 18, don't listen.

Mark O'Meara describes Ray Floyd's level of concentration: "I told him at the Ryder Cup he is the most intimidating player I've ever played against. He plays every shot like it's the last shot of his life. He's like a black leopard stalking the jungle."[44]

OFF-COURSE CONCENTRATION PRACTICE

Let's review a procedure described in the chapter on relaxation, quieting movement, and focused thought through mindfulness. Remember, quieting your thinking will also quiet your nervous system.

As already noted, most of us mentally live in the future, especially during routine activities like grooming, dressing, travel, and so on. Also recognize that if you have a habit of future focus and distraction off the golf course, that is likely going to be your pattern on the course. Concentration is not something you can turn on and off like a light switch. You must practice.

1. Set goals and ignore deadlines. When you have something to complete by a specific time, ignore the clock. Focus all of your thoughts on what you are doing, not how much you have left to do, how much you might not finish, and how much time you have left. Be mindful. All other thoughts will accelerate your nervous system, and impair your performance and mood. Be dispassionate and nonemotional. Accept intrusive thoughts. Allow these thoughts to pass without reaction, and then return your mental focus to the present.

2. Be mindful during your daily routine activities. When you go about your automatic daily routines like grooming or driving your car, be mindful. Focus your full attention to every color, sound, feel, smell, and taste. Focus all of your thinking on what you are doing. Notice how relaxed and in control you feel with this exercise. Again, be dispassionate and nonemotional with intrusive thoughts. Listen to the themes of these thoughts, and note what drives your moods and nervous system. Purposely remind yourself to redirect your thoughts to the present.

3. Practice going from a broad to narrow focus. Practice going from a narrow (specific) focus to broad (general) focus and then return to a narrow focus and then again to a broad attention focus. Spend sixty to ninety seconds in each of these concentration states.

You have the ability to focus on a specific sensation anytime you choose. Think about the feeling of your big toe on your right foot. That information was always being transmitted through your nervous system to your brain. You simply used a mechanism in your brain stem to focus your attention there. This is an example of a narrow focus. The more precise your attention is, the more narrow your focus becomes. Thinking about the sensations of your big toe on your right foot is a narrow focus.

Whether you are practicing a broad or narrow focus, be certain your breathing is deep, diaphragmatic and rhythmic and that you have no sudden or abrupt movement. Your movement should be slow and deliberate.

4. Practice deep diaphragmatic breathing throughout your day. Breathe deeply and slowly sixty to seventy times per day. Consider pairing your deep breathing with daily activities. Let the phone ring at least twice before you answer it. Plan to inhale deeply on the first ring. Breathe deeply when you walk through doorways, when you apply the brakes in your car, when you sit, stand, and so on. Focus on your breathing. Note the flow of air into and out of your lungs.

5. Practice supportive internal dialogue. Talk to yourself as you would a good friend. Supportive conversations with yourself will both encourage and relax you. You will learn about specific techniques for self-reinforcement in the chapter titled "How to Talk to Yourself On and Off the Golf Course."

6. Focus on the present when you have sleep problems. We all have difficulty with sleep at one time or another. Our tendency is to awaken, look at the clock, and then mentally calculate exactly how much sleep we can get if we fall asleep "right now." This tends to set off discussions with ourselves about how much sleep we "have to have" to perform well or not to feel tired. This thinking that is accelerated to the future also accelerates our nervous system, arouses us and keeps us awake. It has the same effect on our "sleep performance" that mentally calculating our score during a round has on our golf performance.

Set your alarm, turn the clock so you can't see the time, and become mindful. If you are concerned that your alarm might not work, set two alarms. If you are traveling, set your alarm and request a wake up call. Feel your body become heavier as you sink deeper and deeper into the bed. Let your arms, shoulders and neck drop into the bed and pillow. Feel the texture of the sheets and the softness around you. Continue this mindful focus as you practice deep diaphragmatic breathing. Become aware of your inhalation and exhalation as you count your breaths.

ON-COURSE CONCENTRATION PRACTICE

What kinds of things can you do on the course to help maintain your concentration?

1. Never add your score until the end of the round. Nothing will take you out of the present faster than becoming score conscious. You have already read what tour players say about a score focus or looking at the leader board. Make a conscious effort to play one shot at a time.

Use your scorecard to rank each shot on a one to ten scale, a "ten" being the best shot you can hit. Set a goal of hitting a "ten" on every shot. The *MIND UNDER PAR* series™ *SCORECARD* provides detailed strategies for using a scorecard to develop focused, one-shot-at-a-time concentration, confidence, a "memory bank" of good and great shots, and an analysis of strengths and weaknesses in your game.

2. Follow the same routine on every shot. A consistent preswing, inswing and postswing routine "cues" the same internal and external behaviors on each shot and ensures that you focus only on the shot you are playing. Practice going from a broad focus as you do yardages, wind, and so on, then narrow your focus from behind the ball into your setup to your target.

3. Stay target focused. Pick a target for every shot you are going to play and keep that target integrated through your entire routine. Maintain that target focus during your swing. LPGA Tour player and US Open champion Meg Mallon says: "When I'm playing my best I know I'm focusing right down to the leaf on the tree I'm aiming at."[45]

4. Never analyze mechanics during a round. Swing mechanics analysis belongs on the lesson tee. If you don't have "it" during the round, remember what Sam Snead said: "Dance with the one you brought." Return to the lesson tee and ask for drills to work on the changes you need to make **after** the round.

5. Practice deep diaphragmatic breathing before, during, and after your round. Deep breathing will keep your nervous system arousal to a minimum and enhance your ability to purposely focus your thoughts on the shot you are playing.

6. Practice quiet movement and mindfulness. Quieting your movement before and during practice and play will help you develop a desired rhythm and tempo that will build a foundation for peak performance. Mindfulness during this quieted movement places you in the present and minimizes distraction. Practice being nonemotional and dispassionate with regard to your performance. Accept the outcome of a shot or situation, and remind yourself to return your thoughts to the present.

7. Practice supportive, reinforcing internal dialogue. Supportive dialogue both on and off the course will teach you to be patient and to manage emotional and physical decay that produces mental distraction and physical arousal.

8. Feel the swing you want to make, then repeat that feeling. Focus your thinking on a feeling of the swing you want to make as you take your practice swings. Focus your thinking on repeating that feeling as you swing. I once heard it stated that you can't think of two things at the same time. I disagree. You can feel the swing you want to make and still hold an image of the target. It takes practice, but you can do it. You are accessing two separate sensory systems simultaneously, feeling and vision. Imagery takes place in the same part of the brain as vision.

Remember, none of these things turn on and off like a light switch. The more you practice them off the course, the more accessible and successful you will be during play. Develop a plan for on and off the course use of these concentration strategies using the format of the examples in the chapter titled "Lift Clean and Place."

NONMECHANICAL FOCUS

Jack Nicklaus reflects on the common mistake of becoming focused on swing mechanics: "If I could get inside the heads of most of the amateurs I've played with in Pro Ams, I'm certain the pictures I'd see would be mostly about club swing and ball striking. That's about as bad a mental mistake as you can make."[46]

Nicklaus began 1994 with a Senior Tour victory at the Mercedes Championship, and then he missed four straight cuts. His fourth missed cut was at the PGA Nestle Invitational in March 1994. He summarized his problems on the course as follows: "I played really well [at the Mercedes] and I suppose it was because I hadn't played any golf when I came out. I hadn't had time to think and really work on my swing. Once I started thinking about it and working on it, I couldn't do it."[47]

PGA Tour champion Johnny Miller describes a similar fate for many tour players, including himself, especially since the advent of video. "It's a common problem for today's pros, even more so because just about everybody uses videotape. Video can kill. Very few guys on tour watched a tape of their swing for the first time and said: 'Wow, I like my swing.' Instead, a lot of them said: 'Geez, I didn't know I did that.' They try to change and then problems begin.

"It happened to me. Everybody said: 'You take it back too far and your left foot hops at impact.' So there I was trying to change my back swing. But if I had it to do again, I'd say, 'Hey, it's my swing. I'm kicking butt. Who cares? My swing must be beautiful because the ball flew beautifully.' Some of the most consistent golfers are guys who know very little about their swings: Billy Casper, Lanny Wadkins, Arnold Palmer, Bruce Litzke..."

Johnny Miller goes on to say: "The secret of golf is not the swing. If you have an ugly swing and hit good-looking shots, you can win major championships if you trust the rest of your game and work on the mental side. The swing is just a part of playing golf.

"I'm convinced that the swing isn't the reason you score well at the professional level. You score well because you're at peace, you have a shot you trust or you just want to go out, play aggressively and make putts."[48] Even the best fall into the trap of ocassionally focusing on swing mechanics.

In 1988, Sandy Lyle won the Masters and two American PGA Tour events plus two of the European Tour's top events, the Dunhill Masters and the Suntory World Match Play. In 1989, sources close to Lyle say that he began to question his swing mechanics. As he watched a tape of the 1987 Players Championship, a tournament he won, he reportedly described his swing as "awful."[49]

This assessment of his swing sent Lyle

from one instructor to another after a lifetime of instruction from his father, Alex, an English teaching professional. He dropped to fifty-third on the European Order of Merit in 1989, his lowest position since turning professional in 1977. That same year he told European Ryder Cup captain, Tony Jacklin, not to pick him for the team. In 1990 he finished 175th on the American PGA Tour money list and fifty-ninth in Europe. Lyle sought the assistance of an Australian sport psychologist, Noel Blundell, who got him off swing mechanics and into targets. In 1991, he won the European Open and finished twenty-second on the Order of Merit. In 1992, he won the Italian Open and the Volvo Masters, and finished eighth on the Order of Merit.[50]

Bob Tway won the 1986 PGA Championship and decided he could do better. He began to work on his mechanics and slid from the top of the money list. Tway halted his slide after five winless years at the 1995 MCI Classic at Hilton Head. Following his win he reflected on his struggle: "In pursuit of getting better, I monkeyed with my swing and got worse. I played poorly for so long I had no confidence at all. I never knew how big confidence was until I didn't have any. Only since last year, as I got back to my natural swing as opposed to connecting the dots, have I done better. I'm just trying to climb the ladder again. No more mechanical thoughts. Just relax and be natural. I'm more of a feel player than I ever thought I was."[51]

Laurie Rinker-Graham joined the LPGA Tour in 1982. She won LPGA Tour events in 1984 and 1986 and the JC Penny Classic team play in 1985 with her brother Larry. She began a search to improve her game consulting some of the top instructors in the country. Her play began to gradually deteriorate. Her final stop was with Mike Adams at the PGA National Academy of Golf in Palm Beach, Florida. Mike reviewed videos of Laurie's setup and swing when she was playing well. He told Laurie that when she played her best, she setup a little right of her target. He said that this setup allowed her to release through the ball better. Sure enough, Laurie resumed her old setup, her ball striking improved, her confidence raised and her scores began to lower.

Many of the tour players and amateurs I work with describe an inswing focus on mechanics at the time of our first meeting. This, I believe, is a primary reason for poor performance. Many of these players had their video recorders with them on the range during every practice session. They would make a few swings, then review the video and analyze their swings. My first request of these players was to put the video recorders away and begin to work on drills that promote a feeling of the swing they want to make.

Swing analysis belongs with the swing instructor. These players lacked confidence in their swings and would go from one instructor to another. My advice: Find an instructor and stay with him or her. There is no such thing as a perfect golf swing. If that is your goal, you won't find it in this lifetime. Most of your time will be spent chasing corrections. If you want to excel, chase your success. The *MIND UNDER PAR* series™ *SCORECARD* provides practice strategies to get you out of focusing on corrections and into practicing success.

PGA Tour player David Frost won the 1992 Westchester Classic in Rye, New York. This was Frost's first win in two years after having won four in the previous six years. To improve his game, he went to a well-known instructor of some of the top tour players in the world. His play quickly deteriorated. His thoughts went from playing shots to having inswing mechanical thoughts. His comments: "I've been very mechanical with my game. I'm trying to eliminate all swing thoughts and play an average game of golf like I was 16 or 17 years old. I'm trying to neutralize the mind. That's the difficult part. It feels great-more natural and less manufactured. The guy who knows the least will probably do the best. The guy who doesn't know much doesn't have too much to think about. The better you get the more things you change to go forward. I got too serious instead of enjoying what I had."[52] Frost's next win came at the Canadian Open in September of 1993, again the following week at the 1993 PGA Tour Hardee's Classic, and the 1994 Canon Greater Hartford Open.

Similarly, Greg Norman described going to the same instructor as David Frost and becoming too mechanical. Norman said that once he dropped the "method" and began to feel as he used to, that's when he got his consistency and steadiness back. This transition back to his old swing began at the Houston Open toward the end of 1991 while working with instructor Butch Harmon. Norman says it took ten to twelve months to get back to where he was comfortable.[53] Then he won the PGA Tour's Canadian Open in September 1992, the Miami Doral-Ryder Open in March 1993 and the 1993 British Open. He finished second on the 1994 money list and led the tour in scoring average. In 1995 he finished number one on the money list and again led the tour in scoring average in just sixteen events.[54]

Butch Harmon discussed his work with Norman: "The first thing we did was get him back to swinging like Greg Norman. He tried a different swing that didn't work for him. It took about six or seven months to get that out of there."[55]

Norman described the effects a mechanics focus had on his game: "...I lost the feel of what I was doing. That's because I was trying to be too mechanical instead of being basic and natural. ...at the end of 1990 I decided to try to get better and improve my golf swing. I should have left the golf swing alone and gone ahead and had a break and started all over working with what I've got, which had been successful for 15, 16 years. So I tried to improve it. I tried a different method. And that destroyed me. That destroyed my natural instincts and feel for the game."[56]

Watch struggling tour players. You will see them working on their mechanics during a round. Between shots you can see them look for the position of their club during a practice swing, sometimes with an imaginary club. This, I believe, is a primary reason for the struggle. You cannot be thinking of mechanics and playing well at the same time. The tendency is for the mechanics thoughts to spill into the swing. A mechanics focus is a formula for disaster.

In 1974, Nicklaus described his early years of work on his golf swing. He said he grew up in the era of Ben Hogan and everything he saw, read, and heard indicated that Hogan had reached mechanical perfection. Nicklaus notes that he felt all he needed was time to work to develop this perfection. Nicklaus commented on his perceptions of those years:

"No matter how much work I did, one week

I would have it and the next I couldn't hit my hat. This is still true today. I am a far better golfer than when I started out on the tour twelve years ago and I feel that I have improved to some degree each year. But that is more the result of maturity and competitive experience than of improvement in the mechanics game."[57]

Former PGA Tour champion and teacher Ken Venturi sums up the mechanics focus quite nicely: "If you're hitting the ball well, don't start fiddling with your swing to make it look prettier. Otherwise, sooner or later your shots will turn ugly...when you start freezing positions, looking in the mirror to see if you're 'perfect,' you become tense and hinder the natural flow of your swing."[58]

Ray Floyd states: "I've had enough of that mechanical stuff, all the swing keys, the pulling and pushing. Now I let the club swing naturally."[59]

All of these examples remind me of the story of the Chinese philosopher who asked the centipede how it could walk with so many legs in such a coordinated fashion. As the centipede began to describe the mechanics of its gait, it stumbled and fell.

Top golfers will tell you that they play their best golf when they have no thoughts regarding their mechanics. Why is that the case? One explanation takes us back to Wiren's, Coop's and Sheehan's description of left and right brain functions. A focus on mechanics is a left brain function that interferes with performance. Another explanation is that you begin to "play swing" and forget the shot. Your goal is to hit the ball to a target. Focus on your targets to the exclusion of mechanics.

Bobby Jones said: "Concentrating on the results of a golf shot to the absolute exclusion of all other thoughts, especially about it's method, is the secret to every good shot I ever hit."[60]

Sam Snead says all you have to do is tell a player his hands are in beautiful position at the top and ask him how he got them there. He says any player who begins to think about his hands will begin to hit balls left, right-everywhere but at the target.[61]

Senior Tour player Chi Chi Rodriguez was asked what he does better now than when he played on the regular tour. His response: "I putt better. If I putted then like I do now, I would have won fifty tournaments. My nerves are better. Putting is a state of mind. I have confidence that I can make the putts; back then, I didn't. I putted OK in the early 70's, then somebody gave me $50 to write an article on how I putt. When I tried to break it down, I couldn't figure it out and I didn't putt worth anything for a long time."[62]

Ed Grant, a lecturer and golf enthusiast, used the following exercise to show what happens when you focus on mechanics during the golf swing. Please do this exercise in the steps presented.[63]

1. Write your name at the top of a piece of paper.

2. Under your signature, copy your name. Look at the length of each line in each letter and copy every curve as you see it. Don't just sign your name again. Look at each stroke of the pen in your signature as you copy your name.

3. Copy your first "copy" again using the same technique.

Notice the progressive deterioration in the quality of your signature from the first to the last signature.

Your golf swing should be as "automatic" as your signature. As you begin to think your way through your swing, it's similar to copying your signature. It's also similar to driving a car for the first time. As new drivers, we had a tendency to over-steer. Our focus was on the steering wheel, brake, accelerator, and a very short distance beyond the front bumper. When you over-steer a golf swing, your performance will deteriorate. When you drive now, your focus is one hundred to six hundred feet ahead of the car. You are looking at your targets. When you steer your golf swing, your focus is on the movements of the swing, not the target. Remember, always think about the target. "Stare at the target and glance at the ball."

THE ANATOMY OF LEARNING

When you trace the development of an infant's brain into its early years of life, it resembles the growth of a young tree. It continues to branch into more and more intricate patterns with age. Recent brain research shows that learning is represented in the nervous system in much the same way. That is, as learning occurs, structural changes evolve in the branching of the nervous system. These structural changes represent many repetitions of simple to complex behaviors.[64]

The following illustration shows the neural structure of the language center of a newborn's brain and that same center at age six years. This illustration shows the effects of learning and development on the neural structures of the brain.

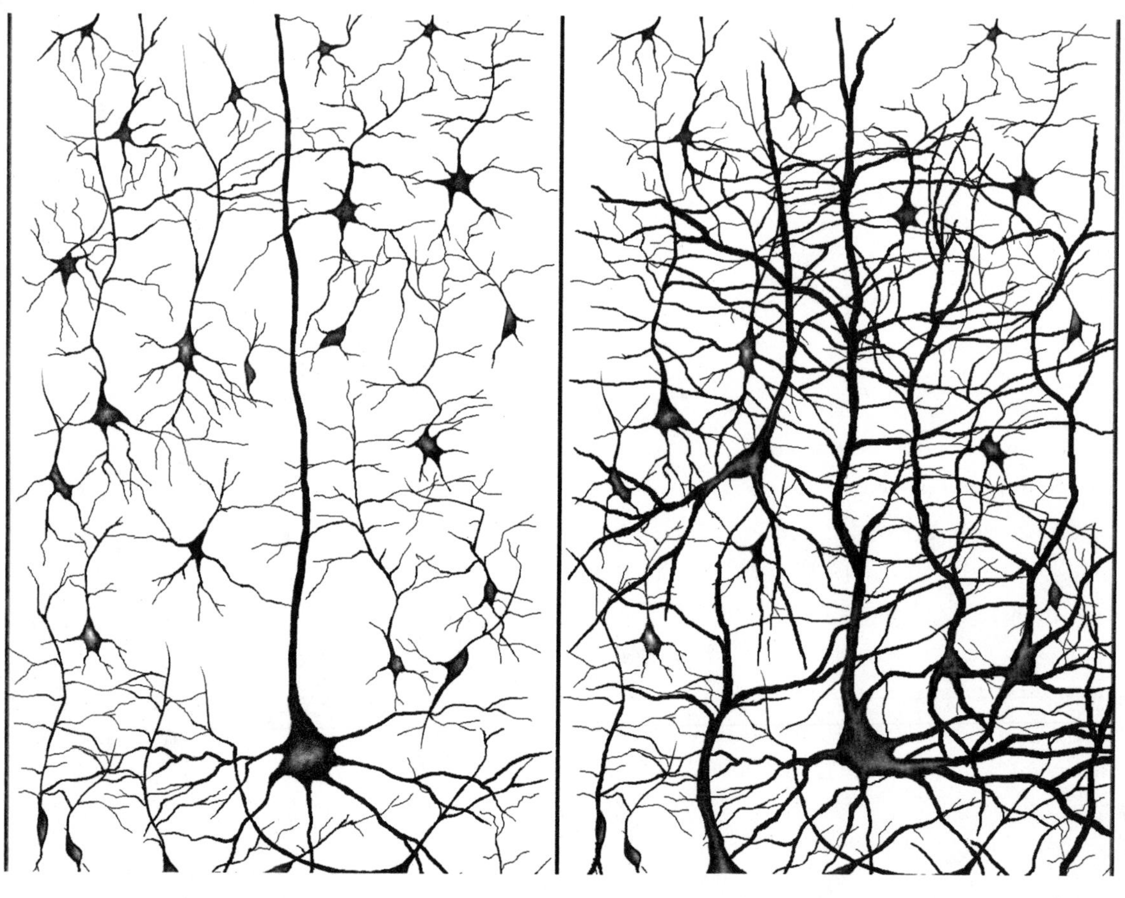

NEWBORN **AGE SIX YEARS**

Neuroscientists suggest that there is a massive flourishing of neural structures from birth to about five years, followed by a pruning of those structures until about age twenty. This flourishing and pruning process involves both learning and development.

Now consider the gradual learning of any motor or mental skill. Performance is dependent upon the "sequential firing" of the correct circuitry. The more repetition through the circuitry, the more learning is ingrained and the more predictable the behavior becomes. Change the conditions in which the behavior was originally learned, and you will create a new path of circuitry. Once the behavior is practiced across a variety of conditions, consistent, predictable patterns of firing will occur and behavior becomes predictable in most conditions.

How many times have you stood on the practice range during a good ball striking period and said: "I've got it!" Anyone who has played golf for any period of time has been on the practice range and concluded he "has it" at one time or another. He is also certain that this "magic bullet" is going to carry him to a higher level of performance the next time he plays.

There are a multitude of reasons why you don't "have it." These reasons all return to the structural, anatomical nature of learning as represented in the brain. This is why lessons that include drills and practice which entails repetition of the desired sequence of behaviors (links) are going to be your best learning strategies for lasting change. This is why it took European and US PGA Tour player Nick Faldo two years to rebuild his swing. He was rebuilding the neural circuitry of the brain. It took Greg Norman six to seven months to return to the old neural circuitry of his former swing.

This is also why you will hear most instructors say that it is easier to teach a beginner than a player of fifteen years who has well-practiced bad habits. These habits have a structural representation in the brain. New circuitry must be built through repeated practice. The "old learning" branches don't "go away" either. Research shows that these unused neural circuits appear to atrophy with age, although they seem to "fire" at the most inopportune times, especially under pressure. The new learning must be rehearsed repeatedly across a variety of situations before it completely overrides the old structural learning circuitry of the brain. There are no magic bullets in learning.

DRILLS: THE PATH TO SWING FIX

As already noted, your nervous system branches like a growing tree as learning occurs. Your swing memory is in these branches. If you are going to make corrections in your setup, inswing, and/or postswing, you have to override old learning that resides in the neural circuitry. This neural circuitry can't be erased or changed in a day or even two or three days. Nervous system branches can't be pruned like the trees in your yard or at your local club.

Daily drills at home and on the practice range are the only way to groove new habits in the nervous system. These drills will reprogram the circuitry of your nervous system through repetition. This is true of both the mental and mechanical routines. If you consider it, it's true of every behavior we learn.

You have never been able to perform a new complex motor skill at your best possible performance level after one or two, or even a series of lessons. It takes practice. Our tendency is to expect maximum performance after a few trials and minimum practice. Frustration follows when we don't experience the expected level of performance.

You can change these undesired learned behaviors. The only way to override this old learning is through daily repetition that grooves "new memory," creating new branching networks in the nervous system. Once learned and practiced in different "states," the learning will generalize or transfer to other conditions, for example, from range, to course, to tournament play.

I have read and heard it stated that it takes twenty-one days and numerous daily repetitions to change a habit. I spent the first eight years of my psychology training in a laboratory setting studying behavior under various learning conditions. I have never seen a scientific study that says it takes twenty-one days and sixty repetitions per day to change a habit. However, I would suggest it's a good guideline. The time it takes to change a habit is going to be dependent upon learning history; that is, how complex are those branches of nerve pathways that are related to the golf swing or similar movement, like a baseball swing? And in how many different "states" have you practiced this swing?

Once you have made the swing changes in a low arousal setting, graduated exposure to on-course situations will transfer this learning to new "states." This is why the person who has a lot of experience in tournament or pressure situations is more likely to play better in those conditions than the person who doesn't. The seasoned player has learned to perform under a variety of different conditions or "states."

Most golfers are familiar with Byron Nelson's 1945 win streak of eleven straight PGA Tour events. Every golf magazine in 1995 had coverage of the fiftieth anniversary of this tremendous feat. Most people don't know that Nelson not only won eleven straight tournaments that year, he won a total of nineteen tournaments and finished out of the top five only one time in 1945 with a stroke average of 68.33.[65]

Byron Nelson began recording his playing performance in a diary in 1935, although his golf career began before that year. In 1935, Nelson played 112 rounds in thirty-one tournaments. He recorded only four rounds in the 60's, three rounds of 69 and one round of 68. He recorded six rounds of 80 or higher and 45 rounds of 75 or higher. His scoring average in 1935 was 74.06.[66] In 1938 Nelson played in twenty-five tournaments and had a scoring average of 74.83[67] In 1942 Nelson's scoring average dropped to 71.02,[68] and in 1944 it fell further to 69.77.[69] Byron Nelson climbed a tall ladder. When you look at his performance over the ten years prior to 1945 you can see his ups and downs and his gradual progress. You can also see he was poised for his 1945 streak.

Every successful competitive golfer has climbed the ladder of competition. Few players experience immediate success as they step onto a new rung from junior golf to high school to college to mini tours, and finally on to the big tour. There are struggles at every rung. The tendency is for these players to lose confidence in their swing and their ability to compete. They begin to focus their concentration on their swings, rather than their targets.

Most of the greatest players in the world don't have "pretty" or one hundred percent technically sound swings. However, their swings are consistent. They repeat the same mechanics on each swing. They aren't searching for the perfect swing or for every shot to be perfect. They can repeat the same swing no matter what the condition. They are not mechanically focused.

In his early years, Bobby Jones was described as a great ball striker but a poor competitor. In the 1923 US Open at Inwood, Jones went into the last round with a three stroke lead until the last three holes where he dropped four strokes to tie with Bobby Cruickshank. Jones won in a playoff.[70]

Again in 1928, he was three strokes ahead of the field in the US Open at Olympia Fields and dropped seven strokes the last eleven holes to tie with Johnny Farrell. Jones lost in a playoff.[71]

One year later at the US Open at Winged Foot, again he was three strokes ahead of the field going into the last day. He took two sevens to drop to a tie with Al Watrous. Again he recovered and won the playoff. With repeated experience Jones learned to compete differently in later years. However, early in his career, anytime he held a lead going into the final round, his pattern was to lose several strokes.

THE PRACTICE SWING: A MEANINGLESS RITUAL?

Your nervous system stores two types of memory: Short-term and long-term. It takes many rehearsals of a skill, verbal or motor, to convert memory from short-term to long-term.

A practice swing does two things for you:

1. It is calling up a swing from your memory.

2. It is providing you with a rehearsal of the "ideal" feeling for a shot.

I see many players practicing on the range, raking and hitting one ball after another. The speed of their practice session spills into the tempo of their swing, and frustration quickly sets in.

I've watched other players take a practice swing on the course during play. However, they don't pay attention to the tempo and feeling, and the practice swing seldom resembles the swing they put on the ball. The practice swing has become a "meaningless ritual" that is part of their routine, however, not used efficiently. Sure, it makes you feel loose and assists you in relaxing before the shot. However, do you feel the tempo? Do you experience and focus on the feeling of your total practice swing? When you play your best golf, do you take a practice swing? Do you have a picture of the swing in your mind?

Let's look at another situation. You play approximately seventy-two percent of your golf game from one hundred and fifty yards in. For the majority of these shots, you won't hit a full club. Do you rehearse the feeling of the swing whether it is fifty-five yards or five yards? You probably won't have the same shot again in that round, or maybe the next two or three rounds. Your eyes "feed" your brain information regarding distance that transfers a feeling of movement to the large muscles. You "feel" the shot as you take practice swings while looking at the target. Most of you will increase the number of practice swings you take on a shot the closer you get to the green. Ideally, when you step up to the ball, your rehearsed practice swing is the swing you make. When you are able to do so, your performance is best.

Why not practice feeling every shot and use your short-term memory to repeat that feeling in your full swing? Mike McGetrick, a friend, PGA teaching professional, and instructor for many LPGA and PGA Tour players, tells me he doesn't let a student hit a ball without first taking a practice swing.

The next time you watch a tour event, notice how both men and women feel the distance on the green as they look at the hole. Notice that they take a practice swing outside a sand bunker before stepping in to hit their shot. They also rehearse their strokes when chipping and pitching and all shots from seventy-five yards in to the green. Any time a player is between clubs, they feel the distance and shot they want to hit.

I recommend you begin taking a practice swing before every shot whether you are on the practice range or during a round. Focus your concentration on the feeling of that swing. If you don't like the way it feels, take another one. Your goal should be to repeat the feeling of the practice swing as you make your swing on the ball. Mentally, maintain your target orientation as you do. You should have no thoughts of mechanics during the swing, only an image of the target and the feeling of the practice swing. The chapter on visualization will show why a feeling and even an image of the swing you want to make are two of the best preswing and inswing thoughts you can have. You will see how this helps construct a performance-enhancing motor program.

I would encourage you to practice feeling the same grip pressure with every shot you hit. If you increase grip pressure during putting, you will "grab" the putter, creating a hitting motion and pull or push the putt. If you increase your grip pressure in the full swing, you will also likely produce a hitting motion. Both of these conditions are created by increased tension. Effort creates tension. Attempting to hit the ball further results in effort in your swing. You will likely find that the day's effort is "working," your short game is off. The accumulated tension interferes with your feel for the short game. Your sense of feel or touch abandons you.

Peak performers will tell you when they are playing well, the feeling is effortless. Remember how effortless the best round you ever played was? Focus on that memory the next time you tee it up with a long hitter. Harvey Penick, one of the greatest teachers of our time, said: "The woods are filled with long drivers."[72] The John Dalys, Fred Couples, Davis Loves and Jim Dents are the exceptions, of course. They are rare; they are world class players. Remember, keep your focus on your targets effortlessly.

In closing this chapter, I want you to recall what Gary Player said: "Concentration takes years of practice to acquire. It's difficult to come by and easy to lose if you let up. An integral part of developing concentration, of course is self discipline-the kind of self-control that teaches your mind to do what you want it to do." [73]

In spite of this practice there are many events that will steal your concentration. It is important that you have as few off course distractions as possible if you are going to play your best.

Tiger Woods shot an opening round 70 to tie for eigth place during the 1996 PGA Tour Championship. At 3:00 A.M. the morning of the second round, Tiger took his father to the hospital and stayed with him until later that morning. Tiger shot a 43 on the front and even on the back to record a 78 on the day, his highest score of his PGA career. Needless to say, Tiger lost his focus that day. His thoughts were with his father in a hospital a few miles from the golf course.

Concentration takes practice. If you are going to heighten your ability to concentrate, I would encourage you to review the on and off course strategies covered in this chapter and begin a daily practice program.

ENDNOTES

1. Jack Nicklaus and Ken Bowden, "My Strongest Weapon," *Golf Magazine* (December, 1993): p. 47.

2. Nicklaus and Bowden, "My Strongest Weapon," p. 47.

3. Jack Sheehan, "Larry Bird," *Golf Magazine* (May, 1995): p. 111.

4 Golf World Staff, "Tour Talk," *Golf World* (June 9, 1995): p. 110.

5. Byron Nelson, *Winning Golf* (New York: A.S. Barnes and Company, 1946), p. 19.

6. Byron Nelson, *The Little Black Book* (Arlington, Texas: The Summit Publishing Group, 1995), p. 148.

7. Gary Player, *Positive Golf* (New York: McGraw Hill, 1967), pp. 16-17.

8. Player, *Positive Golf*, p. 16.

9. Geoff Russell, "Sherri Steinhauer's Major Breakthrough," *Golf World* (August 20, 1992): pp. 40-41.

10. Jerry Potter, "Winning's All in Hill's Head," *USA Today* (August 9, 1994): p. C-10.

11. Golf World Staff, "Venezuelan Whizzes Past Woods," *Golf World* (July 31, 1992): p. 37.

12 Ron Green, "No Brag, Just Fact," *Golf World* (May 21, 1993): p. 40.

13 Bill Huffman, "LPGA Tour," *Golf World* (March 26, 1993): p. 21.

14. Jack Nicklaus and Ken Bowden, *Golf My Way* (New York: Simon and Schuster, 1974), p. 100.

15. Sam Snead and Al Stump, *The Education of a Golfer* (New York: Simon and Schuster, 1961), p. 46.

16. Michael McDonnell, Golf: The Great Ones (New York: Drake Publishers, 1971), p. 86.

17. Snead and Stump, *The Education of a Golfer*, pp. 32-33.

18. Snead and Stump, *The Education of a Golfer*, p. 34.

19. Snead and Stump, *The Education of a Golfer*, p. 44.

20. Bob Rotella, "How to Use Not Lose Your Temper," *Golf Digest* (September, 1992): p. 77.

21. Nicklaus and Bowden, "My Strongest Weapon," p. 45.

22. Charles Price, "Bobby Jones Reveals His Inner Psychology," *Golf Digest* (August, 1989): p. 40.

23. Jack Nicklaus and Ken Bowden, "My Lessons of a Lifetime," *Golf Magazine* (March, 1993): pp. 58-59.

24. Andy Brumer, "Be A Thinking Golfer," *Golf Tips* (May, 1994): p. 38.

25. Gary Van Sickle, "School of Hard Knox," *Golf World* (June 2, 1995): p. 21.

26. John Feinstein, "The Daly Experience," *Golf Magazine* (August, 1994): p. 14.

27. Jeff Williams, "The Golf Course," *Golf Magazine* (October, 1991): p. 73.

28. PGA TOUR Statistics (November, 1995).

29. Nick Seitz, "Corey Pavin: The Most Untypical Star," *Golf Digest* (January, 1992): p. 46.

30. David Barrett, "Major Accomplishment," *Golf Magazine* (August, 1992): p. 92.

31. Monte Scheinblum, Personal Communication (October 31, 1992).

32. Dennis Paulson, Personal Communication (August 20, 1994).

33. Golf Magazine Staff, "Arnie and Jack," *Golf Magazine* (May, 1994): p. 136.

34. Golf Digest Staff, "Peter Thompson," *Golf Digest* (July, 1994): p. 141.

35. Nicklaus and Bowden, "My Strongest Weapon," p. 47.

36. Dave Pelz and Nick Mastroni, *Putt Like The Pros* (New York: Harper Collins, 1989), p. 38.

37. McDonnell, *Golf: The Great Ones*, p. 69.

38 McDonnell, *Golf: The Great Ones,* p. 67.

39 Golf World Staff, "Booth Claims Eighth Title," *Golf World* (October, 1992): p. 44.

40 Bob Robinson, "Suddenly, There's No Doubt About It," *Golf World* (September 18, 1992): p. 34.

41. Golf Digest Staff. "Greg Norman," *Golf Digest* (December, 1992): p. 164.

42. John Hopkins, "Nick Faldo's Mystery Tour," Golf World (July 10, 1992): p. 20.

43. Golf World Staff, "Around The Green," *Golf World* (April 3, 1992): p. 48.

44. Gary Van Sickle, "Man of the Year: Ultimate Warrior," *Golf World* (December 18, 1992): p. 26.

45. Brumer, "Be A Thinking Golfer," p. 38.

46. Nicklaus and Bowden, "My Strongest Weapon," pp. 44-45.

47. Golf World Staff, "PGA Tour," *Golf World* (March 24, 1994): p. 44.

48. Johnny Miller, "Don't Go Changin'," *Golf World* (August 6, 1993): p. 24.

49 Michael McDonnell, "Full Circle," *Golf Digest* (July, 1993): pp. 45-46.

50. McDonnell, "Full Circle," *Golf Digest* (July, 1993): pp. 45-46.

51. Gary Van Sickle, "The Tway We Were," *Golf World* (April 21, 1995): p. 44.

52. Gary Van Sickle, "Just Do It," *Golf World* (July 3, 1992): pp. 11-12.

53. Golf Digest Staff, "Greg Norman," *Golf Digest* (December, 1992): p. 166.

54. Gary Van Sickle, "The Norman Conquest," *Golf World* (November 5, 1995): p. 64.

55. Gary Van Sickle, "New Improved and in the Groove," *Golf World* (July 30, 1993): p. 31.

56. Golf Digest Staff, "Greg Norman," p. 164.

57. Nicklaus and Bowden, *Golf My Way*, p. 22.

58. Ken Venturi, "Do's and Don'ts," *Golf Magazine* (December, 1992): p. 32.

59. John Hopkins, "Floyd Looks at 50," *Golf Illustrated* (October, 1992): p. 40.

60. Price, "Bobby Jones Reveals His Inner Psychology," p. 40.

61. Sam Snead, "10 Point Annual Check Up: Spank That Ball on Its Butt," *Golf Digest* (1992): p. 4.

62. Jeff Williams, "The Golf Course," *Golf Magazine* (October 1991): p. 73.

63. Ed Grant, *Subconscious Golf*, Audio Tape (Phoenix, Arizona: Mind Games Enterprises, 1977).

64. Sandra Ackerman, *Discovering the Brain* (Washington, D.C.: National Academy Press, 1992). pp.124-125.

65. Nelson, *The Little Black Book*, p. 152.

66. Nelson, *The Little Black Book*, pp. 1-19.

67. Nelson, *The Little Black Book*, pp. 51-65.

68. Nelson, *The Little Black Book*, pp. 113-123.

69. Nelson, *The Little Black Book,* pp. 124-135

70. McDonnell, *Golf: The Great Ones,* p. 38.

71. McDonnell, *Golf: The Great Ones*, p. 38.

72. Harvey Penick and Bud Shrake, *Harvey Penick's Little Red Book* (New York: Simon and Schuster, 1992), p. 29.

73. Player, *Positive Golf*, p. 16.

Mike Shelton

5

CONFIDENCE:

Building Mental Toughness From the Ground Up

HOW TOP PLAYERS THINK

Peter Jacobsen tells a story about being paired with Andy Bean and Jack Nicklaus in the 1986 Memorial Tournament at Muirfield Village in Columbus, Ohio. Nicklaus had shot 30 the last round on the back side at Augusta to win his sixth Masters at the age of forty-six a few weeks earlier. Jacobsen, Nicklaus, and Bean were all about even on Sunday after nine holes. The gallery was huge. They were there to follow their local favorite and 1986 Masters Champion. Then Nicklaus birdied 10, 11, 12 and 13. As the birdie string began, the crowd grew.

Their approach shots to the 14th hole left Jacobsen four feet, Bean twelve feet, and Nicklaus fifteen feet from the hole. Nicklaus was obviously away and it was his turn to putt. However, Bean set his ball down, putted first and made his. The crowd applauded. Then Nicklaus turned to Jacobsen and said: "Peter, do you want to go ahead and putt out?" Jacobsen responded: "Why would I want to putt out Jack, you're away." Then Nicklaus said: "Because when I make this putt, the people here are going to go crazy." Nicklaus made the putt and "a deafening roar went up" from the thousands of onlookers.[1]

A similar story was told by Tom Weiskopf. It was the 1973 Ryder Cup. "We're one or two up on the two Brits we're playing when Jack and I both knock the ball close. He's about ten feet away and I'm within five or six feet. Now I'm in Jack's line and about to mark my ball when Jack says, 'Pick it up'. I look at him incredulously and say, 'What?' 'Rack your cue,' he says, 'I'm gonna sink mine.' So I pick up the ball, stand back, and sure enough, he rams it into the center of the cup."[2]

When you ask Jack Nicklaus about putting, he says: "It's all in the mind...Believe you can knock them in the hole and you'll knock 'em in. Believe you can't and you won't."[3]

I would be remiss if I didn't also highlight some of Nicklaus' comments regarding the mechanics of putting. Interestingly he says that: "Achieving equal grip pressure in both hands at address, then sustaining it throughout the stroke, has been a putting key of mine for many years." He also says that you should have your eyes over the target line, putt for distance, find a stroke that is natural for you, stay with your putting style, and don't change.[4]

I couldn't leave you with the feeling that putting is all confidence and no mechanics. As Nicklaus says, a belief that you can putt is important. Two great putters, Dave Stockton and Greg Norman, have both made confident comments about their putting ability. Confidence alone won't change your performance. Confidence is based upon performance and how you talk to yourself about your accomplishments on the greens, tees and fairways. If your thought focus is on the great shots and putts you make during a round or in practice, you'll build confidence. If your thought focus is on your bad shots and missed putts, you will build self-doubt. It's as simple as that. Most players have ingrained habits of focusing on their poor shots and missed putts. As you have already read, what you feed attention grows.

Sam Snead said the following regarding confidence:

"Whenever I've been able to pull myself out of a slump, it's because I didn't forget that breaks always even out, over the long pull, and that the bane of golf-and life in general-is to remember your mistakes and not your right moves. In clubhouses, you'll see men sitting around complaining, going over their bad shots. They should think back to their good shots, then try to repeat them.

"This is the only way to build that feeling called confidence. You can build it - or tear yourself down. The choice is up to every individual. If you know yourself to be a whiner, you'll never play up to your full ability. It takes guts to be an optimist in golf. He who thinks like a winner will win."[5]

European Tour and Ryder Cup player David Feherty made golf his career in spite of the fact that he was never a champion in his youth. His mother stated that what set David apart was blind ambition: "He thought he was better than he was at the time."[6]

During his rookie year in 1990, Robert Gamez was quoted as saying: "I feel I can win any time I tee it up. I don't feel like I'll finish out of the top 20, and that's playing bad. I feel like if I play halfway decent, I'll finish in the top 10 and if I play good, I should win. People see me as cocky because I walk to the tee like I'm better than everybody. I'm just walking with a lot of confidence. If I don't feel like I can win a tournament, I won't play."[7]

Ben Crenshaw ended a two year winless period at the 1992 Western Open. He described his thoughts when he got into contention for the win: "...I realized it was like riding a bike. I just told myself: 'You've been there before. You can do this.' "[8]

Watson won the 1975 British open, and the 1977 Masters and British Open. He described his conclusions and internal dialogue associated with these wins. He said to himself: " 'Maybe you can play this game; maybe you are a quality player.' Obviously the wins helped my confidence. When you are as tight as I am or any player is who is under pressure and you experience that kind of success, you finally start believing in yourself."[9] I would like to see you, unlike Watson, build confidence around good shots and solid putts, not wins.

In an interview with Golf World during the spring of 1992, Payne Stewart said: "My game hasn't been brilliant. There's absolutely nothing mechanical wrong with my game, just confidence and momentum. Once you start playing well, you get that confidence. I still haven't quite got the momentum I need."[10]

On his way to winning the PGA Tour's Canadian Open in September, 1992, Greg Norman made an interesting observation regarding his putting: "I prided myself on that [putting] in the past. I was one of the best putters inside 10 feet God ever put on the planet. This just shows me that all my worries the last 14 months about my putting stroke were ballooned. It's easy to say now, sitting up here after I've won, but my putting stroke never left. It was just a matter of trusting it. Putting had been my downfall all year. You try to fix your stroke and in the end, it's not your stroke, it's probably your posture. I probably fiddled around with it too much."[11]

Confidence is something that is built in small steps. Watson's or Gamez's belief that they can win is based upon a confidence in their total game. Good players have confidence in every shot they make. I believe Sam Snead described the process best.[12] What you feed attention grows. If you focus on your mistakes or poor shots, and take your good shots for granted, you will recall those bad shots when faced with the same or similar situation again. This thinking style will drain your confidence.

HOW CONFIDENCE DEVELOPS

We learn at an early age to practice negative, self-critical thinking. Consider, for example, our parenting styles or the way we were parented. Were we praised for what we did well or more often told what we did incorrectly? Our laws are negative and punitive. Teachers record the number wrong at the top of a corrected paper, seldom the number correct. As children we internalize this communication style; it becomes the foundation of our communication with ourselves. Our internal dialogues with ourselves that become the strategies for our perceptions about the world are shaped from an early age. These events produced our present day thinking habits, especially in our styles of internal communication. Our, negative versus positive perception strategies are learned from how we were parented as children and from the social-interactive world in which we live.

You work at your job for seven hours and fifty-five minutes and things go well. Then, in the span of ninety seconds, you have a problem that becomes apparent to your supervisor. What do you think your supervisor is going to comment on? Will you hear about the seven plus hours of success or the ninety seconds of problem? What will you be thinking about at the end of the day? Will your thought focus be upon the success of the day or the "failure?"

We are unwittingly taught from an early age to take our successes for granted. Self-confidence results from our beliefs and thoughts about our capabilities. If our successes are "taken for granted" and our focus is upon what is wrong rather than upon what is right, our confidence level will be low. Our confidence in our abilities as golfers is equal to our perceptions of our performance.

Everything you do has some form of evaluation by you. You have a habit of paying attention to either problems or successes. I find it interesting and predictable, when working on the practice green with students, that putts roll in the hole and there is complete silence. When a putt misses, there's a comment, a groan, or a frown.

I see the same thing in the full swing: Great shot, not a word; bad shot, and you hear it, sometimes a fairway away; two or three bad shots in a row, look out! When a new student on the lesson tee hits a bad shot he will turn to me and say: "What did I do wrong?" or, "What caused that?" When that same student hits a good shot, I never hear: "What caused that?" That's what I encourage students to ask themselves. Remember, what you feed attention grows. The following are a few examples of what you might say to yourself following a good shot on the range or during play:

- "Contact was solid."
- "I was in balance at setup."
- "I finished the swing in balance."
- "My tempo was good."
- "My setup felt well grounded."
- "I only thought about the shot I was hitting."
- "I planned that shot well."
- "I chose the right club."
- "I was confident I could hit the shot."
- "I had a good image and feeling of the swing I wanted to make."
- "I chose a specific target and stayed focused on the target through my routine."
- "I was relaxed."
- "I thought about the same shot I hit well on my home course last week, I remembered the ball flight, and could picture and feel the swing."
- "I took a practice swing and focused on the feeling of the swing."
- "I was able to repeat the feeling of my practice swing as I hit my shot."
- "Now, I'm going to recall those thoughts and feelings and repeat that shot again," or
- "I'm going to bank that shot so it is available to 'call up' when I need it in the future."

Author and golf enthusiast Ken Blanchard described a discussion he had with Jay Sigel, two-time United States amateur champion, British amateur champion, and the longest-standing member of the Walker Cup Team.

You can never tell from the look on Jay Sigel's face what shot he has hit. He never shows any emotion at all. Blanchard reported Sigel's comments about emotional control: "When I hit a good shot, I tell myself, 'Good Shot,' then respond with an inner smile. On the outside, you wouldn't notice, but there is a difference in the way I respond to a well struck shot and a poor one."[13] Sigel won his first professional tour event in 1994 as a rookie on the Senior Tour.

What do you say and do following good shots and bad shots? Do you talk to yourself about what went well, or do you take good shots for granted and focus most of your attention on poor performance?

I'm sure the concept of a postswing routine is new to most of you, although it exists in every swing. What do you say to yourself after each shot? As I said earlier, you should have an expectancy and belief of hitting every shot you want to hit well. Recognize, after the shot, that the best players in the world hit an average of just under thirteen greens per round and make only forty-five to fifty-five percent of six foot putts.

The greatest players in the world have their problems too. Ray Floyd was contending at the 1994 Senior PGA Championship when he hit two straight shots in the water. Payne Stewart layed up at the 1994 Masters on the 15th hole only to put two straight wedges in the water. Ben Crenshaw took a thirteen on a hole after hitting four straight shots in the water at the 1994 Bob Hope Classic.[14]

As I mentioned earlier, one of the greatest players of the early 1900's was Walter Hagen. He had an interesting strategy for dealing with bad shots. Reportedly, he said he expected to hit seven bad shots a round. When he hit a bad shot, it was expected. It was just another one of the seven. So when he was playing really well and hit a bad shot, it was no surprise and there was no unnecessary emotion wasted on the poor performance that would create tension, a loss of concentration, and so on.

There is one word that will account for sixty to seventy percent of the mental game: That is confidence. When you do anything in your day to day life confidently, you are relaxed and you predict success. You have images of success. Confidence is built on both sides of the golf swing, preswing and postswing, and experienced inswing.

When PGA Tour player Fred Couples was asked how many players on tour are better than he, his response was: "0 [none]. Nick Price had an unbelievable year last year but I don't think he's a better player than I am. I'm part of a group at the top."[15]

Senior PGA Tour player Mike Hill, winner of several regular tour events in the 1970's and two Senior Tour events in the 1990's, says: You have to be "tough in your mental approach, tough enough to stand it when you're not being as successful as you think you ought to be. It takes a certain amount of toughness to win when it's time to come down the stretch and hit golf shots and make yourself do those things. There is a direct correlation between being tough and being a winner...I'm able to draw upon myself to win when I need to...I believe it's the indian, not the arrow."[16]

Confidence carries with it a feeling of being in control. A lack of confidence carries with it a feeling of being out of control. Confidence results from what we tell ourselves about our performance. Consider the following: Your golf instructor follows you for a round of golf and tells you what a great golfer you are every time you hit a good shot. When you hit a poor shot, your instructor says: "Ignore it. All players hit some poor shots." How do you think you would feel at the end of a round? Confident? Probably.

It's important that you are positive with yourself both on and off the course. Most of you wouldn't dare talk to anyone else the way you talk to yourselves. You tend to take good shots for granted and kick yourself in the pants for the poor shots. Consider how you would feel if your instructor ignored your good shots and focused only on your poor shots, or if he told you what an awful player you were.

Johnny Miller described his father's communication with him regarding his golf performance: "One thing that my father always did-and he put in thousands of hours with me-was accentuate the positive and eliminate the negative. He was smart enough to realize that golf is a game of misses, even for the pros, who only hit a couple of shots a day that they would classify as great shots. If you as a parent are always looking for a great shot from your kid, then you're both going to have a lot of disappointment."[17]

Johnny Miller likely internalized this positive communication style from his father and it became a habit of communication with himself. These kinds of habits become the internal dialogue that is the foundation of mental toughness.

Keep one thing in mind: What we feed attention grows!

Like all other habits, this style of internal communication resides in the neural networks of the brain. Given a particular condition, the circuitry is activated or triggered. If the habit pattern is a negative evaluation, that's likely what will be triggered unless you actively intercept this process through conscious thought.

If your style is to negatively and self-critically evaluate yourself, and you choose to change, you will need a written, structured plan and daily practice to change both the behavior and the neuroanatomical basis of the habit. Insight is the first step to change; however, it won't change the long-practiced and reinforced physical structures of the nervous system.

Recent brain research using the PET scanning procedure described in the chapter on visualization showed that people who suffer from depression have a specific neurochemical cluster which non-depressed people don't have. Interestingly, non-depressed people participating in a study were asked to engage in sad or negative thinking. With the onset of negative thoughts, these non-depressed people began to show neurochemical activity at the same site (left frontal cortex) as that found in depressed people.[18] Without question, this study and research in treatment of mood disturbance through cognitive behavior therapy show that negative thinking not only depletes confidence, but also it can affect mood and structural changes in the brain that become the physical foundations of habits.

Psychologists have known for years that a style of negative self-judgment and evaluation creates an emotional state of depression. Cognitive therapists teach their clients to talk differently to themselves by teaching them to discontinue their negative, self-punitive conversations and to substitute supportive, self-reinforcing internal dialogue. I used these strategies for years in my clinical practice to treat a wide range of disorders. These strategies work. If you choose to change, it's going to take time and work. The work includes setting daily goals and practicing new thinking habits daily while recording in a written diary. Strategies for changing your thinking are presented in this chapter and the chapters titled "How To Talk to Yourself On and Off the Golf Course," and "Lift Clean and Place: Applying What You've Learned."

CONSOLIDATION

The neurochemical process of converting short-term memory to long-term memory is called consolidation. Much research has been done over the years on the process of consolidation. Recent studies show that the limbic system, that part of the brain which is the "seat of emotion," plays a major role in the consolidation process. Those events where we experience the greatest emotion are going to be remembered more readily than those events we take for granted or to which we attach minimal emotion.

Where do you respond with more emotion, good play or poor play? Now there is a trap in this process. Too much emotion attached to either good or poor play produces increased arousal. If your personality style is one of an over-aroused player, you run the risk of a loss of focus in the present, increased tempo, and a subsequent deterioration in performance. Acknowledge your good shots quietly to yourself. You know that internal feeling which comes with a good shot. Focus on it. Smile inwardly.

After your round, sit down with your score card and review each hole. Recall your good and great shots. Attach emotion to those shots. Remember, anger and frustration will only serve to set the stage for recall of those bad shots, especially if you continue to emote over one shot.

In this book, you will learn strategies to stop focusing on swing thoughts, to relax, to concentrate, to develop a routine, and so on. One word describes a significant percentage of the natural correction to many of these problem areas. That one word is "confidence." You will be taught strategies to put out the fires of a crisis both on and off the course. However, preventing these crises and developing mental toughness by learning and applying strategies to increase your confidence is a primary goal of this instruction. Learning how to positively reinforce your success is a big step in that direction.

CHANGING YOUR CRITICAL INTERNAL DIALOGUE TO POSITIVE

Gary Player describes the effects of negativity. He refers to comments like: "Gee, I'm unlucky; I never get a good bounce; I know I'm going to land in the water; I work hard and don't get anywhere. These golfers are beaten before they begin. To win, first, you must want to win; second, believe you will win; and third, think only positive thoughts. We create our success or failure on the course primarily by our thoughts."[19]

You say things to yourself you would never say to others. Would you speak to a good friend the way you speak to yourself? Your answer is likely, "No." Why not? Because they wouldn't be a friend for long? Because it would dampen their self-confidence? What's it doing to you? The same thing! As you approach this overview on self-reinforcement, please try to remember the following. Talk to yourself as you would speak to someone you care about:

> ***Encourage, be supporting, counter negativity,***
>
> ***Acknowledge success, and create a positive internal existence.***
>
> ***Be a good friend to yourself.***

The technique of self-reinforcement can be particularly useful in turning around habits of self-punitive or self-critical thinking.

Examples of negative expectations and self-critical thinking might include:

> ***Predicting poor performance in shot making. "I'd better use an old ball here," or "I go right on this hole every time. I might as well set up right."***
>
> ***You evaluate each shot with a focus on your mistakes, errors, or failures. "Missed the green again! That's good for another bogey."***

In day to day life, this thought pattern might follow an eight-hour work day that went well, except for a moment when you made a mistake. If you focus primarily on your mistake instead of the "success" in your day, you will see the day as a failure in general. If you focus only on poor shots, you will see yourself as a bad golfer. Again, please remember, what you feed attention grows.

Examples include:

> ***You evaluate past performance with unrealistic expectations.***
>
> ***You attempt a shot that you aren't capable of executing. You become frustrated with your "less than expected" performance.***
>
> ***You negate positive comments from others verbally or in your thinking: "Not really, I hit it fat," or "It wasn't a bad miss."***
>
> ***If someone compliments you on what a good job you've done, you "undo" the praise by minimizing the importance of the job or talk about the mistakes you made. Or you thank them and focus your thoughts on the mistakes you made or minimize the accomplishment in your thinking.***

Thought patterns such as these are habits. If allowed to increase in frequency, they can virtually immobilize you. If all you notice or pay attention to are your errors and failures, you will begin to feel, "What's the use of trying?" and arousal levels build. This cycle intensifies if you set expectancies that are unrealistic, given your experience and capabilities. Self-reinforcement is a useful technique in interrupting self-critical thoughts.

Don't Blame Me!

There is another style of negativity that many great players use. Tour players have told me that they were instructed as rookies by the better players, "Never blame yourself for poor play." Now, this one was hard for me to take. It is completely contrary to any value I want my children to learn. Of course, you always assume full responsibility for your behavior. Don't blame others or conditions in the environment. Well, I have changed my position, at least my understanding of the principle. My sons will learn of this only if they read this chapter.

If you blame yourself for poor play, you will drain your confidence. If you make a bad stroke on the putting green and tell yourself it was a horrible stroke, you will start to believe you have a problem with mechanics. Begin to search for the mechanics problem and your performance will deteriorate. If it was a spike mark or another player's movement, well, there is no problem with your stroke, just a bad break, and your belief that all is intact mechanically will be retained.

I have heard players overdo the discussion of bad breaks, bad greens, awful playing partners, and the reasons for poor play build and build. It's walking a fine line between retaining confidence and staying positive. I retreat to Walter Hagen's strategy. He said he expected to hit seven bad shots a round. When he hit a bad shot, it was just another one of the seven. And, as Sam Snead said: "...breaks always even out, over the long pull, and that the bane of golf-and life in general-is to remember your mistakes and not your right moves."[20]

As noted, your style of communication with yourself was ingrained at an early age. Not only is it a part of your internal communication, but also it is part of the hard wiring of your nervous system. Like any other habit, it resides as part of the neuroanatomical nervous system structure poised to be triggered by environmental events, the primary triggering event being performance. Performance "lights up" those centers of the brain that ferret out the problem. My swing was too quick, I hit it fat, thin, too high, low, and so on. On those occasions when performance is good, the success is taken for granted.

ATTENTION: A POWERFUL SOCIAL REINFORCER

As a University Professor in a medical school, I wrote several journal articles and made films having to do with the impact of the social consequences of attention on health and illness. These articles included the following case studies:

J.M. was a ten year old boy burned over sixty-five percent of his legs. He was hospitalized several months, made no progress and was facing the amputation of one or both legs. Sammy was projectile vomiting twenty-five to thirty times per day at four years old. Observations of J.M.'s increased pain complaints and refusal to participate in a physical therapy program, and Sammy's vomiting showed that the majority of attention these children received followed the expression of pain and vomiting. When attention was directed to healthy behavior and illness behavior was ignored, these kids got better quickly. The medical and social histories of these children aren't quite as simple as I described; however, the treatment was.[21,22,23]

Attention is a very powerful reinforcer. Whether directed inwardly or outwardly, the things we pay attention to increase in quality and frequency. As already noted many times, what we feed attention grows. It's important to focus our attention on the things we value, things we want to "grow," both on and off the course, especially as related to ourselves.

SELF-REINFORCEMENT

Recall that PGA Tour player Greg Norman says that everybody "...likes to hear words of encouragement as he faces a tough shot, and congratulations after he pulls it off. Unfortunately, unless you play golf with your mother, you can't depend on hearing these things. That's why I talk to myself. Not aloud, but inside my head. The tougher the shot I'm facing, the more I talk. If I'm on the last hole of a tournament, facing a long iron shot to the green and needing a birdie to win, I'll say to myself, 'You know this shot cold, you've knocked it stiff a thousand times, and now you're going to do it again.' I also talk after I hit shots. After a particularly long, straight drive I'll often say, 'Damn, Greg, I'm pretty impressed with that one.' These inner words can be more encouraging than the cheers of the gallery. You don't want to linger too long on your shots-good or bad-but you do want to stamp the good ones on your mind for future reference in pressure situations. Silent self-congratulations is one way to do that."[24]

Strategies for Developing Self-Reinforcing Internal Dialogue

The following are steps for applying self-reinforcement techniques:

Step 1. Listen in on your thinking on and off the course. Keep a diary of your self-communication style. Recognize self-critical thoughts. Behavior follows patterns. Keep a diary of the times and situations in which you practice a negative, self-critical style of thinking and when you practice a positive, self-supporting style. The conditions in which these patterns of internal dialogue occur will become apparent. Once you identify the times and situations for negative, self-critical discussion, discontinue your diary of this negative style. Remember, what you feed attention grows. Keep a diary only of your positive conversations with yourself.

Step 2. Develop "cues" or reminders to focus on self-supporting statements. Place a 5 X 7 card on your mirror or in your desk drawer that you open every morning and evening. Write "Positive Focus, Praise Self" or some similar reminder on this card.

Step 3. Use the techniques for thought restructuring covered in the chapter "How to Talk to Yourself On and Off the Golf Course." Review the consequences of self-critical thinking, e.g., anger, frustration, decreased self-esteem, immobilization, decreased initiative, increased muscle tension, physiology of arousal, sadness, poor performance (and even depression in the more severe circumstances). Use these as reminders to redirect your thinking to mindfulness and a positive self focus.

Step 4. Practice the relaxation strategies and positive imagery you will be learning in subsequent chapters. See yourself being successful. Schedule times daily when and where you will practice the imagery strategies. Focus on your recent success and future goals during these practice times.

Step 5. Consider all the shots you hit well today, rather than the shots you missed, the score, bogeys, doubles, putts, etc. Say things to yourself that will compete with self-criticism. "I played the best I could today. I have the opportunity to create whatever kind of day I choose. I am going to enjoy the rest of the day." Note: The MIND UNDER PAR series™ *SCORECARD* provides the structure for this practice.

Step 6. Keep a daily diary of the positive aspects of your game and your life. Review this diary at least weekly, and visually recall the days and shots.

Research in behavior therapy shows a common denominator for behavior change regardless of what the behavior is. That common denominator is keeping a diary. If you write things down daily, you will begin to see a positive change. Be sure your diary is positive, and review your entries every couple of days. As long as you keep a positive diary, you will continue to experience behavior change. Review your diary weekly on the same day at the same time every week. Notice and record your success in change.

You can begin this process on the course and carry it into your day to day life or vice versa. If you have a resume, review it. Look at what you have accomplished. Don't negate the positive. Recognize and focus on your accomplishments. This is a good springboard to begin your diary.

SUCCESS FOCUS

PGA Tour player Patrick Burke won his second Australian Tour event in December of 1994. He won his first, the Tournament Players Championship, in January of 1994. He contracted a virus at a European Tour event in the spring and was ill throughout the summer of 1994. He missed several PGA Tour events because of health.

Patrick's confidence was beginning to wane due to his mediocre play during his illness. In preparation for returning to Australia to resume the tour in the fall, he began repeatedly watching a video of his January win. He finished second at the first event, Bali, and won the Victorian Open the following week.[25] Seeing yourself succeed builds confidence. If you don't have a video of your past success, recall those successes from memory, and replay them over and over again in your mind.

Recall that Greg Norman describes his postswing routine and how he talks to himself so he can remember and repeat good shots: "I also talk after I hit shots. After a particularly long, straight drive I'll often say, 'Damn, Greg, I'm pretty impressed with that one.' These inner words can be more encouraging than the cheers of the gallery. You don't want to linger too long on your shots-good or bad-but you do want to stamp the good ones on your mind for future reference in pressure situations. Silent self-congratulations is one way to do that."[26]

Focusing on success is a foreign concept to many of you. As noted, most of us take our success for granted, but not peak performers like Greg Norman. A success focus is the very foundation on which confidence is built. Call it self-reinforcement, self-congratulations, positive internal dialogue, or positive self talk, it's all the same. What it is not is taking your success for granted.

I was traveling to a tournament site with my friend and fellow teacher, Derek Hardy. We were discussing the concept of self-reinforcement as part of the postswing routine. This discussion led to the consideration of the kinds of comments a player might make to himself after a good or great shot. These comments are supportive and build confidence in our ability to perform. The following is the list we generated:

- "Great shot!"
- "Terrific!"
- "OK."
- "I can't be stopped."
- "It's mine."
- "Yes."
- "Awesome."
- "Felt great."
- "On line all the way."
- "That was solid."
- "Easy."
- "I'm playing well."

- "Super!"
- "Outstanding."
- "Good show."
- "Beautiful!"
- "I'm good."
- "Boy, can I putt."
- "I know I can do this."
- "This is mine."
- "It's a walk in the park."
- "Here I come!"
- "I have a great short game."
- "I've hit every drive solidly."
- "The fairways are 200 yards wide."
- "Smooth!"
- "What a shot."
- "Just as I called it."
- "Perfect."
- "Excellent."
- "That's a 10."
- "Piece of cake."
- "Pure!"

This list is an ideal. These comments will be performance enhancing. Remember, what you feed attention grows. I don't suggest that you announce any of these to your playing partners, only to yourself. There's a feeling that only you will experience when you hit a good shot. Savor that feeling. Recall the ball flight and the feeling of the swing. Smile inwardly. Never let your eyes drop below the horizon.

There's a fine line between being self-supporting and building confidence, and being obnoxious. You don't need to say these things to others; your performance will speak for itself. When you are complimented by your playing partners, just say: "Thanks." Don't negate the compliment, regardless of how uncomfortable it may make you at the time. Don't allow yourself to undo the compliment in your thinking. Say: "Thanks" and tell yourself to accept the compliment. It's like changing your grip or putting your underwear on backwards. It's uncomfortable at first, but you get used to it and in time it feels natural.

Peak performers have an internal dialogue of confidence that sustains them. After winning his first Senior PGA Tour victory at Dearborn, Michigan, 1991 Ryder Cup Captain Dave Stockton said of the nine foot putt he had to win: "I wouldn't want anyone else to putt that. I was born being able to putt."[27]

Lee Trevino won his fifth Senior Tour title at the Bell Atlantic Classic in May of 1992. After that win, he had three top ten finishes and thumb surgery in December of 1992. He played his first 1993 tournament in mid March and had only one top ten finish in his first five starts. He finally got into contention again at the 1993 Bell Atlantic Classic where he was defending his title. He finished that tournament tied for third. He won the following week at the Cadillac NFL Golf Classic by two shots. He said of his climb back to the top: "I didn't expect to do anything last week and then when I got in the lead I was as surprised as anybody. But I came into this week expecting to win."[28]

Peak performance for world class players and the mental toughness attitude that they can win are not something with which they are born. The internal dialogue and associated confidence are learned through a focus on their successful experiences. Many people have success; however, in this success their focus is still on what went wrong, not what went right.

PGA Tour Player Rocco Mediate described an event that changed his outlook and expectancy when he is playing poorly. He relates the story: "It happened at Bay Hill this year [1993]. I was six over par after 11 holes the first day. Six over, I just doubled the 11th. I'm standing on the 12th tee. It's windy and it's tough. I got up and told my caddie. 'If we can just get two or three birdies, shoot 75 or 76, OK, I can handle it.' Hey, I just miss birdie at 12. I birdie 13. I get up and down at 14. I birdie 15, eagle 16, birdie 17 and 18. When I got done, I looked at my caddie and said, 'What did I shoot?' He said, 'Even par.' I couldn't believe it. That changed my outlook on golf. I feel like now, no matter where I am, I can come back from adversity. I may not do it. But I know I've done it already."[29]

Senior PGA Tour player Larry Gilbert won the 1994 Vantage Championship. His best finish prior to that win was a second in December, 1993 when he lost to Ray Floyd in a playoff. He had earned over one million dollars on the Senior Tour despite not having won. He said the following regarding his climb to victory: "I couldn't convince myself that I was good enough to compete with those guys. Confidence is 90 percent of the battle against these guys. If you think you can beat 'em, you just might."[30]

After winning the 1993 Bob Hope Chrysler Classic, Tom Kite attributed his impressive play over the last year to confidence: "It's just confidence in my game. A little bit of maturing. Now when I look at the guys around me there's not many I say, 'Boy, that guy's better than I am' "[31]

FAILURE FOCUS

Even world class players have periods of poor performance that deplete their confidence in one part of their game, often putting. Ray Floyd finished third in a field of four greats that included Chi Chi Rodriguez, Arnold Palmer, and Jack Nicklaus at the 1993 Senior Skins game. Floyd won $60,000 with birdies at the first, fourth and sixth holes, and then his putting went sour and he was shut out over the last fourteen holes (two playoff holes). "I just lost confidence in my putter. When you miss a few it just gets into your mind."[32]

In 1986, Lee Trevino said of Bob Tway: "If you're looking for the next superstar, there he is. That guy can golf his ball." In 1993, Golf Digest's Michael Bamberger interviewed Bob Tway during The Colonial, a Texas PGA Tour stop. He had missed seven cuts in a row, shooting two rounds of 81 and four rounds in the high 70's. His last win was the Las Vegas Invitational in 1990. He finished 179th on the PGA money list for 1992.

Tway spoke candidly about his slide from the top: "The problems started off mechanical and then they got mental. I started driving the ball bad, and then I reached a point where I'd get to a tee and say, 'Where's this one gonna go?' My confidence level changed. When you're playing good you have a lot of inner calmness, your mind is working very, very slowly. When I'm feeling confident, everything is so slow. When you're playing poorly your mind is bombarded with thoughts."[33]

Bob Tway didn't like the way his swing felt after a successful year in 1986. Sound familiar? Recall Sandy Lyle, David Frost, and Greg Norman. So, Tway turned to mechanics and began to make changes. He had a "handsy but rhythmic hook swing, the swing that won the [1986] PGA Championship."[34]

His thoughts the year following his PGA Championship win are interesting: "Your expectations change. So you go out the next year and kind of expect to keep playing that way. What you don't realize is that everything was going very good for you to do that. So when things aren't going that way, it's like, 'What's wrong? How come I can't keep doing what I did before?' Our expectations and the level of play, it's not reality. Reality is to keep plugging along."[35]

Tway worked on mechanics and began to show improvement. Instructor David Leadbetter summarized Tway's plight: "Technically, he has a better swing now than he did in '86, but in tournaments it's almost as if he has the yips with the driver. Making good swings on the practice tee doesn't mean diddly when you have no confidence."[36] In the end, Tway returned to the "feel" that won the 1986 PGA championship, his old swing.

Tway made a significant breakthrough when he won the MCI Classic in April 1995 in a three-way playoff with David Frost and Nolan Henke. He commented that the win was a boost to his confidence.

In spite of the slow climb back to the top Bob Tway experienced before his 1995 win, his comments reflected interesting insight during his struggle: "Let's say your confidence is low, but your ball striking is starting to get better. Your mind hasn't caught up to your ball striking. You've got to hit more good shots to get those bad shots out of your mind. I've actually been hitting the ball better lately, but I'm not as comfortable and as relaxed as I should be because I still have a lot of memory of hitting crummy shots. You've got to hit a lot of good shots in competition until you can get relaxed. I can't really brainwash myself and say 'OK, you're gonna hit good shots.' People say, 'Relax and let it go.' It's easy to let it go when it's going good. But if a couple shots go right and a couple left, it's not so easy."[37]

The brain research discussed in the chapter on visualization suggests that a focus on an image of poor shots "lights up" the brain in areas to produce that same poor performance.

Johnny Miller reflected on Bob Tway's swing changes: "...when I think of Tway, I think of the one piece of advice I'd give every serious golfer: Use your own darn swing and tell everybody else to shove it. Tell them to keep their swing thoughts to themselves. Why? Because more players get ruined by trying to improve their swings instead of just going with the swings that won them all those junior and college tournaments."[38]

Expectancy also played a role in Tway's dilemma. European and US PGA Tours player Seve Ballesteros has won eighteen straight years on the European Tour. He is well known for hitting tee shots "everywhere" and still making birdies and pars from the rough, from behind trees, out of bunkers, and even from an occasional parking lot. Ballesteros expects to hit some tee shots "sideways;" then he finds his ball and the next target. During his search for the perfect swing, Tway expected to hit his tee shots in the fairway. When he didn't, he described a loss of confidence and poor play.

The majority of you likely take your good shots for granted and direct most of your attention to your poor performance. What do you think about after a round? Do you think about the great drives, fairway shots, chips and putts, or do you think about the bad breaks, and the hooks and slices, or shots into the hazards? The following is a list of preswing and postswing statements that will deplete your confidence, cause you to be distracted, frustrated and angry, increase tension, promote bad swing mechanics and create poor performance.

Preswing

- "I can't."
- "This is a big carry."
- "I wonder if this is enough club."
- "I need this..."
- "I have to..."
- "I'm playing over my head!"
- "Keep your head down/Straight left arm/Don't look up."
- "If I go par, par this will be my best score ever."
- "Don't hit it left."
- "I hate this hole/shot/club."
- "I may as well kick it; I can't putt."
- "Don't be short/long."
- "The last time I had this shot I hit it dead (left, right and so on)."
- "The hazards are short left and long right."

Postswing

- "What's wrong with you!?"
- "Those lessons haven't helped!"
- "That stinks!"
- "I may as well give this game up!"
- "That was awful!"
- "Stupid!"
- "You suck!"
- "Why don't you think you idiot!?"
- "You @#$% %^ @&*(*@ !"
- "You should play left-handed."
- "You belong on the red tees."
- "Your mother is better than you are."
- "If you could putt, that would only leave woods and irons to work on!"
- "That was a 300 yard drive: 200 yards up and 100 yards out."

POST SWING STEAM

There is a difference between being complacent with poor performance and self-critical as in the previous examples. Sam Snead referred to it as letting off steam, while at the same time knowing when to shut off the steam valve. However, he did not endorse verbally beating yourself up. Great players intuitively know that a self-critical posture will deplete their confidence, and indifference takes them no where.

Regarding indifference, Sam Snead said: "Show me the fellow who walks along calmly after topping a drive or missing a kick-in putt, showing the world he is in perfect control yet burning up inside and I'll show you one who is going to lose."[39]

Similarly, Lee Trevino described the close of 1992 and his depleted confidence: "I had no confidence. It's not easy walking around with spring in your legs when you're making bogeys. I want to win...I've got a lot of killer instinct in me and if people expect me to jump up and down when I'm shooting 75, well, that just isn't me...You show me a guy who smiles when he's shooting 75, and I'll show you a guy who's broke."[40]

There is a fine line to walk in learning to be self-supporting in your internal dialogue, while at the same time learning to quickly vent frustration. Determine how much "venting" of frustration improves your play and how much causes a deterioration in performance. It varies from one player to another. The content of the venting is also important. If your comments are self-punishing, your confidence will be drained.

This is a good time to recall Walter Hagen's strategy for dealing with poor play. Remember, Hagen expected to hit seven bad shots a round. When he hit a bad shot, it was just one of the seven. Walter Hagen was one of the greatest players to play the game. How many bad shots a round should you expect? Some of you may see Hagen's style as indifferent. It was, but it doesn't mean he didn't care. He knew what getting upset can do to a score. In addition to Hagen's style, you can also learn to be a good internal coach.

Be a good motivator: "Com'on, you can play better than this! Get focused! You are much better than you are playing!" This internal dialogue is not self-punishing. It's being an internal motivator, a good coach. The emotional states of anxiety and anger are incompatible. Similarly, this "good coach" internal dialogue will help override any anxiety you might experience with poor play. Just keep that supportive, no nonsense, aggressive dialogue going. Be patient. The chapter titled "Lift Clean and Place: Applying What You've Learned" provides several examples of how to redirect your internal dialogue to improve performance.

I'm going to refer back to one of Sam Snead's comments that says it all:

"Whenever I've been able to pull myself out of a slump, it's because I didn't forget that breaks always even out, over the long pull, and that the bane of golf-and life in general-is to remember your mistakes and not your right moves. In clubhouses, you'll see men sitting around complaining going over their bad shots. They should think back to their good shots, then try to repeat them.

"This is the only way to build that feeling called confidence. You can build it-or tear yourself down. The choice is up to every individual. If you know yourself to be a whiner, you'll never play up to your full ability. It takes guts to be an optimist in golf. He who thinks like a winner will win."[41]

Remember, we recall things to which we attach emotion. Review your good and great shots following a round, and attach emotions to those shots, not your poor shots. It is important to remember that your nervous system is storing experiences with every event and golf swing you make. If you are negative and focus on your mistakes, your confidence will be low. You don't have to get overly excited with good shots, just note them and focus on them immediately following the shot and after your round.

You will build confidence in small steps. The first step is to begin to "listen" to your thinking and how you talk to yourself both on and off the course. If you are negative and self-punishing off the course, you will be negative and self-punishing on the course.

I have a standing rule for students attending our golf schools at Pelican Hill Golf Club and Resort at Newport Coast, California: If you call yourself a name on the range or during play, that becomes your name for the remainder of the school. We've had some interesting people come through our schools. "Oh God, No!" joined me on the first tee one weekend and "Jesus Christ" picked up our group on the twelfth hole. "You stupid #@%^&#$!!" usually attends a school once a month.

The next time you tee it up with your foursome, adopt the *Mind Under Par* rule: If you call yourself a name, it becomes your name for the remainder of the round. This rule will help you become more aware of your verbal self-abuse and add humor to your round.

STRATEGIES FOR A SUCCESS FOCUS

Let's look again at several ways you can begin to make changes.

Pick out what was right about a shot. Don't take anything for granted.

- "Felt solid."
- "Tempo was good."
- "It was on line."
- "Good distance feel."
- "Right club selection."
- "I am mindful and focused in the present."
- "My routine is becoming more and more automatic."
- "I'm feeling more relaxed with deep breathing and quieted movement."
- "I'm playing one shot at a time and think about score only after the round."
- "I'm being patient and mentally tough. I'm managing my anger."
- "I'm really into my targets. I'm seeing every shot. I'm even able to recall similar shots I've hit well and use that ballflight memory for visualization. I play so much better when I am able to see what kind of a shot I want to hit. That really helps me stay narrowly focused."

Pick out what is right about off-course behavior.

- "My intent was good."
- "I gave one hundred percent."
- "I did what I felt was right."
- "I did a good job."

- "I am being more positive and I feel better about me and life."
- "Being more positive makes errors less emotional and easier to correct."
- "I'm being more assertive and I am free of a lot of my distressing thinking."
- "Being positive and complimenting others makes me and them feel good."
- "When I eliminate negativity about others, I feel better about them and myself."
- "I like myself."
- "I am good at this."
- "That's a big positive change for me."
- "I feel relaxed."
- "I feel good."
- "This stuff really works."

Develop written reminders or "cues" to keep a positive focus and record these thoughts in a daily diary. Talk regularly to someone close to you about your goals and review them regularly. Write down your successes only. I ask the players I work with to write down what they did well after each round.

PRACTICE TO BUILD CONFIDENCE

PGA Tour champion Gary Player established practice goals that required a specific performance before he discontinued practice. He described some of these practice routines in a 1967 book: "I wouldn't leave that bunker until I'd holed five shots. I'd just stay there until I'd done it, even if it took two or three hours. ...I had my own private self imposed goals; I had to chip five into the hole before I'd quit."[42]

Player also says if you think: "I'm going to get this chip close enough for one putt," it is the wrong attitude. He says you should focus on holing out every shot.[43]

Nothing will build your confidence faster than successful performance, especially if you will focus your attention on your successes. There are a number of strategies you can use to focus on success while practicing.

Set specific, measurable practice goals. Be sure you can succeed at the first level. Once you succeed, gradually increase the difficulty level. The goals of the tour player and low handicappers are going to be much higher than the fifteen index player. The tour player who holes out bunker shots and chips in from the fringe will have goals to hole a set number of shots before moving to the next drill.

The following are a list of successive approximations for practicing shots from greenside sand bunkers for the higher index player. Regardless what your playing level is, adopt the same strategy of setting goals.

A. Get five of ten shots out of practice bunker.

B. Get seven of ten shots out of practice bunker.

C. Get nine of ten shots out of practice bunker.

D. Get ten of ten shots out of

practice bunker.

E. Get five of ten shots within ten feet of hole.

F. Get seven of ten shots within ten feet of hole.

Your entry level may be at step F for this drill or you may enter at ten of ten within five feet of the hole. You can always get closer. Finally, you will be holing out one of ten and so on. As noted, the tour player will set goals for holing shots. You must, however, set realistic goals. Realistic starting goals simply mean you are capable of having success relatively quickly.

If during your practice sessions you go from step B (seven out of ten shots out of practice bunker) to step C and don't have success, one of two things has happened.

1. ***The step between B and C is too big and you need to break down the step further, or***

2. ***You have reached your maximum performance capability.***

If you have reached your maximum performance capability, it's time for a lesson. In fact, it's a good idea to have a lesson on putting, chipping, bunker shots, and so on before you set practice goals. There's no substitute for good technique, especially with trouble shots and shots that are going to help you score, in other words, the short game.

These techniques will also give you a good idea of your proficiency level across a variety of shots and give you realistic performance expectancies. If you are hitting seven out of ten bunker shots within ten feet of the hole during your practice times, there is no reason to expect anything less than that during play. In fact, both during practice and play I would like for you to see the ball land and roll into the hole before every shot. Use your practice success level (seven out of ten bunker shots within ten feet of the hole) as a postswing expectancy evaluation. You should be satisfied with every shot within your practice success range.

Always practice with a purpose and a specific goal. Set practice goals and keep a diary so you can follow your progress. Jackie Burke, former PGA Tour Champion, once told me that he would not leave the practice green in the evening until he made one hundred straight three footers. If he missed one, he started over. He set balls in a circle around the hole. There is a different putt on every stroke. This is called a clock drill. Jackie said when it came to making a three footer under pressure it was just another one of the one hundred.[44]

If you start this drill, depending on your entering skill level, you might begin at five or ten in a row and gradually build to a level that meets your time allocation for practice. Remember, the bigger the performance goal, the longer the time allocation.

No matter what shot you practice, if you practice with a purpose and set goals, you will be more confident when you have that shot during a round. Note: the *MIND UNDER PAR* series™: *Setting Practice Goals For Golf*, provides a comprehensive program for developing shot proficiency and building confidence.

Another practice strategy to build confidence is to play from closer tees. If you are accustomed to playing from the regular men's tees, play the ladies' tees for a few rounds. If you usually play from the men's championship tees, play a few rounds from the men's regular tees. You will not only be playing a shorter course to build confidence, you will have different shots to the green than usual. Forget about what people think when you play from the closer tees. In fact, if you are concerned about what people think, play from the red tees, and practice quieting your internal dialogue and becoming focused in the present. You can work on two goals at once, building confidence and setting aside thoughts of what others might be thinking. Perform for yourself and nobody else.

Lastly, during play rate each shot on a one to ten scale. Record only the eight, nine, and ten shots on your scorecard. If you hit a shot you judge to be seven or less, don't record it. Review your eight, nine, and ten rated shots at the end of each round. Think about and picture each shot. Feel and see the swing that produced that shot. Focusing only on your success will help you build confidence. The MIND UNDER PAR series™ *SCORECARD* presents a comprehensive summary, examples for building confidence, and practice strategies to recall good shots for future rounds.

GENERALIZATION

Let's assume you practice swing changes on the range and have success. When you attempt to take those swing changes out to the course to play, your performance begins to deteriorate. Your thoughts go to the mechanics of your swing and the deterioration is amplified. When you return to the range you are able to perform well again. The "state" or situation of the range, where learning originally occurred, promotes the repeated good performance. This is called "state dependent" learning. The original learning occurred in the "state" of the relaxed, non-demanding environment of the range. It's easily repeated when you return to the range.

The range is relaxed, non-threatening, and provides no performance demands. You likely hit several shots in a row with the same club. Overall, arousal on the range is low. You have never had to perform your swing changes with an internal state of high arousal. You go out to the course to play and the range performance abandons you.

Many players ask: "Why can't I hit on the course the way I can hit on the range?" The answer is you don't practice the way you play. When you practice the way you play, you will be able to repeat your range performance on the course in increasingly more competitive or stressful situations. This means hitting only one shot at a time with one club on the practice range. Go through your full routine on each shot and start to practice the way you play. Choose targets and practice deep diaphragmatic breathing and mindfulness between shots. With repeated practice the way you play, you will be able to take the swing you make on the range to the course successfully.

LPGA Tour player and US Open champion Meg Mallon describes her practice strategies under the direction of PGA instructor Mike McGetrick: "The thing I've learned from Mike is that routine is such a big part of the shot. ...Every time I hit a shot on the range, I step back and line it up. I go through the same routine I go through on the golf course."[45]

Mallon also described how she gets a "new shot" to a point of confidence so she can take it into a tournament round: "I love to go out on the course on practice holes and hit over and over again the shot I've been learning. This shows me I can do it on the golf course."[46]

Give yourself different lies on the range. Practice with a head wind and a tail wind. Compete with your friends hitting to a target on the range. Play a practice round and play two balls. Play your worst ball on each shot. That means if you hit your first shot to the green to within ten feet of the pin, you must hit it within ten feet to have at least that shot. Asian, Australian and PGA Tour player Dennis Paulson says he plays the worst ball game frequently. He indicates that it's the best way to prepare for a tournament. He notes: "You find yourself thinking a lot like you do during a tournament and you begin your breathing and thought restructuring and working on staying focused on one shot at a time."[47]

A story is told about Sam Snead betting Doug Sanders $500 that he would play worst ball and not make more than a bogey on any one hole. Sam lasted three holes before he lost the bet.

Now you enter a tournament. Your arousal is high. You have never used the "new swing" in an atmosphere of high internal arousal. You begin to notice remnants of your "old swing" surface again. Your swing tempo quickens. Why? The transfer of training from the range to casual play to tournament play is called generalization. This transfer of training occurs only through repeated exposure to high arousal states during play. Many teachers will encourage early, repeated exposure to high arousal conditions so there is "habituation" to the effects of stressful situations. That is why many teachers advocate gambling on the course, no matter how small the bet. Repeated exposure during play to having something "on the line" provides a learning opportunity during various arousal states.

Practicing one shot at a time while going through your full routine is the first step toward improved on-course performance. The next step is to play in the easiest performance situation you can and gradually increase the stressful conditions over time. Compile a list from easiest to most difficult playing conditions for you.

For example:

1. Playing alone.
2. Playing with players whose handicaps are higher than mine.
3. Playing with friends who have the same handicap.
4. Playing with players better than I.
5. Playing in a tournament scramble format, best ball, and so on.
6. Match play tournament.
7. Stroke play tournament: Club, school, city, state, US amateur, mini, Nike, PGA, and LPGA Tours.

Consider this list a ladder to climb and each step a rung. Your starting level on this list may not be item number one. You will find plateaus in your performance at various rungs. It simply means you need to participate at that level longer. If the plateau is prolonged, it may be time to look at setting goals for practice that are performance based.

Every club champion has experienced plateaus on different rungs. Every PGA Tour player has experienced plateaus and periods of adaptation on the rungs of this ladder. Remember, the range is filled with scratch golfers. Take it from the range to the course.

Establishing practice criteria that promote high arousal is another strategy. For example: "I will leave the putting green only after I make thirty consecutive three foot putts. If I miss a putt, I'll start over." Or, "I will leave the range only after I hit ten straight wedges within five feet of the flag. If I'm outside five feet on any one shot, I start over." You can imagine how much pressure and frustration you would begin to experience after missing your twenty-eighth putt or your tenth wedge shot. As you have success at each stage, you increase the criterion to thirty-five, forty, seventy-five, one hundred putts or twelve, fifteen, twenty, thirty wedge shots until you experience pressure. Range contests with other players can also add competition and pressure that is good practice exposure.

This is why the experience of competition seasons a tour player or competitive amateur. The frequent "state" of intense competition provides an opportunity for learning, both mental and mechanical. After years of repeated experience in the "state" of competition, a player learns mental and mechanical strategies that hold up well under pressure.

SITUATIONAL CONFIDENCE

Our confidence changes depending on the conditions of play, with whom we play, and how we perceive these conditions as related to our past success and experiences. When faced with situations in which we have performed well in the past, our confidence rises.

Lanny Wadkins was five shots off of the lead going into the final round of the Greater Hartford Open, Sunday, August 2, 1992. In an interview prior to that round, Wadkins, when asked if he thought he had a chance to win, responded: "Maybe if it got windy and I shot 65." He was paired with Billy Ray Brown, another good wind player. On the practice tee Sunday morning, the wind began to blow. Wadkins turned to Billy Ray Brown and said: "Hey, we have a chance." Wadkins shot 65 and won the tournament.[48]

On July 11, 1993 Lanny Wadkins was tied for the lead following the third round at the PGA Tour Anheuser-Busch Golf Classic at Williamsburg, Virginia after shooting a 64 on Saturday. The heat index was as high as 140 and a minimum of 115 during that weekend.

Wadkins was interviewed following the third round. His response to his lead on Saturday was a bit different from the year before. "There's one more day to go. Still time to screw it up." Perhaps the conditions of the heat, being in the lead, his evaluation of his performance, or just not wanting to sound too confident produced that response.

However, it was a self-fulfilling prophecy. On Sunday Wadkins shot a one under par 70 to finish the tournament three shots behind the winner, Jim Gallagher, Jr. Following the Sunday round, Wadkins summarized his impressions of his play: "It was a bad day for me. I'm totally disgusted with the way I played."[49]

Different situations or conditions promote different degrees of confidence or lack thereof. The best players have the greatest number of conditions that promote confidence and the fewest number that create self-doubt. Those players who have the most mental toughness believe they can perform well regardless of what the conditions are or what their recent performance has been.

The following are a few examples of conditions that will cue an attitude of confidence or one of self-doubt:

- Weather: wind, rain, sun, hot, cold
- Start round well, or poorly
- Bogey or series of bogeys
- Birdie or series of birdies
- Someone else's poor play/good play
- Casual round versus practice round versus tournament round
- Playing with good/better players
- One, two (three/four, etc.) three putt greens in a row.
- Club to be used (1, 2, 3 iron, driver, fairway wood, etc.)
- Water hazard, trees, sand, etc. between you and target
- One putt from outside six feet two greens in a row
- Make four three footers in a row
- Left to right putts
- Right to left putts
- Fairway or greenside bunker shot
- High score/low score on the last round you played
- Hit good/bad shot the last time you played this hole
- Played well in same tournament last year
- Played poorly in same tournament last year
- Playing "home course"
- Hard/soft greens
- Consecutive "bad" shots
- Consecutive "good" shots
- Hit poorly on the range before play
- Hit well on the range before play
- Putt poorly on the practice green before play
- Putt well on the practice green before play

and the list goes on...

Johnny Miller won the 1994 AT&T at Pebble Beach making it his third time to win that title (1974, 1987, and 1994). Miller had some interesting observations regarding his 1994 win: "I wasn't suppose to win. I'm retired. I'm a golf announcer. I don't play more than twenty-five rounds of golf a year. I don't practice...I don't know what it is but something about this course makes me hit it good. I feel like I play young when I come to Pebble Beach."[50]

The best players will focus and capitalize on confidence building events and situations, and minimize their attention to problems, with the exception of practice to overcome deficits.

During a 1992 interview, Fred Couples was relating the effects that comments from Tom Watson had on him: "... when someone like Tom Watson says something good about you, it can have a big effect on you.

...he told me, 'You're a great player, keep doing what you're doing and it'll happen.' "[51]

When Nick Price won the 1992 PGA championship at Bellerive CC in Saint Louis, he made an interesting observation: "Tom Kite winning the Open at forty-two helped me a lot. I figured when you're in your mid to late 30s, you'd better start winning. With older guys like Raymond Floyd winning, that gave me the confidence there was time left for me."[52]

Most people think that once an athlete in one sport experiences pressure, he won't have problems with pressure in other sports. Not so. This is true only if that athlete has had repeated exposure to "pressure" in both sports.

Miami Dolphins quarterback Dan Marino was playing in a shootout with nine PGA pros during the spring of 1992. In an interview with Golf World Magazine, Marino said: "Yeah, I was nervous. The worst part was the tee shot. That's as hard as anything I've done. I was happy because I didn't hit nobody."[53] This is the same person who played in the Super Bowl on national television in front of millions of people.

Your comfort zone and your confidence zone are determined by you and your prior experiences in those situations and your perceptions. With repeated exposure to those conditions, Dan Marino would likely have little difficulty with what Sam Snead called "first tee jitters."

PGA Tour player Patrick Burke played his first major at the US Open in Pebble Beach, California in June of 1992. I met him on Thursday morning prior to the first round. I had never seen him so revved up internally. He said he had played a practice round and noted, as is customary for the US Open, the roughs were high, the fairways were narrow, and the greens were quick. Patrick informed me that he had removed two of his wedges and replaced them with one wedge and a cleek (5 wood-railer) so he could escape more easily from the deep rough. He had also changed his putter because of the quickness of the greens. The first round he struggled. It was painful to watch. In spite of the cleek, he still had problems with the rough. He shot 79 the first day and his play was well below his capability. After the round, he remarked that his greatest problem was getting close to the pin since he didn't use his normal wedges which he knew well and with which he was confident.

During dinner, we discussed the obvious, returning to the full set of clubs he usually played. The second day, with an eagle and two birdies, Patrick was four under after nine holes. He brought it in even on the day after two double bogeys. He missed the cut and the rest is history. This was an important lesson for Patrick. The "situation" of his first major affected his confidence in his ability to perform in US Open conditions. His second day took care of all the doubts.[54]

MENTAL TOUGHNESS

In 1988, Matt Biondi was a member of the US Olympic swim team. Many predicted that Biondi would repeat Mark Spitz's feat of seven gold medals. Biondi won a bronze and siliver his first two events. Television announcers began to prepare the public for continued "sub gold" perfomance. Onlookers didn't have expectations for gold in Biondi's subsequent events. Biondi responded with five consecutive gold medals.

Why was Matt Biondi able to turn his performance around? Prior to the Olympics, Matt Biondi was given false feedback by his coach on the one hundred-yard butterfly. His actual time was 50.2 seconds, he was told his time was 51.7 seconds. Biondi was asked to rest and repeat the event again. The second time he improved to 50.0 seconds, better than his actual first time.[55] It is not surprising that Matt Biondi was able to come off bronze and silver medals and turn in a golden performance. When faced with negative feedback, he turned things up a notch, stayed focused, and performed better. Matt Biondi is mentally tough.

Brad Faxon won over 1 million dollars on the PGA Tour in 1996 to finish eigth on the money list and he was ranked twenty-fourth in the world. 1996 PGA Tour statistics showed that Faxon was ranked 170th in average driving distance, 142nd in total fairways hit,134th in greens in regulation and first in putting with an average of 1.709 putts per hole. He played in twenty- two tournaments and made twenty-two cuts. His peers will tell you that he scores well with these statistics for two reasons. The first is reason is obvious. When you can putt like Brad Faxon, you can score. Secondly, they will tell you that Brad Faxon can hit the ball 100 yards off line and you would never know he had hit a bad shot. He simply finds his ball and his next target. The key to scoring well is to have a strong short game and the mental toughness to negate a loss of confidence with poor play.

The next time you start to miss fairways and greens or hit the ball off line, think about Brad Faxon. Be mentally tough and a good internal caddie.

European and PGA Tour player David Feherty made an interesting observation about the importance of how you handle adversity. He said: "...It's not what happens to you that matters in the long run. It's your attitude. That's what determines how you cope with the next experience that comes along...Quite often it's how you deal with failure that determines how you achieve success...The mental process is like building a muscle. It's not letting your whole framework of thinking fall down around you. It's having the resolve and mental toughness to take it on the chin, keep your head up, and feel good about yourself for having done that. You can either feel bad because you failed or good because of your positive reactions to it. That will give you the armor to cope with it the next time."[56]

Also recall what Sam Snead said about giving up: "In tossing in your cards after a bad beginning you also undermine your whole game, because to quit between tee and green is more habit forming than drinking a highball before breakfast."[57]

We think in pictures. If you are confident and mentally tough, you will see success. If you are fearful, don't believe you are capable, or interpret poor perfomance as "not having it today," you will give up and see failure. The next chapter describes the role these pictures have on performance.

ENDNOTES

1. Peter Jacobsen and Jack Sheehan, *Buried Lies: True Tales and Tall Stories from the PGA Tour* (New York: G.P. Putnam's Sons, 1993), p. 33.

2. George Peper, "The World's Best Putter," *Golf Magazine* (September, 1994): p. 12.

3. Jack Nicklaus and Ken Bowden, "All About Putting," *Golf Magazine* (September, 1994): p. 34.

4. Nicklaus and Bowden, "All About Putting," pp. 36-38.

5. Sam Snead and Al Stump, *The Education of a Golfer* (New York: Simon and Schuster, 1961), pp. 243-244.

6. Tim Rosaforte, "Running to the Horizon With His Arse on Fire, " *Golf Illustrated* (July, 1992): p. 37.

7. Jim Moriarty, "Playing the Hot Hand," *Golf Digest* (June, 1990): p. 44.

8. Geoff Russell, "Won From the Heart," *Golf World* (July 10, 1992): p. 29.

9. *The History of the PGA Tour*, Film (Jacksonville, Florida: PGA Tour Productions, 1990).

10. Gary Van Sickle, "Waiting for a Wave," *Golf World* (May 22, 1992): p. 48.

11. Gary Van Sickle, "PGA Tour," *Golf World* (September 18, 1992): p. 15.

12. Snead and Stump, *The Education of a Golfer*, pp. 233-234.

13. Ken Blanchard, "Practice With a Purpose," *Golf Tips* (October, 1993): p. 49.

14. Golf Digest Staff, "Moments of the Year," *Golf Digest* (January, 1995): p. 66.

15. Jeff Williams, "Fred Couples," *Golf Magazine* (May, 1994): p. 93.

16. Golf Digest Staff, "The Hill Brothers," *Golf Digest* (May, 1992): pp. 90-91.

17. Johnny Miller, "Child's Play," *Golf Illustrated* (April, 1993): p. 47.

18. Sandra Ackerman, *Discovering the Brain* (Washington, D.C.: National Academy Press, 1992), p. 41.

19. Gary Player, *Positive Golf* (New York: McGraw Hill, 1967), p. 17.

20. Snead and Stump, *The Education of a Golfer*, pp. 243-244.

21. David Wright, Ph.D. and Richard Brown, Ph.D., "Remission of Chronic Ruminative Vomiting Through a Reversal of Social Contingencies," *Behavior Research and Therapy* Vol. 16 (1978): pp. 134-136.

22. David Wright, Ph.D., Henry Slucki, Ph.D., and Beverly Benetti, R.P.T., "Elimination of Pain Behavior in a Burned Child Through a Reversal of Social Contingencies," *Journal of the American Academy of Behavioral Medicine* Vol. 1 (1983): pp. 34-44.

23. David Wright, Ph.D., and George Bunch, M.D., "Parental Intervention in the Treatment of Chronic Constipation," *Journal of Behavior Therapy and Experimental Psychiatry* Vol. 8 (1977): pp. 93-95.

24. Greg Norman and George Peper, "Greg Norman's Instant Lessons," *Golf Magazine* (April, 1993): p. 52.

25. Patrick Burke, Personal Communication (December 6, 1994).

26. Norman and Peper, "Greg Norman's Instant Lessons," p. 52.

27. Jack Berry, "Rydin' in Style," Golf World (June 19, 1992): p. 22.

28. David Coates, "Thumbs-up," *Golf World* (June 4, 1993): p. 21.

29. Gary Van Sickle, "Like a Rock," *Golf World* (May 14, 1993): p. 56.

30. Chris Millard, "Smoke 'Em if You Got 'Em," *Golf World* (October 7, 1994): pp. 13-14.

31. T.R. Reinman, "PGA Tour," *Golf World* (August 13, 1993): p. 20.

32. Norm Guenther, "The King Lives," *Golf World* (February 5, 1993): p. 22.

33. Michael Bamberger, "The Golden Boy Who Turned to Stone," *Golf Digest* (August, 1993): p. 92 and p. 94.

34. Bamberger, "The Golden Boy Who Turned to Stone," p. 92 and p. 94.

35. Tom Callahan, "Win a Major Go to Hell," *Golf Digest* (July, 1994): p. 79.

36. Bamberger, "The Golden Boy Who Turned to Stone," p. 92 and p. 94.

37. Bamberger, "The Golden Boy Who Turned to Stone," p. 92 and p. 94.

38. Johnny Miller, "Don't Go Changin'," *Golf World* (August 6, 1993): p. 24.

39. Snead and Stump, *The Education of a Golfer*, p. 82.

40. Golf World Staff, "Talking Golf With Lee Trevino," *Golf World* (June, 1992): p. 96.

41. Snead and Stump, *The Education of a Golfer*, pp. 243-244.

42. Player, *Positive Golf*, p. 2.

43. Player, *Positive Golf*, p. 18.

44. Jackie Burke, Personal Communication (July 27, 1990).

45. Andy Brumer, "Be a Thinking Golfer," *Golf Tips* (May, 1994): p. 38.

46. Brumer, "Be a Thinking Golfer," p. 38.

47. Dennis Paulson, Personal Communication (August 20, 1992).

48. Gary Van Sickle, "Take Your Best Shot," *Golf World* (August 7, 1992): p. 13.

49 John May, "Those Are the Breaks," *Golf World* (July 16, 1993): p. 14.

50. Johnny Miller, "Paul Harney or Bust," *Golf World* (February 11, 1994): p. 21.

51. Golf Digest Staff, "Fred Couples," *Golf Digest* (July 16, 1992): pp. 116-117.

52. Gary Van Sickle, "From Last Out to In First," *Golf World* (August 7, 1992): p. 22.

53. Golf World Staff, "Tour Talk," *Golf World* (March 20, 1992): p. 44.

54. Patrick Burke, Personal Communication (June, 1992).

55. Martin Seligman, *Learned Optimism*, (New York: Knopf, 1991), pp. 163-165.

56. Golf Digest Staff, "David Feherty," *Golf Digest* (November, 1992): p. 111.

57. Snead and Stump, *The Education of a Golfer*, p. 34.

HOMEWORK

Confidence

Listen in on your thinking off the golf course. Focus on your evaluations of yourself. Begin a daily diary. Are you supportive? Are you encouraging when faced with adversity? Do you give up easily? Are you negative? Are you tense? Do you predict or expect failure or success? Do you "call up" past success, problems or failures when faced with difficulties? Review your diary after one week. Write a plan for change and record your success daily.

OFF COURSE DIARY

SUN ____________________

____

____

____

MON ____________________

____

____

____

TUE ____________________

____

____

____

WED ____________________

____

____

____

THURS ____________________

____

____

____

FRI ____________________

____

____

____

SAT ____________________

____

____

____

Listen in on your thinking on the golf course. Again, what is your evaluation of yourself and your performance? Are you supportive and encouraging when faced with a difficult shot? Do you give up after a few bad holes, bad swings or bad breaks. Are you negative? Are you tense? Are you easily frustrated? Do you predict or expect success or failure? Do you "call up" similar good shots or do you recall bad shots during your round? Make copies of this page and use the following key words and phrases as reminders for your diary. Review this diary after four or five rounds and make a plan for change. Keep a diary of your successful changes.

Did you have a success focus? Were you confident? ______________________________

____

Recall similar good shots? ______________________________

____

Nervous or tense? ______________________________

____

Predict success or failure? ______________________________

____

Supportive or encouraging? ______________________________

____

Self critical? ______________________________

Give up after a few bad shots or bad breaks? ______________________________

____

Frustrated or angry? ______________________________

Focus on good shots or bad shots after round? ______________________________

____

Did you have fun? ______________________________

Did you talk to yourself positively after good shots? ______________________________

____

SELF REINFORCEMENT DIARY OFF THE GOLF COURSE

BEHAVIOR	goal	Sun	Mon	Tue	Wed	Thur	Fri	Sat
I became determined and positive when I was frustrated, angry, or faced with a difficult situation.								
I encouraged myself in my thinking throughout the day. I was positive and predicted success in my thinking in everything I did.								
I practiced breathing and slowed movement for relaxation ____% of my day.								
I practiced focused concentration strategies and mindfulness when I awakened and before I got out of bed.								
I practiced focused concentration strategies and mindfulness when I drove my car. I practiced broad to narrow focus skills.								
I practiced focused concentration strategies and mindfulness during the evening. I practiced broad to narrow focus skills.								
When I was faced with adversity, fear or apprehension in a difficult situation, I recalled past success in a similar condition. I remained mentally tough and determined to overcome the situation								
I praised my children, mate, friends and/or coworkers.								
I was accepting of my self and others without judgment.								
I caught myself engaged in a negative, self critical evaluation and redirected it to a positive, supportive comment.								
I successfully redirected my frustration and anger and put myself back in control emotionally.								
When working, I stayed focused on what I was doing and redirected thoughts of deadlines and urgency to finish.								
I practiced diaphragmatic breathing and slowed movement for relaxation ___times during the day.								
My eyes were at or above the horizon ___% of my day.								
When I felt down, nervous, angry or frustrated, I quieted my thinking, used diaphragmatic breathing, mindfulness and an "as if" posture to redirect my thinking and mood.								

SELF REINFORCEMENT DIARY ON THE GOLF COURSE

BEHAVIOR	HOLE 1	2	3	4	5	6	7	8	9	10	11	12	13	14	15	16	17	18
I redirected anger and negativity to a positive focus.																		
I recalled past similar good shots ___% of the time during my round.																		
I remained focused and determined when faced with bad shots or bad holes.																		
I was able to "let off steam" then get focused on the next shot without allowing my frustration and anger to affect my concentration or performance.																		
I had a solitary focus on one shot at a time for ___holes/shots with no expectations.																		
I totaled my score only after the round. The only score I thought of was to hit a 10 on the shot___% of the time.																		
I was able to balance my emotions with success, bad shots, and bad breaks. I never got too excited or overly frustrated.																		
I redirected fear/aprehension by focusing on past success in similar situations.																		
I was a good internal coach when I was faced with a tough shot.																		
I was encouraging and supportive in both my preswing and postswing routines.																		
I used my practice swing to feel the shot I wanted to hit with a focus on the entire swing.																		
My inswing routine was nonmechanical. My focus was on an image of the target or a feeling of the swing I wanted to make on ____% of my shots.																		
I stayed with the same positive routine on ___% of my shots.																		
I stepped off the ball when I had negative intrusive thoughts over the ball ____% of the time.																		
I practiced recalling my good shots on the practice range ___% of the time before and after I played.																		
I went through my full routine on every shot I hit on the practice range and with every putt I rolled on the practice green.																		
I practiced diaphragmatic breathing and slowed movement during my range practice and on the golf course.																		

-Get golf tips

-Visit the golf clinic

-Visit the Birdie Boogie

-Email Dr. David Wright

and much more...

www.mind-under-par.com

19th HOLE
STARTER
COUNTRY CLUB
MALL
LIBRARY
THEATRE
E BOOGIE
POST OFFICE
BOOKSTORE
GOLF SCHOOL
GOLF CLINIC
REALAU

Mind Under Par
D
Mike Shelton

Par
Mike Shelton

6

VISUALIZATION

Pictures = Performance

IMAGES: THE TARGETS OF THE NERVOUS SYSTEM

In 1974 Jack Nicklaus described the importance of visualization in his game: "I never hit a shot, even in practice without having a very sharp, in-focus picture of it in my head. It's like a color movie. First I 'see' the ball where I want it to finish, nice and white and sitting up high on the bright green grass. Then the scene quickly changes and I 'see' the ball going there: its path, trajectory, and shape, even its behavior on landing. Then there's a sort of fade-out, and the next scene shows me making the kind of swing that will turn the previous images into reality. Only at the end of the short, private, Hollywood spectacular do I select a club and step up to the ball."[1]

Senior Tour player Dave Hill has won ten regular tour events, three Senior Tour events, a Vardon trophy, and played on three Ryder Cup teams. He says of visualization: "Imagination is very important in shot making. If you can't picture it, you can't do it."[2]

During a 1993 interview, Paul Azinger noted that he was reviewing the computer statistics of his record. He said he began to play well in 1987, the same time he began to use visualization during play. He won one tournament a year through 1994. His record was interrupted in 1994 due to a bout with cancer.

WE DO WHAT WE SEE

We think in pictures. Describing the putt or shot you are about to make paints a mental picture of the outcome. As we approach difficult situations, we picture the events in our mind's eye. We visualize, in detail, the sequence of events that we anticipate.

This visualization of the "expected events" is often negative. We tend to visualize the consequences of a poor shot, and we focus on the hazards or unfavorable judgment by others. We also play out the dialogue of these visualized situations in our thinking.

Most players have a hole or two on a course which they play often where they know they are going to hit a great drive, no matter how poorly they may have hit on other holes. Most players also have a hole or two where they are going to hit poor tee shots, no matter how well they are hitting the ball. When these players walk on the tees, their images are of their past performance. They either expect to hit a good shot or a poor shot.

If you have a habit of emoting over and analyzing bad shots, you will have clear images of poor past performance. If you accept poor performance and recall only your success after each round, you will have images and an expectancy of good performance.

Remember the story about Jack Nicklaus giving a clinic at a tournament site when he was asked how to cure a shank. He said he didn't know because he had never hit one. A clinic participant spoke up indicating the tournament, day, and hole on which Nicklaus had shanked a shot. Nicklaus responded something to the effect of: "Maybe I did but I don't remember it."

Peak performers, both on and off the course, focus on the shot they hit well in the past or the positive way they handled a situation. This positive focus prepares you to perform in a confident, relaxed manner. A negative focus prepares you to perform in a negative, tense state. Negative visual anticipation prepares the nervous system to perform an "error" and produces an undesired arousal state that increases the chance of poor performance.

Remember what Greg Norman says: "... I talk to myself. Not aloud, but inside my head. The tougher the shot I'm facing, the more I talk. If I'm on the last hole of a tournament, facing a long iron shot to the green and needing a birdie to win, I'll say to myself, 'You know this shot cold, you've knocked it stiff a thousand times, and now you're going to do it again.' "[3]

PGA Tour player Fred Couples never hits a shot without "calling up" a similar shot he hit well in the past.[4] We think in pictures. When you approach a difficult shot, do you think of a shot you hit well in that situation before, or the shot you hit poorly? If you are like most golfers, you will likely recall the shot you hit poorly. If you have a difficult situation in your day to day life, do you think of the time you handled that situation well, or do you focus on all the possible negative outcomes? Most people focus on all the possible negative outcomes.

Research in the areas of internal dialogue and visualization suggests that the brain cannot tell the difference between real and imagined experience. Learning takes place in the nervous system and is stored in its neurochemical network. This learning results from both real and imagined experience. This concept is presented pictorially later in this chapter.

Sam Snead recalled an experience with imagery in his 1960 book: "It was at the Masters Tournament long ago that I discovered how mental images can be planted in the brain-particularly by the golfer himself, which is self needling. Playing with Jim

Turnesa one day, I was intently studying his actions on the tee. Turnesa pushed his drive into timber to the right. The image of everything Turnesa had done was so strong in my mind that I stepped up and my muscles followed the image and I did the same thing, landing almost exactly in the same spot in the jungle as Jim. After that, I watched my opponents only casual-like."[5]

LPGA Tour player Marta Figueras-Dotti and PGA Tour player Brad Bryant won the JC Penney Classic team play championship December 4, 1994. Marta said she stood on the 17th tee, a par 3, the last day of the event with a 5 iron. She said: "I felt so good in my routine I knew I was going to hit a good shot. I hit it right over the flag stick and landed it ten feet from the hole. Then on the third playoff hole we were back on seventeen. I said to myself: 'You were just here an hour ago. Just set up and hit the same shot.' I had the same feeling in my setup and this time I knocked it four feet."[6] Marta and Brad won the tournament on the fourth playoff hole.

CHANGING PREDICTIONS AND IMAGES

Consider the following situation. You have just taken a seven on a hole. As you step to the next tee, you see water right and out-of-bounds left. You begin to recall times in the past when you have hit both shots. As you recall these events, your mind begins to paint vivid pictures of these past errant shots. You're on the tee. What do you think the outcome of your shot will be?

Negative predictions and associated thoughts are of no assistance. These negative predictions work against you. When a single negative prediction is repeated frequently in thoughts and images, it becomes established as a belief. Remember, these images create neuroanatomical changes with repeated practice. Like other thought themes, these habit patterns can be changed with repeated, daily practice of alternative thoughts. If you don't implement a strategy to change this negative style, the patterns become more deeply ingrained with repeated use and the environment is in control, not you. It is your choice.

The mental preswing chain presented in the chapter titled "Routine" includes a link of describing the shot you want to hit. This is the same process. Predict a positive outcome. The more positive information your brain has to work with, the more likely positive performance will result and the more confident, relaxed, and effortless you will feel. You can start by looking at your good performance, and reinforcing and replaying that positive information in your mind for future reference. This will give you both confidence and a positive "motor program" when you need it.

Recall how Greg Norman talks to himself so he can remember and repeat good shots: "I also talk after I hit shots. After a particularly long, straight drive I'll often say, 'Damn, Greg, I'm pretty impressed with that one.' These inner words can be more encouraging than the cheers of the gallery. You don't want to linger too long on your shots-good or bad-but you do want to stamp the good ones on your mind for future reference in pressure situations. Silent self-congratulations is one way to do that."[7]

This strategy works in day to day life events

as well. Bank your successes and call upon that positive history when faced with a difficult life situation.

"BANK" SUCCESS: YOURS AND THEIRS

Byron Nelson reflected on his caddying days as a way of developing a good swing: "The great thing about caddying was that you watched people and saw good players and bad players and so forth. So you got a feeling in your subconscious and in your mind of how a good swing looked. It was an accumulation of what you saw over a period of time that made you become a good player. I know Ben Hogan has said that a man he caddied for, Ed Stewart, had some influence on him in his early days, and I'm sure he did. Ed was a long hitter; he had a long, high hook and that's what Ben had. You know, I was influenced by my caddying because there weren't many books about golf, and there was no photography of golfers playing."[8]

Johnny Miller advocates finding a pro model you like and imitating his swing. I refer to this as banking or storing the memory of a swing in your nervous system. Johnny Miller says he used images of different pros, depending on whether he wanted to fade, draw, or hit a straight shot. Miller said he modeled Cary Middlecoff's swing in developing his swing in his youth.[9] Similarly, PGA Tour player Vijay Singh watched Tom Weiskopf's swing on television as a child and modeled what he saw. His father taught him the basics. He had no formal instruction other than watching Weiskopf's swing.[10] Interestingly, Tom Weiskopf says he learned by watching Sam Snead and Tommy Bolt. He also noted that he learned by watching and competing with Jack Nicklaus.[11]

Johnny Miller says he always enjoyed playing with guys who were leading a tournament because he was able to learn from those situations by watching how others performed under pressure.[12] He further noted that when you pass your prime and you're under pressure, you have to "dial back" to a time when you were a younger player dealing with pressure, and then reproduce those feelings and behavior.[13] I suggest you can "dial back" at any time and think of past success when you want to improve your performance.

PGA Tour player Andrew Magee says that the best time to practice is when you're striking the ball well. He says that at these times he doesn't try to analyze his swing. Instead, he says he uses this practice time to commit to memory what his best swing feels like. He also practices after a round if he has played exceptionally well. This practice time he uses to "bank" the feeling of this good swing.[14]

Remember, Fred Couples never hits a shot without recalling a similar shot he has hit well before. He states: "When I'm over the ball I picture the shot I'm trying to hit and I think of a shot that I hit-might be seven years ago, might be the day before-that was successful...but one thing you don't do is think of bad things when you're over the ball. People might think about bad shots, but I don't, even on shots I might be scared to hit or whatever. Now I visualize things like the 6 iron I hit at Riviera under pressure against Davis [Love III, on the 14th hole in the playoff at the '92 Nissan Los Angeles Open]. It won the tournament for me. I didn't hit it one foot away, it was ten to twelve feet away. When I'm on the 18th tee at Augusta, I think of Riviera...[I say] 'Here I am, 18 at Riviera' and I picture the ball fading. Every shot I do that. Joe

[Couples' caddie] gives me the yardage and I get the club. I immediately think of a shot-like now with the 9 iron, I'll think third hole at Augusta where I hit it eight inches."[15]

European and PGA Tour player Seve Ballesteros says he paints "positive pictures of smooth swings and successful results in my mind's eye."[16] He uses this particular strategy not only to visualize a positive outcome, but also to calm his nerves.

Most amateurs will recall the missed shot into the hazard off the tee or fairway, or difficulty recovering from a trouble shot the next time they have that shot, especially on the same hole. Jack Nicklaus described a similar recollection on his way to winning the 1993 Senior Open on the 12th hole of the final round: "As I was lining up the putt I realized that this was the exact same putt I had in the final round of the 1960 Open. I was five under then, too, but I missed it." Nicklaus also missed that putt on the 12th hole, but he went on to win by one stroke over Tom Weiskopf.[17]

This example amplifies the point that we tend to remember content that is triggered by similar conditions (both US Opens and both putts were on the 12th hole). We also remember situations to which we attach the most emotion. Interestingly, these conditions not only triggered the memory of the missed putt on Number 12 in 1960, they also triggered the memory of playing the last six holes three over par. In response to this recollection, Nicklaus turned to his caddie, son Jack, and said: "We're not playing the last six holes like I did then." In fact, this determination led him to one under on the last six holes leading to the 1993 Senior Open Victory.[18]

During the 1960 US Open at Cherry Hills, Arnold Palmer was seven shots behind leader Mike Souchak going into the last round. Palmer stepped onto the first tee of the final round and drove the green of the 346 yard par 4. He shot 65 that day and won the Open by one shot. As Palmer stepped onto the first tee of the 1993 Senior Open at Cherry Hills thirty-three years later, his thoughts were still on that memorable shot: "I certainly couldn't ignore the fact that everyone in the gallery was thinking about it. I'm no different, I was thinking about it, too."[19]

The next time you have a tee shot, a chip, a putt, or shot to the green, recall a similar shot you hit well. Picture the shot and your swing, and experience the feeling of the swing, your tempo, and balance as you do. Put that feeling into the shot. You will be pleasantly surprised at the outcome.

Jack Nicklaus summarizes this process well. He says: "Thinking of past successes instead of failures will help you. If your situation suggests a shot that you've never hit successfully before, reject it and recompute less ambitiously, choosing a play that you've already pulled off brilliantly. Replay that success in your mind as you step up to the ball...If you keep your mind this busy, you won't have time to get tense and pressured."[20]

Nicklaus also says: "Visualize. First see that brilliant previous achievement, then the shot now facing you behaving identically; picture yourself taking the club that will pull it off, then executing the necessary swing. As you finalize your setup, say to yourself, 'Okay, I'm ready now, just do it' and go."[21]

PICTURES OF VICTORY

We all have periods where our thoughts and images drift to other times and places. These periods are called daydreams. When we are relaxed and comfortable, we tend to drift into places that are representations of our goals and fantasies of the future or to a more reinforcing place.

In the sixth game of the 1993 World Series, Toronto was leading Philadelphia three games to two. The score was six to five in the bottom of the ninth. There were two out and two men on base, with two strikes on Toronto's Joe Carter. Philadelphia was one strike away from winning game six. Carter hit the next pitch over the left field wall; this won both the game and the 1993 World Series. During an interview following the Series Carter said he had lived that fantasy behind his father's gas station as a boy: Two outs, two strikes, one run down, and hitting a home run to win the World Series.

You'll find numerous quotes from tour players describing their thoughts during putting practice in their years prior to the tour: "He needs this putt for a birdie to win!" Gary Player describes his thinking during practice: "Always when putting, I'd imagine I was about to win one of the major tournaments, saying to myself: 'This one's for the US Open, Gary...the British Open,' and so forth...I believed then-and still do-that your wildest dreams come true."[22]

Part of Gary Player's daily preparation for the 1965 US Open was to see his name next to the number one spot every time he passed the leader board the week of the Open. "I was walking past the master scoreboard, which includes the names, lettered in gold, of all the previous winners...with space alongside for that year's winner. Then suddenly I saw it-my name lettered in that space. I really saw it! It was bright gold just like the others. All during the Open I visualized myself winning."[23] Set long-term and immediate performance goals, and begin to "see yourself" accomplishing them.

We all have daydreams. Many of these images reflect our fantasies and goals. That's not to say if you have a performance fantasy, reality will always follow. If you daydream or night dream, you visualize. Why not load all of your daydreams and fantasies with success? These images promote confidence and prepare you for positive experience. Set goals and see yourself achieving them.

PROCESS AND OUTCOME VISUALIZATION

There are two types of visualization, images of outcome and images during the process of performance. Outcome images are the easiest for you since they are already a part of everyone's daydreams. Hopefully, these outcome images are seeing yourself succeed. An example is Gary Player seeing his name in the number one position on the leader board each day prior to the 1965 US Open. He won the Open that year. Seeing yourself succeed, no matter what the event, on or off the course, is outcome visualization. You set a goal and then see yourself succeeding at that goal.

Many players set themselves up for mediocre performance. For example, the Tour rookie will set his sights (images) on making the cut. He finds himself on the bubble week after week, making or missing the cut by a stroke or two. Set your goals for peak performance and see yourself attaining those goals.

Positive process visualization is much more difficult to master since most players tend to be very mechanical (negative process) in the way they approach their swings. Positive process visualization is just like positive outcome visualization, except you break the large goal into a shot at a time, and see successful swing and ball flight or roll outcome on every shot. For example, Gary Player says: "I've conditioned myself to visualize the path of my shots before I play them. I always believe in positive thinking. To me it's all part of concentration."[24]

During the shot or stroke, your goal is to repeat the feeling of your practice swing and to hold a picture of the target, ball flight, or ball landing in your mind's eye. At the very least, one of these images should be your last focus as you start the club back. Let's look at a few strategies that will enhance both your process and outcome visualization skills.

YES, YOU CAN!

I have had many players tell me: "No matter how hard I try, I can't see the line, ball flight, target, the ball landing, and so on." There are many reasons you can't or at least think you can't. The first is your expectancy. You will probably never have a crystal clear picture. If you try too hard, the picture is going to be fuzzy at best.

Describe the Number one hole at your home course. Is it a par 4 or par 5, or perhaps even a par 3? Is it a dog leg or straight? Are there reachable hazards off the tee? If so, is it sand, water, brush or trees? Is there an out-of-bounds left or right off the tee? What was the fairway like the last time you played? Lush? Brown? Is the fairway wide or narrow? Can you see mower tracks in the fairway from the first tee? Is there a flat landing area, uphill, downhill, or sidehill? Is there rough? Are there homes along the fairway?

The last time you played, did you hear sounds of traffic, voices, cart noise, birds, maintenance crews, music from a fairway home, construction noise, the voice of the starter over the public address system, or other sounds on the first tee?

Now let's return to the first tee, still considering the last time you played. How many players were in your group? Were you relaxed, confident, and comfortable, or nervous, tense and concerned about getting your first shot in play? Were your thoughts on the shot, on what the other members of the group would think, on the hazards off the tee, your target, or on something unrelated to your game?

What club did you hit off the first tee? Did you have a specific target in the fairway? Did your drive go straight, fade, draw, hook, or slice? Was your shot high or low? What did the ball flight look like? How would you rate your drive on a one to ten scale (one would be the worst drive you could hit and ten the best)? Is this a shot you would want to commit to memory so you can "call it up" on the first tee the next time you play?

Let's go to the fairway for your approach shot? What kind of lie did you have? Was it in the fairway or rough? Was the ball above or below your feet, or was it a level lie? Were there obstacles between you and the green? How far were you from the green? What club did you hit? If it was a par 5, did you lay up or go for the green? Did you have a specific target? What was your shot like? Was it high, low, left, right or straight? What did the ball flight look like? What's your rating on a one to ten scale? Is this a shot you would want to commit to memory so you can "call it up" the next time you have a similar shot?

Let's go to the green. How far were you from the cup? How many putts did you have on the green?

You think in pictures with the exception, sometimes, of calculations and rote memory. As you answered the questions about the last time you played the first hole at your home course, you visualized. You had a picture in your mind of the first tee, the fairway, the hazards, the colors and sounds. You likely saw the flight of your tee and approach shots, and perhaps even the roll of your putt(s) on the first green. Simply stated, you visualized. Yes, you can!

In a 1994 Golf Magazine interview, Jack Nicklaus described a golf course, a particular tournament round, a hole and the shot he hit in 1975.[25] Several years ago, I would sit around listening to players discuss their round and a particular shot. I often wondered how they could remember so well. Now I can remember golf rounds and shots I hit years ago. The more focused you are during a round, the better your recall will be. You have the ability to selectively recall your good and great shots, and to use those shot images to "ready" your nervous system to perform the same swing again.

Visualization will allude you when you try too hard to picture your swing or ball flight, or when you are under stress. The more stressful the situation, the more difficult it is going to be to visualize. On the other hand, the more relaxed you are, the clearer the images will be. The chapter titled "Fine Tuning Your Nervous System" describes what happens during stressful periods when you try unsuccessfully to visualize a shot or see the line on the green.

Johnny Miller gives one of the best examples I have heard in his description of the effect of anxiety during play. He states that the arousal produced by pressure "...heightens your awareness; your brain gets knocked up a notch or two; it speeds up...and the way you process data is messed up. You've got all this information coming to you real fast, and you're not used to it, so you get confused. You have to take deep breaths to slow your heartbeat; or sing a slow song or walk more slowly. I've done all those things...I've likened pressure to tuning in a radio...Get too excited, tell yourself you want it badly, and it's static time. You can't let the moment overwhelm you and hold you captive."[26]

If you will follow the relaxation strategies outlined in the chapter "Fine Tuning Your Nervous System" off the course, they will be well-practiced habits available to you on the course. In particular, when you are standing over a putt trying to see the "line," take a couple of deep diaphragmatic breaths behind the ball. Think of a similar putt you made in this or a previous round. Recall the roll, the tempo, and the feeling of the stroke. Describe to yourself the path the ball will follow into the hole and you will begin to notice the image of the path the ball will take to the hole.

DEVELOPING AND IMPROVING VISUALIZATION SKILLS

You can develop and improve your visualization skills by setting practice goals, scheduling and doing a few imagery exercises daily, and keeping a diary of your progress.

1. Breathing: The importance of breathing for relaxation and increased concentration has been described in the preceding chapters. For a review of this content, turn to the chapter titled "Fine Tuning Your Nervous System." In summary, deep diaphragmatic breathing quiets the nervous system and stems the flow of input to the brain, permitting a more focused concentration. You will achieve the best results by combining breathing and focusing your thinking only on the shot or activity in which you are involved.

Diaphragmatic breathing will increase your success with the following visualization practice exercises.

2. Burning in Images: Hold a small bright colored object at eye level and focus your attention on the detail and color for fifteen seconds. Close your eyes and note that you have an "after image" of the object. Take a deep breath and continue to hold this image. Review the details of the object as you hold the image.

3. Recall Your Past Success: When you arrive at your ball and determine the shot you are going to hit, think of the last time you hit that shot well. Picture the ball flight, and see and feel the swing that produced that shot.

After your round, sit down and review your good shots you hit on the course. The *MIND UNDER PAR* series™ *SCORECARD* provides a format for this summary that you record during play. After your round, it is easy to sit down and review only your good shots. It is much easier to call up one of these shots once they are reviewed and committed to memory.

4. Describe the Flight of the Ball (Call Your Shot): Have you ever noticed that when you are playing and tell someone the shot you are going to hit, you often hit the exact shot you described? Start describing the ball flight and landing of the ball to yourself. You think in pictures. Describing the shot you are going to hit prepares the brain for successful performance. Get in a habit of describing to yourself every shot you hit during practice and play from putting to driving. If you have played much golf, you have likely hit the very shot you are playing well at some time in the past. The best image to have is a replay of the shot you hit well. It's much easier to call up a past experience than to create a new one.

Stay focused on your target and off mechanics during this practice. If your thoughts are on swing mechanics when you describe your shots, you will meet certain failure. Thoughts of mechanics during your swing is a sure formula for disaster. Describing each shot to yourself and staying focused on your targets during swings is a sure formula for success.

5. Define Clear Specific Targets: Be certain that the targets you are picking during play are specific. For example, if you are putting, your target may be a spot over which you want to roll the ball or a spot in the back of the cup, a precise area on the green where you want to land your irons, a rake in a distant bunker you can't reach, the corner of a chimney on a house on the horizon, or a specific small area in the fairway as a landing area off the tee. Always hold a clear picture of your goal.

If you have a destination to drive in your car, you have a clear picture of your objective in your mind. You aren't just driving "somewhere" down the street. Your goals in life are the same. The more specific your targets in life or on the course, the more successful you will be at reaching your goals.

6. Hold the Image: Practice looking at objects in the distance with your eyes open. Then turn your head, with your eyes open, to a neutral area like a wall. See how long you can hold the image of that distant object. Your best images will come when you have the sensation that you are staring through the wall, not looking at the wall. See the image, not the wall.

Once you are able to see the image consistently "through the wall," place a golf ball at your feet as though you are setting up to hit a shot. Assume your stance and posture. Again, find an object, this time a bright object like a cola can. Stare at the object for five to ten seconds, then turn your eyes back to the golf ball. Stare "through" the golf ball, as you did the wall, and hold an image of the object for as long as you can. Once you are able to hold the image for five to ten seconds, begin to practice with objects from five to one hundred fifty yards away. When you are able to look "through" the golf ball and hold these distant images for five to ten seconds, you are ready to take your visualization skills to the practice range and the golf course.

7. Start With Putting and Chipping: If you are going to work on visualization, the best place to begin is with putting and chipping. Practice finding the line the ball is going to take to the hole for your putts. Look at the hole as you make your practice strokes, feeling the distance to the hole. Find a spot over which the ball will roll, and hold an image of that spot as you repeat the feeling of your practice strokes.

Sam Snead said the best putting round he ever had was when he found a spot three and one-half inches in front of his ball.[27] Be sure you feel the distance to the hole. You will find that your putts are short when you hold an image of a spot short of the hole. Your feeling for distance comes through your visual sense. Find a spot the size of a spike mark on your line and the same distance as or in the hole. Look at that spot as you feel the distance; then hold an image of the spot through your stroke.

The best players I work with hold one of three images through the swing or stroke: Ball landing, ball flight, or target (for putting it would be line, ball rolling in hole, spot over which you want the ball to roll, or spot in or around the cup).

For chipping, estimate the distance you want the ball to fly onto the green. Find a spot or discoloration in this landing area and read the rest of the distance to the hole just as you would for a putt. Find the line the ball will take to the hole. When you set up over the ball, look at the spot on the green where you want the ball to land, make three or four practice strokes as you look at that spot, feeling the distance as you do, and then hold an image of that spot as you make the stroke. Many players hold an image of the ball rolling the last few inches into the hole and even hear the ball hitting the flag stick as they stroke the chip.

Harvey Penick, instructor of many PGA and LPGA Tour players over the years, said the following regarding thoughts and images during putting: "I believe your mind should be on the cup and your touch..."[28]

Once you are proficient at holding images of your targets in chipping and putting, extend your practice to wedges, then mid and long irons, and finally the driver. Work on holding these images as you look through the ball, from the time you start your stroke or swing to the completion of your follow-through.

After you describe the shot, feel and see the swing you want to make from behind the ball, and glue your eyes to the target as you deliberately move back to the ball.

Keep looking back and forth from the ball to the target. Burn the image of your target into your mind as you look back and "through" the ball.

If holding an image of the target is difficult, you might have more success seeing the ball flight or ball landing during your swing.

8. Have a Picture and a Feeling of Your Swing: The best swing advice I can give you is to have one instructor and one swing. It is important to have a picture of that swing in your mind. When you set up to a shot, make a practice swing and feel the whole swing. Your goal is to see the swing, feel the tempo and balance of your practice swing, and repeat that feeling when you set up to the ball.

The first paragraph of this chapter is a quote from Jack Nicklaus regarding his visualization in his preswing routine. As part of his visualization, he describes seeing himself make the swing that would produce the shot he visualized. Later in this chapter, you will read about how important these images are in building a positive motor program in the nervous system.

9. Hole Every Shot: Many players play to get the ball close. I want you to hole every shot, whether it is a putt, a chip, or a 7 iron from one hundred fifty yards. See every shot all the way into the hole. You should have these images of making the shot from behind the ball. Once over the ball, hold the image of your primary target, ball flight, or ball landing. If you are playing to get close, that's exactly what you will do. If you play to "hole out" every shot, you will start to chip in more often.

10. Rate Clarity of Image: You will find that the clarity of your images during visualization will vary from one shot to the next. As noted, you will have your best visualization success if you work with the strategies to quiet your nervous system and describe to yourself the shot you are going to hit. The other thing you will find is that the clearer the image, the better your performance. The better your concentration, the better your image will be. Recall that Nick Price says he holds an image of the target during his swing. He says the clearer his image of the target, the better his shot will be.[29]

11. Plan Your Targets in Advance: In his prime, Ben Hogan would start at the 18th green, walking each hole from green to tee identifying his landing areas. He chose his targets based on the best landing areas and what club he wanted to hit to each green or from each tee. This is a good time and place to practice your visualization on the course. There is no substitute for good course management, and what better place to begin than walking the course, developing a game plan, and visualizing success with each shot as you do.

12. Play the Course Before You Play: Once you know what clubs you are going to use from the tees and where your ideal landing areas are, visualize your round the night or morning before you play. See every hole in order of play, and see every swing and shot hit perfectly. Take a short break every three or four holes until you finish playing the course in your mind. Give yourself errorless performance before you play. Establish a game plan and stick with it .

Harvard psychologist William James made the observation that "we learn to skate in summer and play tennis in winter." One author and brain researcher, Dr. Richard Restak, interpreted James' comments as meaning that we rehearse motor skills through mental imagery. He suggests that when periods of relaxation are used to mentally practice that this mental rehearsal probably encodes a program in the higher brain.[30]

If you have never practiced visualization before, you will meet certain failure if you try to visualize ball flight, a swing, and target during your swing the first several times on the course.

It is a reasonable expectancy, and good practice, to get comfortable picking out specific targets and eliminating the internal dialogue (chatter) of swing mechanics. If you try to force images of targets, ball flight, and so on, you will become tense and discard visualization as something that isn't for you. It will take you between three and twelve months, depending on the intensity of practice on and off the range and practice green before you are ready to put a full routine together on the course that "comfortably" and automatically includes visualization of ball flight, swing, and target during play.

This probably sounds like a lot of work, and it is. It's no more work, however, than "mindlessly" beating balls on the range. You will find these exercises fun, especially as you become more and more proficient. A comment I frequently hear from players is how much they enjoy practicing and mastering the visualization exercises. Each player is amazed at the improved accuracy he experiences with this strategy. Remember, the mental mechanics take as much practice as the swing mechanics.

IMAGES FROM THE INSIDE OUT

I have presented you with the practical side of visualization with comments from tour players about their use of this important mental strategy. The scientific part of me can't resist taking you one step further inside the brain to explain why visualization works. I have purposely included this section at the end of this chapter for those of you not so inclined to ask, "Why?," or those of you who don't need to understand before you follow the exercises listed.

I don't fit either of these categories. If someone tells me I should do something, I need to understand why. Once I understand, I give one hundred percent. I won't follow directions until I know I am on relatively firm ground. For those of you who share this trait, I have included the following summary of the nature of visualization in the brain. As you can imagine, this is a complex subject. I have made every effort to simplify this content inclusive of pictures. Now, let's move on, and see how the brain processes and uses these visual images.

We use the same part of the brain to visualize as we do to see. This area of the brain is called the visual cortex. Recent research on visualization shows that when we picture ourselves doing some kind of physical movement, the part of the brain responsible for initiating movement, the motor cortex, also shows activity.

Neuroscientist Dr. Peter Fox of the Brain Imaging Research Center in San Antonio, Texas had a group of volunteers perform a simple physical movement while he monitored brain activity. Then he had these same people visualize the physical movement they had performed. His research showed brain activity in the same areas for visualization as it did for physical movement, with the exception of that part of the brain responsible for initiating movement, the motor cortex. The motor cortex showed activity only when the actual movement was performed.[31]

Dr. Fox's study was replicated in 1995 at the Institute of Neurology in London where Dr. K.M. Stephan and his associates had volunteers physically move a joystick, and then visualize themselves moving the joystick while he monitored brain activity. The brain scans showed that the volunteers "turned on" about eighty percent of the brain circuitry when they visualized, as compared to the scans of actually physically moving the joystick.[32]

These research studies show that visualization activates a significant percentage of the same parts of the brain as physical movement. Two things are happening:

1. ***The nervous system is being primed to perform the behavior being visualized. The neural circuitry is firing or "warming up" in the same patterns it will when the behavior occurs.***

   Regardless of whether the image is a successful shot or a shot to a hazard, visualization prepares the nervous system to perform, assuming the circuitry is not broken by competing images.

2. ***When the neural circuitry is firing, structural changes or learning is occurring in the nervous system.***

This "warming up" phase of brain activity prior to some voluntary movement is a phenomenon that was discovered in the 1970's and referred to as the "readiness potential." Subjects were asked to move their index finger. There was brain activity for 1.5 seconds prior to the finger movement. The initiation of movement took 0.1 seconds. The brain takes fifteen times longer to prepare for novel, voluntary movement than it does to initiate that movement.[33] The part of the brain where this "readiness potential" appears is the same location where Dr. Fox found activity during visualization of motor behavior, the supplementary motor area (SMA). This area "builds" a motor program, a nervous system program that prepares the brain to initiate a behavior.

Research with a device called a positron emission tomography (PET) scan has enabled neuroscientists to see how the brain works under a variety of different conditions, in this case visualized movement.

First, let me briefly explain what a PET scan is, and then we will look at a PET scan of brain activity during a visualization experiment. A PET scan is similar to MRI (Magnetic Resonance Imagery) and CAT scan (Computerized Axial Tomography). The MRI and CAT scan show x-ray pictures that are very thin sections of the body part being scanned. These pictures are as thin as 1.5 to 2.0 millimeter sections and, when input into a computer, they can be viewed a number of different ways.

The PET scan shows an image of the brain following the injection of a radioactive substance that is "taken up" in the brain. When a part of the brain is used, the radioactive material "lights up" that part of the brain where there is activity. Using a similar technique to the CAT and the MRI scans, the section of the brain being studied can be isolated, sectioned, and viewed as a picture of activity.

Let's look at a photograph of brain activity

for actual and visualized movement. The pictures you are going to see are from Dr. Peter Fox's laboratory at the Brain Imaging Center at San Antonio, Texas. The images are photographs of a PET scan. The first picture shows the neurochemical activity in the brain when someone moves his tongue. Note the center line and activity on both sides of the brain.

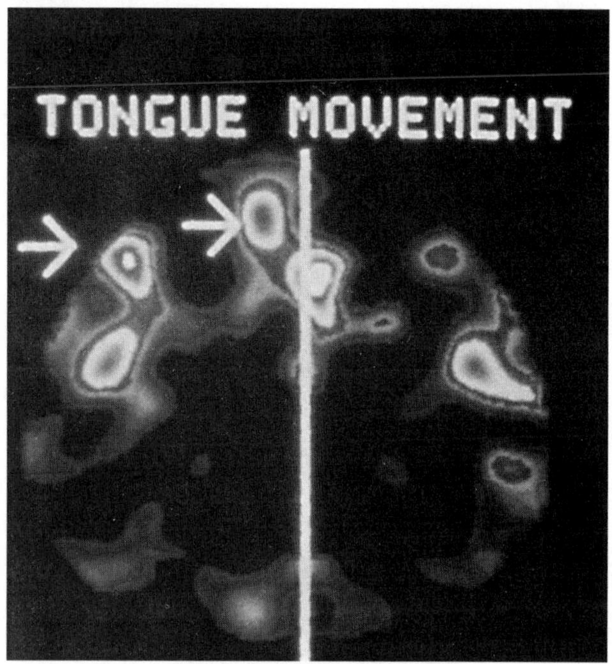

Tongue Movement

The next picture shows a burst of neurochemical activity when this person moved his right hand. Notice the designation of the SMA (supplementary motor area) with the small yellow center and green wall. This area shows the organization of sensorimotor information in preparation to initiate a behavior. This is the area where the brain integrates information for a brief period prior to the neural circuitry firing the initiation of behavior.

To the left is a larger and brighter area of activity labeled sensorimotor cortex. This area is the final integration of sensorimotor information as the neural circuitry fires and behavior occurs, in this case, right hand movement.

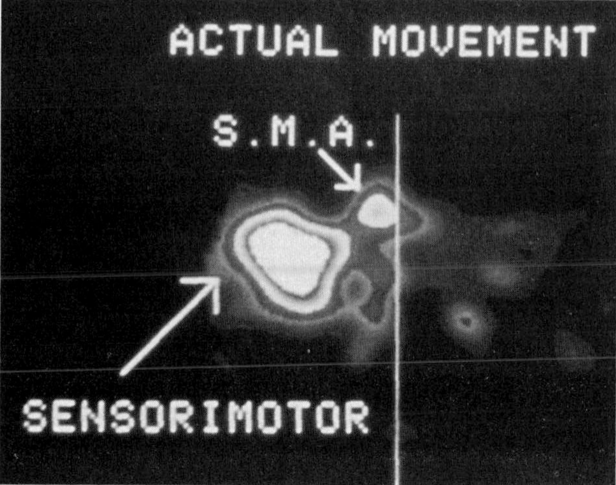

Right Hand Movement

The last picture shows imagined or visualized right hand movement by the same person. Note the area marked SMA (supplementary motor area). Also note the similarity of the SMA in both the actual and imagined movement.

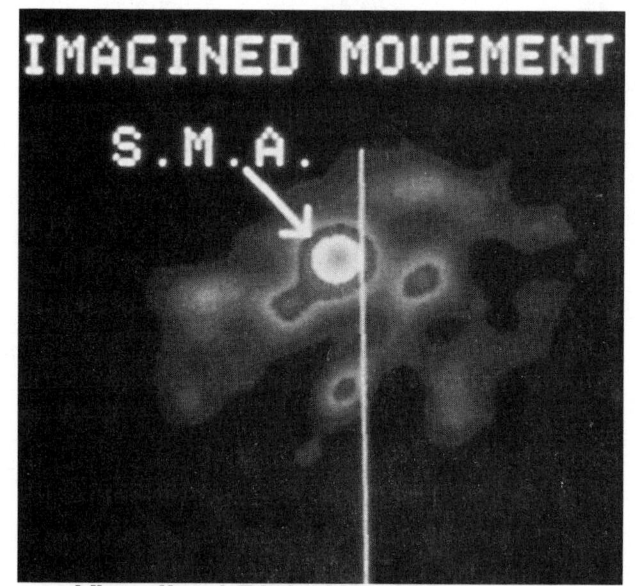

Visualized Right Hand Movement

Recall that the 1970's researchers monitoring brain waves described a "planning period" or "readiness potential" that took place in the brain prior to voluntary finger movement. This was also referred to as motor programming.[34] In the PET scans shown, the motor programming area is identified by

(Please refer to the end of this chapter for color illustrations of the PET scans.)

an arrow and the letters SMA (supplementary motor area). As already noted, research suggests that the readiness potential or motor programming occurs, in part, in the SMA portion of your brain. The brain lights up for both actual and imagined movement in the supplementary motor area. This brain activity prepares the program that initiates movement.

The activity of motor programming in the SMA exemplifies the importance of a consistent, repeating routine. The more consistent and repeating the pre-performance behavior (routine) is, the faster and more consistent the motor program will be.

When a player approaches a shot and says, "Just don't hit it right into those trees," and has images of the trees, water, sand, out-of-bounds, and so on, what kind of a motor program is the brain preparing? What kind of a shot will likely follow? The likely shot is into the hazard or an overcompensation, for example, a sweeping hook.

When a player approaches a hole or lie he hasn't been playing well and he begins to think of all those bad shots he has hit in that situation, what kind of motor program is he building? That is the neurophysiological reason why images of poor shots produce poor shots. The brain does what you tell it to do.

This is also why it is so important to focus on where you want the ball to go (your targets), or to recall good and great shots you have hit on a hole or in a given situation. When you approach a shot or a hole you haven't been playing well, think back to a time when you hit that shot well. Focus on your target, see the ball flying to and landing on your target, and rolling into the hole. Picture and feel the swing that will produce that shot.

Remember, when Johnny Miller wanted to work the ball left to right or right to left, he pictured the swing of a player who naturally hit the shot he needed. Miller said he modeled Cary Middlecoff's swing in developing his swing in his youth. He described it as a "...big, high backswing with lots of knee action and lateral movement." In his later years, he copied the swings of Tony Lema and Lee Trevino. He used images of Tony Lema's swing when he wanted to hit a draw, and Lee Trevino's swing when he wanted to hit a fade.[35]

The information you provide your brain is what you will use to build a motor program. The more positive the information is that you process, the more probable your performance will be as desired.

Many players are focused on swing mechanics or broad focus information. They don't see ball flight, nor do they have a narrow focus on target. This sets the table for mixed performance outcomes. The best players in the world process information about what they want to do and their targets. Again, provide your nervous system with details of information regarding desired performance and related outcomes, and you will see a marked improvement in performance.

THE PHYSIOLOGY ASSOCIATED WITH IMAGERY

Psychologists who use biofeedback in therapy know distressing thoughts produce increases in heart rate, blood pressure, breathing rate, muscle tension and decreased skin temperature and digestive activity. What happens to your physiology with neutral thoughts and images?

Take a moment and picture a yellow, ripe lemon cut in half and laying face up on a plate. The lemon is soft and juicy. Now, pick up the lemon, place it in your open mouth, bite down, and begin to suck. Hold that image and continue to suck as you taste the sour flavor and feel the juice trickle over your lip. Take another big bite and feel the sour juice squirt into your mouth. Hold that image and sensation. Continue biting and sucking for ten seconds before proceeding.

Are you salivating? Most of you are. If a neutral image like sucking on a lemon can produce the physiological response of salivation, imagine what potent images of failure or conflict are doing to your nervous system.

Now, whatever you do, don't think about that lemon. Don't take another bite and suck on the lemon and taste that sour juice. Don't squeeze the juice into your mouth and pucker your lips. Notice the increased salivation again? Your physiological response to the thought is the same. The "target" thought is still the lemon. When you tell yourself, "Don't think about the water," or "Don't recall the last time you hit it out-of-bounds here," or "Don't think about how much you have been struggling in greenside bunkers," you only amplify the clarity of the negative focus.

When you say to yourself, "Don't hit it right into the trees!", the trees become your target. Your muscles tense, and your nervous system arousal increases. Your tempo will likely increase, and you will have a tendency to steer your shot. You have built a motor program to hit the shot. You either hit into the trees or overcompensate and pull the ball left. So, what should you do? Think only of your targets and what you want to do. The hazards and out-of-bounds aren't going anywhere.

Hit your shot with a focus on your target and the swing it is going to take to get it to that target. Call up your past success. Think about the last time you hit that shot well. See the ball flight, and picture and feel the swing you made to hit that great shot. Step up and make that same swing. These images of past success provide increased confidence, a narrow focus, and arousal levels conducive to good performance.

Additionally, these images of past success are lighting up that part of the brain (SMA) that prepares the nervous system to perform (positive motor program). If your thoughts and images are only on successful past performance and current desired targets, you are preparing yourself for successful performance. If your images are of past problems and failures, and the hazards of present (negative motor program), you are preparing yourself for poor performance. Interestingly, this same process translates to off-course behavior as well.

In summary, the most recent brain research suggests that visual images which precede the golf swing serve as a "readiness potential," also known as a motor program. Recall that this "readiness potential" for voluntary movement takes fifteen times longer to prepare for the behavior than it does to initiate the movement. Psychologists have discussed the importance of a preswing routine, and visualization of the shot and swing you want to make for years. Research strongly supports the need for a consistent, repeating routine with positive visual predictions of performance and outcome to maximize peak performance.

Ken Venturi sums up the use of visualization quite nicely: "Take the time to visualize the perfect shot before you swing. When the mind can see the shot required, the body is more likely to make the necessary swing."[36]

There is no question that positive visualization is an important link in the preswing and postswing mental chains. It's a link that requires as much active practice as the golf swing.

MEASURE YOUR SUCCESS

If you are going to practice visualization skills, consider measuring your success as you do. Rate each shot you hit on a 1 to 10 scale. A rating of 1 equals the worst shot you can hit and a rating of 10 is the best shot you can hit. Next, as you hit each shot, hold an image of your target through the swing. Rate the clarity of your target image on each shot. A rating of 1 equals little or no image and a 10 rating is a clear image of your target through the shot.

When you begin this practice, start with short shots, like a chip or a pitch. As you become proficient, extend your practice to longer shots. If you struggle with an image of target through your swing, try an image of ball flight or ball landing.

The illustration below is a sample of a form I use in teaching students to visualize. Sandra Palmer, LPGA Tour player, hit ten consecutive shots. Each shot was hit with a five iron at a different target. The first rating you see is the quality of the shot. The second number directly under each shot rating is the clarity of the target image through her swing.

Note the relationship between the shot rating and the clarity of the image. High shot ratings show up with clear target images. Low shot ratings are paired with poor target images. Recall that Nick Price says he holds an image of the target during his swing. He says the clearer his image of the target, the better his shot will be.[37]

Name SANDRA PALMER **Date** 2/17/95

Club 5 iron **Condition** VARY TARGET— Image of target through the swing

shot	1	2	3	4	5	6	7	8	9	10
rating	8	7	10	10	10	9	8	6	7	10
clarity	8	6	9	10	10	9	8	5	6	10

The illustration on the following page shows the same conditions for PGA Tour player Patrick Burke. Once again notice the relationship between the ratings on the shots and the ratings on the image of the target through the swing. The higher the shot rating, the clearer the image. Low shot ratings were paired with low image ratings. This is not an unusual result when I do this drill with players on the range. You cannot be focused on an image of a target and focused on the mechanics of your golf swing at the same time. You may not have the same visual picture as Patrick or Sandra, however, the more narrow and precise your target, the better your performance. The broader your target focus, the worse your performance.

Name PAT BURKE **Date** 5/13/93

Club DRIVER **Condition** Image of Target through swing

shot	1	2	3	4	5	6	7	8	9	10
rating	8	9	10	10	6	8	9	3	10	8
clarity	9	9	10	10	7	8	8	4	10	7

ARE YOU A *FEEL* OR VISUAL PLAYER?

The following illustration shows the results of a drill with LPGA Tour player Laurie Rinker-Graham. Laurie took rehearsal strokes to feel each chip shot. In this illustration, clarity refers to the feeling of the shot compared to the rehearsal stroke. The more closely the feeling of the shot resembled the rehearsal stroke, the higher the clarity rating. The "0" rating in the clarity row indicates that there was a loss of concentration and feel on that shot.

This illustration also shows the distance from the hole the chip shot finished. A "0" in the "dist" row means the shot was made. For example, Laurie made the fifth chip in this series. Note the shots where there was a "0" retention of feeling of the rehearsal stroke, the distances from the hole were the highest (five and ten feet respectively). With the exception of the third shot, the better the retention and replication of the rehearsal stroke, the closer the ball was to the hole. Laurie's average distance from the hole in this shot series was 2.8 feet.

Name LAURIE RINKER-GRAHAM **Date** 10/29/94

Club________ **Condition** chip to 10 targets - feel in rehearsal stroke - Goal = repeat feel

shot	1	2	3	4	5	6	7	8	9	10
rating	9	7	8	9	10	7	6	9	10	5
clarity	8	7	5	8	10	4	0	8	8	0
dist.	1'	3'	1.5'	2'	0	4'	5'	1'	6"	10'

28'

average distance= 2.8'

Laurie chipped another ten balls using a visualization strategy. In this ten ball sequence she held an image of the ball hitting the flagstick through her stroke. The results of her use of imagery with each chip are shown in the following diagram. Again, Laurie rated each shot on a 1 to 10 scale, the clarity of her image of the ball hitting the flagstick on a 1 to 10 scale, and I stepped off the distance of each shot from the hole. The results of these ten chip shots is shown in the diagram below. As in the preceding sequence, the distance from the hole is shown in the third row labeled "dist.". Again a "0" in the distance row denotes that the chip was made. In this chipping exercise, Laurie was an average of 8.4 inches from the hole. She made three of ten chips.

Club________ **Condition** chip to 10 targets - hold image of ball - hitting flagstick through stroke

shot	1	2	3	4	5	6	7	8	9	10
rating	9	9	10	10	8	10	9	10	10	10
clarity	9	9	10	10	9	10	8	10	9	10
dist.	1'	18"	0	1'	18"	6"	1'	0	1'	0

7'

FEEL SWING CORRECTIONS

Autralian, Asian, and PGA Tour player Dennis Paulson has always been a visual player with great touch. When he becomes immersed in mechanics or swing changes, like most players, he struggles. Dennis' best performances have been when he has had a strong visual image of ball flight through his swing. He made a swing change in early 1996. He had been turning, lifting and crossing the line at the top of his back swing. Dennis was attempting to shorten his swing to eliminate this problem. As long as he held a thought of "shorter" his swing would remain at the desired length and his ball striking was much improved. When he held an image of ball flight through the swing, his swing returned to turn, lift, cross the line at the top and the quality of his ball striking diminished. The following shows ten shots with an image of ball flight through the shot at a lesson during the time Dennis was making this swing change.

Name Dennis Paulson **Date** 1/23/96

Club 7 **Condition** Image of Ball flight thru shot

shot	1	2	3	4	5	6	7	8	9	10
rating	8	10	8	8	7	6	8	9	7	8
clarity	10	10	10	10	7	7	8	9	8	10

Note that Dennis rated good visualization using image of ball flight. His results weren't bad, but they weren't on a caliber with what he wanted in ball striking.

The Next sequence of ten balls shows Dennis taking a practice swing until he felt the swing he wanted to put on the ball. Then, he held a feeling of the practice swing through each shot. In this condition, Dennis' rating of clarity represents how well he thought he reproduced the feeling of the practice swing. His rating of the shot was based upon the feeling of impact, ball flight and proximity to target.

Name Dennis Paulson **Date** 1/23/96

Club 5 **Condition** Feel Swing – Repeat Feel of Practice Swing

shot	1	2	3	4	5	6	7	8	9	10
rating	10	10	6	9	10	9	10	10	8	10
clarity	10	10	10	10	10	10	10	10	9	10

In the next ten ball sequence, Dennis was again making a practice swing and feeling the swing he wanted to make. Note that he was able to reproduce the practice swing at a "10" level on every shot. The only difference in this ten ball sequence and the preceding one is that he used a different club on every shot. I randomly selected the club. Dennis set up, made a practice swing, then hit the shot. Notice the higher shot ratings for shots where he felt the swing he wanted to make versus seeing the ball flight through the swing.

Condition Practice Swing feel – Repeat feel Rotate Club after each shot – Random

shot	1	2	3	4	5	6	7	8	9	10
rating	9	10	8	10	10	10	9	10	9	10
clarity	10	10	10	10	10	10	10	10	10	10
club	7	9	3W	2	SW	8	2	D	6	D

Visualization is important, however, if you are making swing changes, focus on the feeling of the total swing through the shot. You should still stand behind the ball and see the ball flight you want to hit to your target. In time, you will be able to integrate both the feeling of the swing and an image of your target or ball flight through the shot. Remember, you can have input from two sensory systems at once. In this case, one is visual and the other is feel. Work with both independently before you try to blend them.

INSIDE OUT VISUALIZATION

Picture the most pleasurable, exciting event you have ever experienced. Take a moment and gather a mental picture of that event. Now, picture the most distressing event you have ever experienced. Again, take a moment and gather a mental picture of that event.

As you pictured yourself in these two conditions, were you standing at a distance watching yourself or were you seeing these events from inside yourself? Now change your perspective and repeat the exercise. If you were watching from a distance, change your mental image perspective to inside and vis versa. Did you notice any emotional or physical changes in your body? I have never done this exercise with someone who reported a clear image who did not experience an increase in physical and emotional sensations when they were "inside" experiencing the event, good or bad. Similarly, if they were observing themselves from a distance, their physical and emotional responses were much less.

I have seen a number of variations on how people approach this exercise. Some players report they watched the good event from outside and the bad event from inside and vis versa. They always report a greater physical and emotional response to the "inside" experience.

What does this mean? If you are going to visualize yourself playing a round of golf, making a swing, seeing ball flight, and so on, do it from the "inside," not as a passive observer. The brain scans in this chapter would look very different if the volunteers in the study watched themselves from a distance rather than from "inside."

This phenomenon suggests that learning and visualization of pending performance is most efficiently accomplished from an "inside" perspective as opposed to observing yourself from a distance. When you practice visualizaton as part of a learning process or when you are building a motor program for optimum performance, be yourself, not a passive observer.

ENDNOTES

1. Jack Nicklaus and Ken Bowden, *Golf My Way* (New York: Simon and Schuster, 1974), p. 79.

2. Golf Digest Staff, "The Hill Brothers," *Golf Digest* (May, 1992): p. 87.

3. Greg Norman and George Peper, "Greg Norman's Instant Lessons," *Golf Magazine* (April, 1993): p. 52.

4. Golf Digest Staff, "Fred Couples," *Golf Digest* (July, 1992): p. 114.

5. Sam Snead and Al Stump, *The Education of a Golfer* (New York: Simon and Schuster, 1961), p. 233.

6. Marta Figueras-Dotti, Personal Communication (December 4, 1994).

7. Norman and Peper, "Greg Norman's Instant Lessons," p. 52.

8. Eric Alpenfels, "Interview with Byron Nelson," *Golf Tips* (October, 1993): p. 63.

9. Johnny Miller and T.J. Tomasi, "Shaping Your Shots," *Golf Illustrated* (September, 1992): pp. 22-25.

10. Robinson Halloway, "Fiji's Finest," *Golf Magazine* (September, 1993): p. 51.

11. Glenn Monday, "Tom Weiskopf: Still on Target," *Golf Tips* (September, 1994): p. 96.

12. Johnny Miller, "Pressure on the Prowl," *Golf Illustrated* (May, 1989): p. 26.

13. Miller, "Pressure on the Prowl," p. 27.

14. Andrew Magee and T.J. Tomasi, "Practice Like a Pro," *Golf Illustrated* (May, 1992): p. 28.

15. Golf Digest Staff, "Fred Couples," p. 114.

16. Ed Weathers, "Nerves," *Golf Digest* (October, 1994): p. 75.

17. Chris Millard, "Bear With Us," *Golf World* (July 16, 1993): p. 10.
18. Millard, "Bear With Us," p. 10.

19. Golf World Staff, "Tour Talk," *Golf World* (July 16, 1993): p. 30.

20. Jack Nicklaus and Ken Bowden, "How to Beat Tension," *Golf Magazine* (July, 1993): p. 90.

21. Nicklaus and Bowden, "How to Beat Tension," p. 90.

22. Gary Player, *Positive Golf* (New York: McGraw Hill, 1967), p. 2.

23. Player, *Positive Golf*, p. 15.

24. Player, *Positive Golf*, p. 15.

25. Golf Magazine Staff, "Looking Back on the PGA Tour," *Golf Magazine* (August, 1994): p.54.

26. Miller, "Pressure on the Prowl," p. 26.

27. Snead and Stump, *The Education of a Golfer*, p. 144.

28. Harvey Penick and Bud Shrake, *And If You Play Golf, You're My Friend* (New York: Simon and Schuster, 1993), p. 98.

29. Bob Rotella and Bob Cullen, *Golf is Not a Game of Perfect* (New York: Simon and Schuster, 1995), p. 58.

30. Richard Restak, M.D., *The Brain* (New York: Bantam Books, 1984), p. 181.

31. Peter Fox, M.D., Personal Communication (June 8, 1993).

32. K.M. Stephan, G.R. Fink, R.E. Passingham, D. Silbersweig, A.O. Ceballos-Baumann, C.D. Firth, and R.S.J. Frackowiak, "Functional Anatomy of the Mental Representation of Upper Extremity Movements in Healthy Subjects," *Journal of Neurophysiology* (January, 1995): pp. 373-386.

33. Restak, M.D., *The Brain*, p. 181.

34. Restak, M.D., *The Brain*, p. 83.

35. Johnny Miller, "Child's Play," *Golf Illustrated* (April, 1993): p. 48.
36. Ken Venturi, "My Best Tips," *Golf Magazine* (January, 1994): p. 27.

37. Bob Rotella, Ph.D. and Bob Cullen, *Golf is Not A Game of Perfect*, p.58.

As already noted, the common denominator for behavior change, whether your goal is weight loss, exercise, developing confidence, changing your thinking habits, or learning visualization skills, is setting goals for change and keeping a diary of your progress. Weight loss programs require that a diary of everything eaten be written down. Exercise program diaries list the exercise, the number of sets and repetitions of each exercise. The diary is filled out as the exercise program is done.

Make copies of all of the diaries in this book and use them to plan change strategies and evaluate your success. Change is a gradual process. Repetition of desired behaviors will override the old habits ingrained in the neural structures of your nervous system. Insight is the first step toward change, however, insight alone won't produce change. You will most likely make behavior change when you establish a plan, set realistic goals, keep a diary of your progress, review your diary daily and change your goals in successive approximations toward a final goal.

This chapter provides exercises for developing visualization skills. To become proficient with these skills, you must practice. Review pages 158 through 161 and do the visualization exercises. The following page is a diary form for you to set goals and record your practice success. Make copies of this form and use it daily.

Week of ___/___/___ VISUALIZATION SKILLS PRACTICE

BEHAVIOR	goal	Sun	Mon	Tues	Wed	Thur	Fri	Sat
BREATHING								
BURN IN IMAGES								
RECALL PAST SUCCESS								
CALL YOUR SHOT								
DEFINE PRECISE TARGETS								
HOLD THE IMAGE								
SPOT OR BALL ROLLING IMAGERY WITH PUTTING PRACTICE								
SPOT OR BALL HITTING FLAG IMAGERY WITH CHIPPING PRACTICE								
PICTURE AND FEEL YOUR SWING (FROM THE INSIDE--ASSOCIATIVE IMAGERY)								
HOLE EVERY SHOT								
RATE CLARITY OF IMAGE								
PLAN YOUR TARGETS IN ADVANCE								
USE YOUR VISUALIZATION SKILLS TO PLAY THE ROUND THE NIGHT BEFORE OR MORNING BEFORE YOU PLAY								

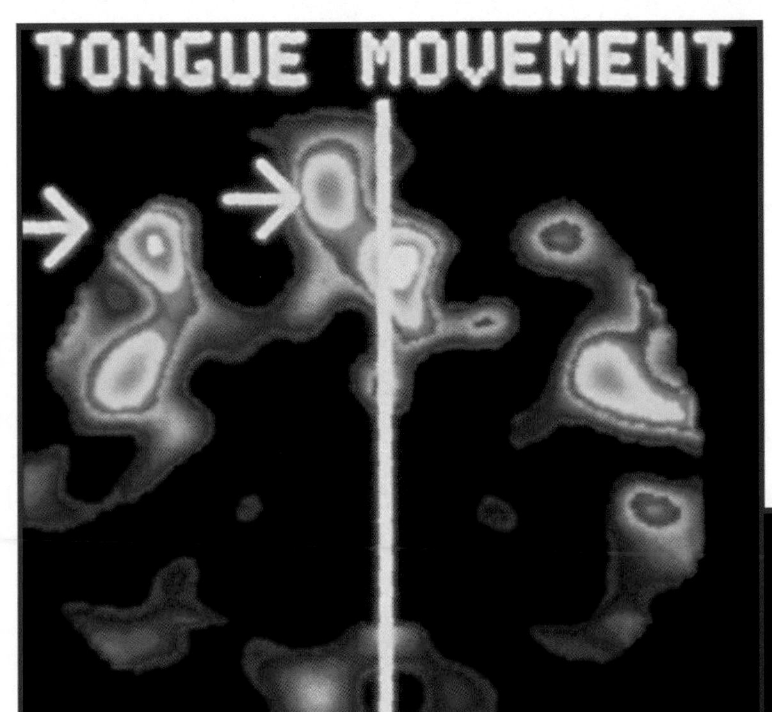

Tongue Movement

ACTUAL MOVEMENT
S.M.A.
SENSORIMOTOR

Right Hand Movement

IMAGINED MOVEMENT
S.M.A.

Visualized Right Hand Movement

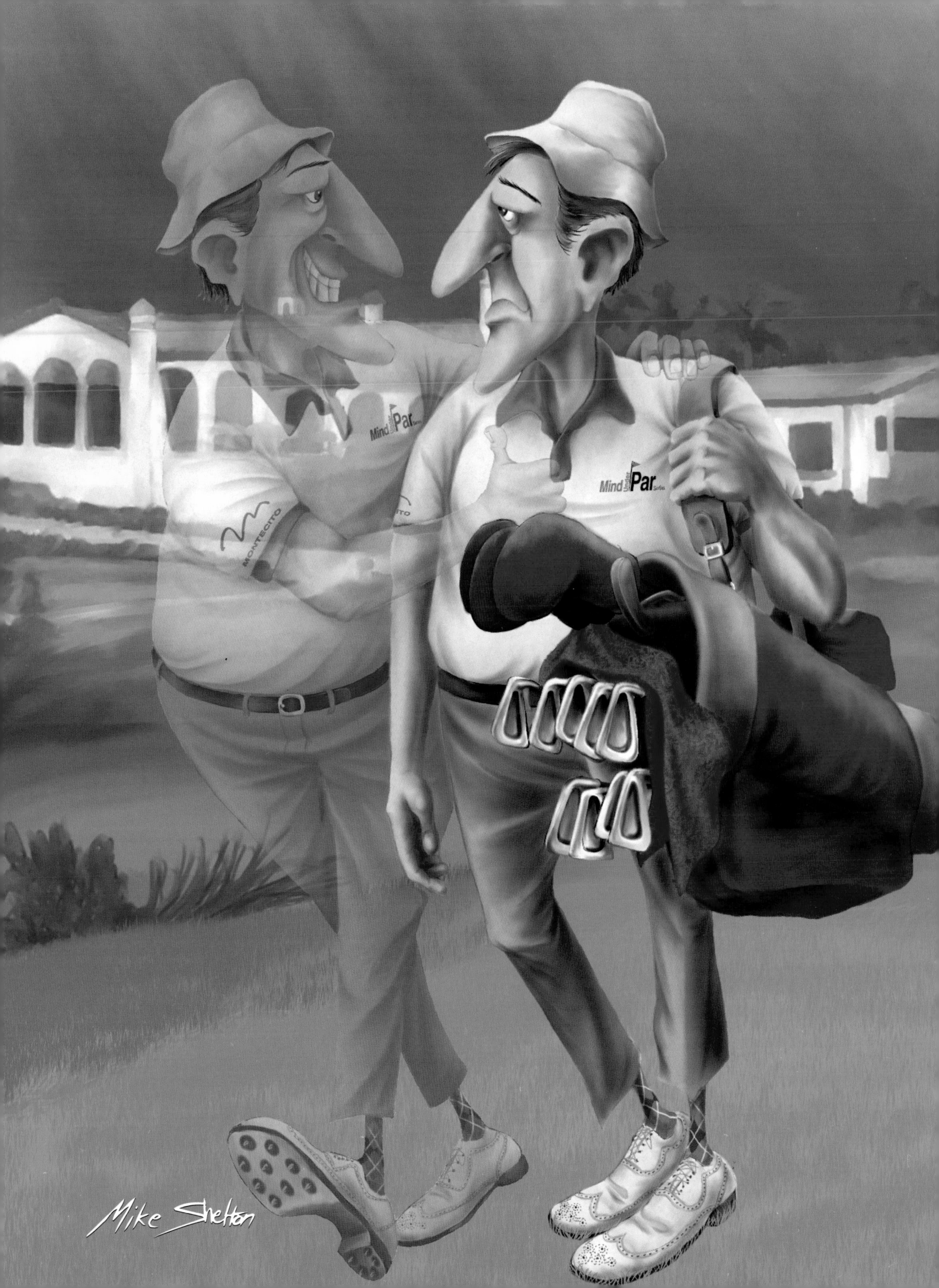

Mind Par
MONTECITO
Mind Par
Mike Shelton

7

HOW TO TALK TO YOURSELF ON AND OFF THE GOLF COURSE

European and PGA Tour player David Feherty pointed out that "...the World's Number One tennis player spends 90 percent of his time winning, while the world's Number One golfer spends 90 percent of his time losing. Probably more than that. Golfers are great losers. You have to be. The genuine failures that you have, and there are many of them, make you into a more resilient specimen."[1]

Senior PGA Tour player Tom Weiskopf was known for his temper when he played on the regular tour in the 1970's. He reflected on his past: "Whenever I was playing good, I'd think something bad was bound to happen." Upon winning the 1995 U S Senior Open, Weiskopf commented on the changes in his thinking: "...I've never played better. I never got mad, I never lost concentration, I never thought about the next shot, and I immediately forgot about the last shot."[2]

Harvey Penick, past instructor to many successful PGA and LPGA Tour players, says: "You should make birdies with your good breaks, but your bad breaks must not be allowed to mess up your thinking and poison your attitude. Leaving the breaks out of it, what causes the bleeding is what is going on in your mind during the five or ten minutes between shots... Are you thinking ahead to future holes? Perhaps you are thinking: 'I'll knock this wedge stiff for a birdie, then par that long hard hole, reach the 17th in two for a cinch birdie-and par on the final hole will pay me a great big fat check.' Not only are you living too far in the future to be playing a sharp game of golf, you have let the thought of gold enter your mind... You reach your reward stroke by stroke. You must be mindful of each stroke as it is played. Golf is played in the present. If you can wash your mind clean each time while walking to your next shot, you have the makings of a champion."[3]

This chapter will present you with strategies to restructure your thinking so you can "wash your mind clean" between and prior to each shot and in day to day life. Clinical psychologists call the procedures in this chapter cognitive behavior therapy. The next chapter provides examples of how these strategies are used in a variety of situations on and off the golf course.

As Jack Nicklaus once said: "Correct thinking plus a measure of self-control will not only tame tension, but actually make it work for you."[4]

HOW TO THINK ON THE COURSE

The chapter titled Routine: The Links to Success presented ideal mental (thinking) strategies to incorporate as part of the preswing, inswing, and postswing routines. These "ideal" thoughts create a present focus in the preswing and inswing routines free of swing mechanics. Recall that the routine is a step by step process that takes you from a broad focus of relevant information about the shot to a creative, narrowing focus on ball flight, and a narrower focus on shot outcome or target.

The postswing routine summary emphasized the importance of effective use of internal dialogue and images following shots. In particular, anger as a performance enhancer versus a performance deterrent was discussed. To repeat these "ideal" internal dialogues would be redundant. Suffice it to say, those mental strategies are the desired thoughts for peak performance on the course.

Prior to play, it is important to develop a game plan. Know what club you are going to hit and where you want to place your ball off the tee on every hole. If it is a course you haven't played, ask your playing partners what your targets are. Ask which mower track or discolored area in the fairway is your target. Redirect or ignore discussions of areas to avoid. Ask what the carry is to your target and choose a club. Just because it is a par 4 or 5 doesn't mean it's a driver from the tee. If you know the course, play it in your mind the day or morning before you play. Use your past experience and success on the course as a guideline. This is covered in more detail in the chapter on visualization.

Both Jack Nicklaus and Johnny Miller describe the importance of finding a swing key that is working on the practice range prior to play. Miller describes these keys with the acronym "WOOD": Works only one day.[5, 6]

Once you settle on a swing key, focus on the associated feeling in the swing, and stick with that key and feeling the entire round. Don't change or search for other keys during play.

PGA Tour player Tom Watson once said: "I know when I am playing my best I am not thinking of very many things, maybe not even a swing thought. Just whatever the shot requires."[7]

Bobby Jones also said: "... after taking your stance there should be no room for worry."[8] Jones described the secret to every golf shot he hit as a focus on the outcome of the shot to the exclusion of everything else. I would expand this to say that as soon as you start your routine, stepping off your yardage, your thought focus should be nothing but positive and on the anticipated success of the shot you are about to hit.

The procedures described in the following pages will assist you in developing techniques to increase your mental toughness by restructuring and changing thoughts that lead to poor performance. Use these strategies and your on-course performance will improve. If you also use these techniques off the course, you will have a happier, less stressful, and more productive life.

This instruction will also give you a better understanding of the automatic nature of thinking and how many of us fall prey to nonproductive and sometimes self-destructive, automatic thoughts. It's important for you to recognize that you have control over your thinking. All you need to do is assume that control. As a part of this change, you will begin to notice positive on-course performance and enjoyment as you begin to apply these strategies.

THOUGHTS AS HABITS

The nervous system consists of billions of neurons. As we experience thoughts and images, these neurons begin to communicate at lightning speed. The pathways of these neurons fall into a patterned circuitry and are triggered by conditions in the environment. These patterns are the physical structure of learning. Your thinking tends to follow a predictable set style. It's like turning on a light switch. You flip the switch and the current causes the lights to come on. Conditions in the environment around you trigger a particular style of thinking in much the same way. Thought styles are habits

If you are going to learn to control your thinking, the first step is to understand what conditions trigger thinking when you perform your best, and what conditions trigger thinking that hinders performance.

All of this from thinking? Yes. Thoughts play a major role in both your mood and internal physical state. The more aware you become of your thoughts, the more you will be able to actively control your physical self and your mood. These changes will positively affect your performance.

THE NEUROPHYSIOLOGY OF HABIT

Brain researchers have identified and "photographed" biochemical representations of mood states. For example, a group of depressed individuals showed a particular use of a radioactive tracer (glucose) in their brains that non-depressed people did not show. When non-depressed people were asked to engage in negative thoughts, a cluster of use of the radiotracer identical to that of the depressed individuals began to appear in the brain images.[9] Similar findings were made with individuals suffering from panic disorder and obsessive-compulsive disorder, both anxiety-related problems.[10]

A variety of treatments were attempted across three groups of individuals with obsessive-compulsive disorder. One of these procedures was cognitive therapy (thinking therapy), a significant part of the content of this chapter. Changes in brain chemistry were monitored through an imaging procedure described in the visualization chapter, a PET scan. Interestingly, as the obsessive-compulsive symptoms diminished, the brain chemistry, as shown from the imaging, also changed to a "normal" state. One of the most effective treatment strategies used was cognitive therapy. This is the same therapeutic style used in the treatment of depression.

Cognitive therapy can just as easily be used to change thoughts that interfere with performance on and off the course. For example, we all worry, some of us are just more proficient than others. The first thing to recognize is that this "future focus" or nervous, anxious anticipation is represented in the brain as neurochemical patterns or clusters. These clusters are triggered by a variety of environmental conditions and represented in thoughts that make up a particular thinking style, for example, worry. Changing patterns of worry is just as involved as changing negative thought patterns that fuel a mood of depression. A dedicated effort that includes a daily diary of success is important for sustained change.

Bobby Jones described worry in golf like worry anywhere: "It's a fear of the future which is pointless. There isn't anything you can do about something that hasn't happened yet." He further stated: "The ability to play the shot you visualized and let trouble take care of itself is a rare quality in a golfer, one the average player should strive for more than perfection in a swing..."[11]

AUTOMATIC THOUGHTS AND BEHAVIOR

It is important that you understand the concept of an "automatic habit" or "routine" as related to your thinking. The automatic habits that make up a good part of our day to day routines include our thoughts. Sometimes these thought habits promote desired performance. Other times these thoughts interfere with performance.

The golf swing is "cued" by the conditions in our internal and external environment. The external environment is lie, wind, target, and type of play (tournament, casual round, etc.), and the internal environment would be our thoughts and physiology. Let's look at how thoughts are cued both on and off the course.

Few of us recognize that we can exercise voluntary control over our thoughts. Becoming aware of your "thought patterns" is not easy. Our thoughts and thought patterns are learned, much like most of our behavior patterns. In fact, ninety-nine plus percent of all behavior is automatic. Behavior occurs without direction by thinking. The movement of your eyes across this page is automatic. The way you hold this book, take a drink, open a door, and so on, is automatic.

Automatic behavior means that you don't actively think through each step of a particular behavior. For example, as you take a drink, you don't say: "Now I need to extend my right arm, open my hand, grasp the glass, bend my elbow, etc." This behavior was learned as a habit, and is produced without thought.

THINKING AND PERFORMANCE

1981 British Open Champion Bill Rogers also won three times on the PGA Tour that year. PGA Tour player Bruce Litzke reflected on Rogers' stature during the early 1980's: "For a period of time, he dominated the World." His record certainly reflects that. Then he began to struggle. By 1988, he had made three cuts in fifteen tournaments and had won only $5,482. When he left the tour, he still had three years left on his exemption for winning the World Series of golf. In 1993, he talked about his struggle in the 80's: "I think I was motivated for a lot of the wrong reasons. Not wrong necessarily, but reasons that were shallow and prideful. 'How am I stacking up? What do people think?' Stuff like that."[12]

When describing his win at the 1992 British Open, Nick Faldo indicated that he wasn't discontinuing his search for perfection; he was just not being so hard on himself when he didn't achieve it.[13]

You answered questions regarding conditions and thoughts that promote poor performance at the beginning of this book. Let's review them again. How do you think and behave when you play your worst rounds of golf? Do you feel focused on the game? Are you relaxed? Do you expect to be successful? Are your movements and swings relaxed, automatic, fluid and non-mechanical? Do you follow the same routine on every shot? If you are going to improve performance, it's important that you recognize internal (thoughts) and external routines which contribute to good and poor performance both on and off the course.

What type of thinking promotes poor performance in your day to day life? Consider the following. You awaken in the morning and selectively focus on problems with your family, difficulties at work, the many things facing you that appear to be insurmountable, what you failed to accomplish yesterday, and so on. These thoughts are negative, and, unless restructured, will create an undesired mood, loss of concentration, acceleration of your nervous system, irritability of movement and thought, impulsive judgment and action, and subsequent poor performance. When you take this emotional/physical state to the golf course, it results in poor performance there as well.

When you awaken and begin to worry about how you will pay your bills, or you anticipate the disapproval of others for something you have done, or you worry about your children or other family members, or you begin to think about the big tournament, your mood is most likely going to be anxious. This selective focus is a habit many people begin upon awakening. This mood adversely affects your performance both on and off the course.

What kinds of thoughts promote enhanced performance? Top athletes from a variety of sports were asked to describe their mental state during their peak performance periods. Their descriptions included the following:[14]

1. ***There is a one hundred percent concentration in the moment on what they are doing.***

2. ***A state of total relaxation exist.***

3. ***A feeling of confidence that they can "do anything" is present.***

4. ***There is a perception of every thing moving in slow motion.***

5. ***A feeling of one hundred percent control and a totally effortless, automatic state surrounds them.***

6. ***During their event, they are void of thoughts of anything other than that which they are doing.***

7. ***They don't bring the mental or emotional experiences of other parts of their lives with them to the event.***

8. ***These top athletes don't perform for anyone but them selves, not the crowd, their family or others. They perform for the personal enjoyment they experience.***

9. ***They assume full responsibility for their errors. They don't blame equipment, conditions, etc.***

10. ***They all describe a routine they follow as a pre-performance behavior pattern. These routines are both external behaviors and internal (thoughts and physiology) behaviors.***

Item number nine fits my value system quite well. I personally believe that we should all assume responsibility for and the consequences of our actions. My work with top golfers contradicts this ethic. As I noted in the confidence chapter, I have had some great players tell me they were told by other great players: "Don't ever let it [bad shot or bad break] be your fault." Again, if you assume full responsibility, your confidence will begin to fade.

In practice, I counsel that accepting or not accepting responsibility for poor play is a fine line to walk. I have had good players tell me they aren't putting well because the greens are bad, and so on. I remind them that the entire field is putting on the same greens. Their usual retort is, "Yeah, but the greens aren't spiked-up at the times they play," and so on.

The conversation always returns to questions of whether they are doing their putting drills, what their routine is like, and what thoughts they are having "in stroke." Additionally, we discuss whether they have purposely or inadvertently change their posture, grip, alignment, their eye position, or if they are following the putter blade back or the roll of the ball with their eyes, and so on. It is easy to rationalize poor play when you don't assume responsibility. Don't blame and get down on yourself if you can honestly say you have been working hard on the mental side and not thinking mechanics. If you don't experience success with a solid mental practice program, it's time to look for help. Have your PGA or LPGA professional check your setup, the fundamentals of golf.

When you consider it, thinking is the foundation of the majority of the ten characteristics of top athletes. As noted, your thinking is ingrained in a neuroanatomical structure that is predictable across any number of situations. Each time you change a situation, your behavior changes. The situation "triggers" different behaviors. It's like walking into a room and turning on a light switch. The room is prewired to turn on a light. Your nervous system is prewired to respond differently in different situations. This wiring is laid down during development and learning. If you want to change your behavior, you have to re-route the circuity of your nervous system. Rewiring or rerouting the behavioral circuitry of your nervous system is accomplished through repetition.

For the majority of players, the more aroused you are, the more "interference" you will experience in your thinking and performance. Your thoughts don't have a life of their own. You can gain active control of your thinking. However, due to the neurophysical and neurochemical foundations on which these predictable thought patterns evolve, extensive practice or repetition is necessary to change these physical, neurochemical structures.

POSITIVE VERSUS NEGATIVE THOUGHT THEMES

Most of us have heard about the importance of being positive from our coaches, teachers, peers and/or parents. We acknowledge, agree, and most of us return to our themes of negativity. Why? The automatic thoughts we learned as children were most likely negative. Negativity varies from complaints about weather or health to judgmental or critical comments regarding others. Negative themes in thought and discussion produce frustration, anger, unhappiness, and depression. As you begin to listen in on your thinking, note how many of your thought themes are negative. Set goals to change. I've heard stories and read that Gary Player would leave a room if he heard any negativity at all. Listen in on your thoughts as suggested on the following pages, and see for yourself: Negative?

People who are judgmental of others tend to be most focused on how others perceive them. If you want to decrease your concern regarding how others perceive you, the first step is to set a goal to be non-judgmental of others.

The following pages provide an overview of thought restructuring procedures. You will learn, for example, to discontinue patterns of worry, and anticipation, or to control anger and frustration, and develop patience and a more positive focus on both yourself and others.

The purpose of this chapter is to teach you internal communication strategies that will enhance your mental toughness and make you more resilient when faced with difficulty or when you have thoughts that set you up for failure.

THOUGHT TRACKING

The first step to assuming active control over thinking is an awareness of thoughts. Thoughts occur as habits or routines, and repeat in patterns. We look at these internal behavior patterns, like external behavior, as a chain. Thought one is the first link in the chain. Thought one serves as a cue for thought two, the second link in the chain which cues thought three, the third link, etc. This behavior chain is like the one I presented in the overview on routine and the physiological chains of relaxation and arousal.

THOUGHT CHAINS AND THEMES

Your first task is to develop an awareness of these "thought chains." As presented in the overview on confidence, listen in on your thoughts and record them in a diary format. As you become aware of these patterns, ask yourself:

- ***Are these the kinds of thoughts I want to have often?***
- ***Should I increase or decrease these thoughts?***
- ***Are these thoughts helping or hindering me?***
- ***Will these thoughts make me calm, comfortable, and happy, or***
- ***Will these thoughts make me nervous, tense, sad, or angry?***
- ***How do these thoughts affect my***

performance on the course?

- ***How do these thoughts affect my performance off the course?***

The following are a few of the various themes of thoughts:

Positive Thought Themes	**Negative Thought Themes**
Confident	*Pessimistic*
Calm/Controlled	*Anxious/Worried*
Self-Supporting	*Self-Critical*
Happy/Comforting	*Sad/Depressing*
Caring/Loving	*Critical/Judgmental*
A present focus	*Future/Past Focus*
Relaxing	*Tension Producing*

Once you determine the themes, you can decide whether your thoughts are something you choose to continue or end.

Thoughts can be "tracked" very easily. Thought tracking will help you become aware of both positive and negative themes in your thinking. It is a procedure where you begin to "listen in" on your thinking. Take the following day to day life situation as an example:

You awaken in the morning, lie in bed, and begin to think of all the things you need to do today. You begin to feel a sense of urgency and an internal agitation. A pattern of thoughts begins. Thought one leads to thought two, and so on.

What theme do you think would characterize your thoughts as you lie in bed considering your day in this example? Remember that each person is different; the chain of thoughts that evolves in the situation presented would vary from one person to another.

Your answer was probably something like:

- **negative**
- **nervous/anxious/worried**
- **anticipatory**
- **tension producing**

Is this theme going to help you? What will happen to you physically with a thought theme like this?

What were your thoughts when you played your best rounds of golf? Were you focused on bad shots? Were you angry? Were your thoughts supportive? Were you thinking about hazards or targets? Were you worried or thinking about off-course things like family, finances, or work? Were you thinking about how much money you were winning or losing?

You have a "bank" of thoughts and behaviors to draw upon from your past peak performances. Your goal should be to practice internal and external behaviors that draw upon these memory banks to reproduce this state. You should also consider your physical and mental preparation (preround) prior to these peak performance periods.

Recall that Gary Player "quieted his movement" in everything he did in preparation for the 1965 US Open.[15] You can practice focused concentration during day to day life by being mindful during all routine activities.

THOUGHT TRACKING EXERCISE

Now it's your turn to try thought tracking.

It's 10:00 P.M. the night before a big tournament. You are preparing for bed. What are your thoughts and images? Please list them as they occur.

What was the theme of your thoughts?

What were your thoughts and images prior to the best rounds of golf you ever played? Please list them here.

1

2

3

4

5

6

7

What was the theme of your thoughts?

What were your images and thoughts during the round?

How did you handle frustrating situations, bad shots, bad breaks, bad conditions, and so on?

____
____
____
____
____
____
____

You are on the first tee of a big tournament. There are ten to fifteen people gathered around the tee waiting. It's your turn to tee off. What are your thoughts and images? Please list them as they occur:

1 _______________________________________
____
____

2 _______________________________________
____
____

3 _______________________________________
____
____

4 _______________________________________
____
____

5 _______________________________________
____
____

6 _______________________________________
____
____

Next, identify the theme(s) of your thoughts:

____
____
____

Are these thoughts/themes supportive and comforting and confidence building? Will these thoughts "cue" good or poor performance? Do you need to consider a plan to change this thought pattern at the beginning of your next round or tournament? Do you see a similar pattern of thinking in your off-course behavior where you can begin to change these patterns?

Note the interlocking circles (chain) of thoughts used in each example so far. Thought one serves as a cue for thought two that cues thoughts three, four, and so on. Behavior can be changed by simply learning strategies to break behavior chains. You learned for example in the chapter titled Fine Tuning Your Nervous System that you can break the chain of arousal by quieting your breathing, slowing down your movement and relaxing your muscles. Similarly, you can learn to substitute chains of desired behavior. You are ready to discover ways to break the chains of the behavior of thinking.

CHANGING UNDESIRED THINKING CHAINS

Let's look at how you can begin to change undesired thinking. Remember that a chain breaks when a link is removed. Therefore, if you catch the chain at the beginning, you can interrupt and avoid the rest of the chain. It is likely that you will be close to the end of the chain the first few times before you become aware of the thought pattern. However, with repeated practice and a plan for change, you will be avoiding the undesired pattern altogether.

When you become aware of the early signs of predictable thoughts, note the associated behavior patterns that evolve. These patterns are predictable. Learned patterns are repeated in the same or similar situations. An undesired chain of thoughts on the first tee is automatic and might be something like the following for some players:

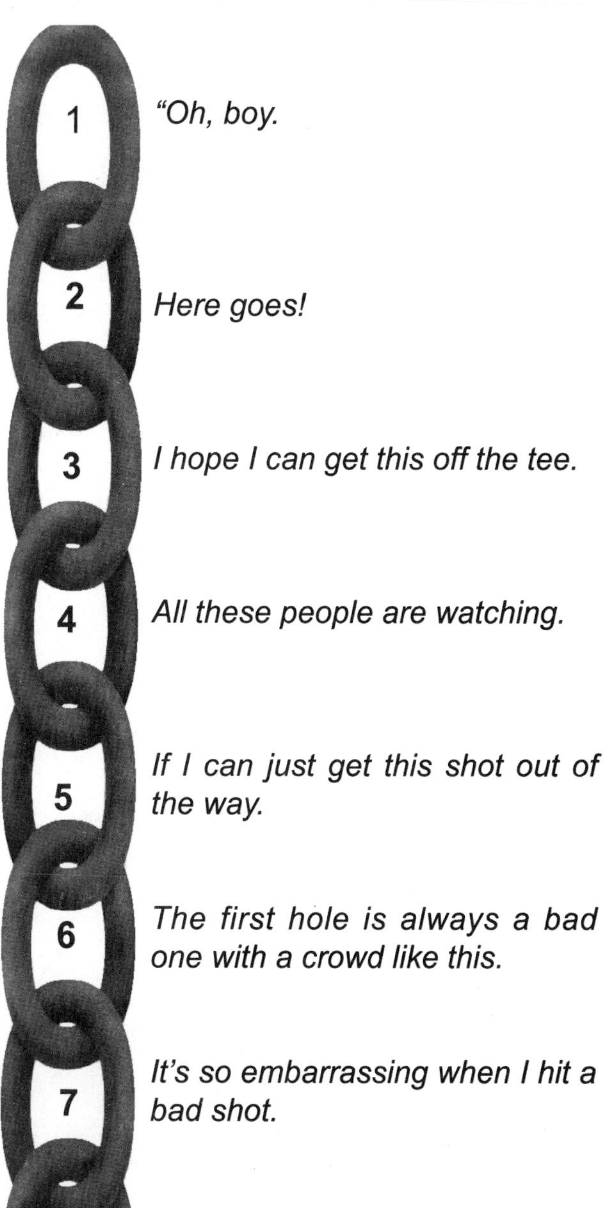

Remember, the nervous system consists of billions of neurons. Your thinking follows a predictable set style. This style is automatic and will not change unless you do something to break the behavior chain. The first step you will learn to break the unwanted behavior chains is called *Thought Stopping.*

THOUGHT STOPPING

Dawn Coe led the LPGA money list in March of 1992 after recording her first victory in eight years. She attributed her new found success to learning to block out distractions.[16]

Thought stopping is a cognitive therapy procedure used to block thoughts that serve no purpose other than to result in undesired physical, emotional, and performance consequences. What thoughts would fall into this category?

Suppose you find yourself repeatedly thinking about a decision you made, about what you "should have done" in a recent situation, or what you "should have said," or your club selection two shots ago, your score, or what others are thinking about you. Or, you may have some intrusive thoughts in the middle of your routine, for example, "Do I have enough club?"

Thought stopping is a strategy you can use in all of these examples. Let's assume you are set up to hit a shot and begin to think about the shot you hit into the hazard your last round on this hole. The following is a summary of the *thought stopping* technique you could use in this situation.

Step 1. Step off the ball. Begin diaphragmatic breathing (deep breathing) slowly. Inhale through your nose and exhale through your mouth. Note the increased relaxation as you exhale. Exhalation should take twice as long as inhalation. Purse your lips to slow down your exhalation if necessary. Do a body scan as you exhale. Purposely slow down your physical movement. Step off the ball if you are in the middle of your routine.

Step 2. Say to yourself subvocally: "STOP... RELAX" or "KNOCK IT OFF!, SHUT UP!, BE QUIET!, RELAX!" Each time you say "RELAX," concentrate on that relaxed feeling. Each time you exhale, say to yourself: "RELAX." Slow down your pace. If you are aroused, you have likely quickened your movement and this will be expressed as a faster than normal swing pace. Slow down your walking pace and breathe deeply.

Step 3. Once you have stopped the undesired thoughts and feel more relaxed, bring yourself into the present. Feel the club in your hand and the ground under your feet. Develop a one hundred percent here and now, present focus. Confidently tell yourself what you are going to do in this situation.

Recall the same shot you have hit well in the past. Experience the feelings and images of that shot. Visualize your success as you describe the shot you are about to hit. Once you have successfully input the confident images, bring yourself back to the moment as you move deliberately through your preswing to setup position.

Anne Marie Palli won the LPGA 1993 Atlantic City Shoprite Classic in a playoff against Laura Davies. Anne Marie had knocked her second shot to three feet on the par 4, and Laura had bogeyed the hole. As Anne Marie stood over her putt, she said: "This would be embarrassing if I miss this." Then she stepped back and said: "Shut-up! Just stay in your routine and knock it in the hole." She resumed her routine, saw the ball roll in the hole, set up, made the putt for birdie and won the tournament.[17]

In other situations:

Step 1. If you are applying *thought stopping* in your day to day routine, and you are involved in a project that does not permit you to use imagery, focus all of your attention on that project. If the undesired thoughts return, repeat the procedures.

Step 2. At bedtime, when thoughts interfere with sleep, begin counting backwards from one hundred. Visualize each number painted on a wall as you say it to yourself. Use deliberate, slow movement as you begin counting and visualizing. Relax your head, neck, shoulders, chest, back, stomach, legs, and feet as you feel each area sink into the mattress. Use slow, deliberate movement as you position yourself in your bed. Be mindful of the sensations and comfort of your bed.

If you have the *MIND UNDER PAR* series™ *Routine: Guided Practice in Developing Consistent Performance,* listen to one of the arousal reduction tapes and repeat the phrases to yourself.

RATIONAL DIALOGUE

Our internal dialogue can be considered either rational-enhances performance-or irrational-disrupts performance. *Rational dialogue* is a technique that is used instead of or in conjunction with *thought stopping.* This technique will help interrupt and redirect thought patterns that are negative (irrational). Let's move directly to the steps involved in *rational dialogue,* and then consider an example of how this technique could be applied to specific thought themes.

The steps to *rational dialogue* include:

Step 1. Awareness or recognition of the irrational and nonproductive thoughts you are experiencing.

Step 2. Begin diaphragmatic breathing (deep breathing) slowly. Inhale through your nose and exhale through your mouth. Note the increased relaxation as you exhale. Exhalation should take twice as long as inhalation. Purse your lips to slow down your exhalation if necessary. Do a body scan as you exhale. Purposely slow down your physical movement. Step off the ball if you are in the middle of your routine.

Focus on the relaxed feeling. Repeat the relaxation procedures in movement, breathing, and heaviness again and again, until you are experiencing a relaxed sensation.

Step 3. Remind yourself of the consequences to you if you continue this irrational, nonproductive thinking. For example, there will be no change in the situation. Irritability, loss of concentration, and inability to improve or deterioration in performance will be the outcome. This is the time to be a good internal coach: "Com'on! You can still have a decent round. Get back in this shot and forget about those bad breaks."

Step 4. Actively REDIRECT YOUR THOUGHTS and images to success in your next shot. Again, recall similar successful shots of the past, and the associated feelings and images of those shots. You can use *thought stopping* at this point if you are having difficulty keeping a positive focus. Continue using relaxation and positive imagery as you approach the next shot and during your preswing routine. Continue deliberate movement and moment to moment focus. Again, be an aggressive, supportive coach: "Stop crying and play! You are too good to behave like this! Get your head back in the game! You have this shot! Feel it, get into your target and knock it stiff."

If you experience distressing or disruptive thoughts during day to day life situations, use the following strategies:

Step 1. Make an appointment with yourself to "worry." Remind yourself: "I can't do anything until 9:00 A.M. Monday. I'll take care of it then. Life is too short not to enjoy each moment to its fullest. I'm going to assume control and enjoy it now."

Step 2. Remind yourself that you have control over your thoughts! All you need to do is assume that control.

APPLYING COGNITIVE THERAPY PROCEDURES FOR IMPROVED PERFORMANCE

Now, let's consider how you might apply these techniques to a specific situation.

You are on the 10th tee. You decided to apply the recommendation of not adding your score at the turn (after nine holes). A well-meaning fellow competitor tells you your score. You are two strokes lower at the turn than in any previous round.

You can feel the excitement in the thought of having a career best round.

The speed of your thoughts accelerates. You can see your score as it's totaled in the clubhouse. Unbeknownst to you, your heart begins to beat faster and muscle tone increases (tension) moderately. You are so occupied with the events nine holes from now, you lose track of the fact you are on the tee, until you hear a voice from beside you say: "You're Up." You are startled back to the present.

You take your driver to the tee, then realize it's a 300 yard sharp dogleg right, and you don't need a driver. You "quickly" return to your bag, "grab" a 3 iron, and "hurry" back to the tee so you don't hold up play. The speed of your swing and quickened movement on the tee matches the acceleration of your heart and breathing rate. You hook your tee shot into the trees. By the time you recover, you take a double bogey on the hole.

As you approach the 11th tee your thoughts are as follows:

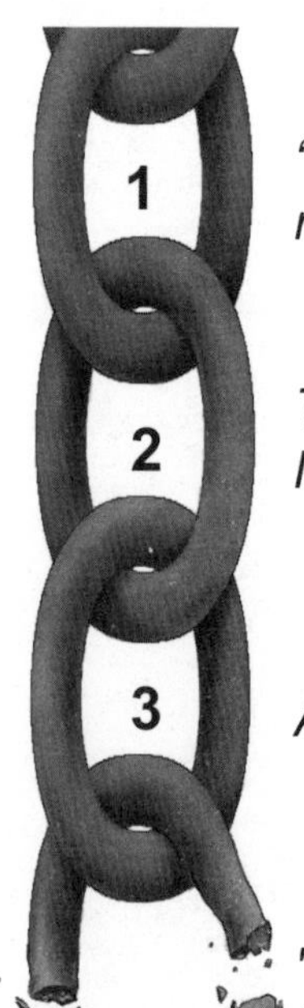

"I can still have a good round."

That double brings me back a little, but I can still recover.

All I need is a few pars and..."

*"**BE QUIET!**," you say, "**KNOCK IT OFF!**"*

1. *"You are moving too quickly and focused on score."*
2. *You stop your physical movement and breathe deeply-long exhalation. You regroup and say:*
3. *"Ok this is a 425 yard par 4.*
4. *The flag is in the back left and I can see my approach shot to the elevated green.*
5. *I recall the same shot I hit well on the 4th tee. I recall the feeling and image of the swing, and I picture the ball flight.*
6. *I'm going to hit my first shot to the shady area in the right center of the fairway.*
7. *Breathe deeply, slow down my movement.*
8. *I can feel the head cover as I slowly, deliberately remove my driver from the bag. I am one hundred percent in the present.*
9. *I move deliberately and comfortably as I place my ball on the tee.*
10. *I feel the ground under my feet and my club in my hands, as I walk slowly behind the ball.*
11. *I breathe deeply with a feeling of control.*

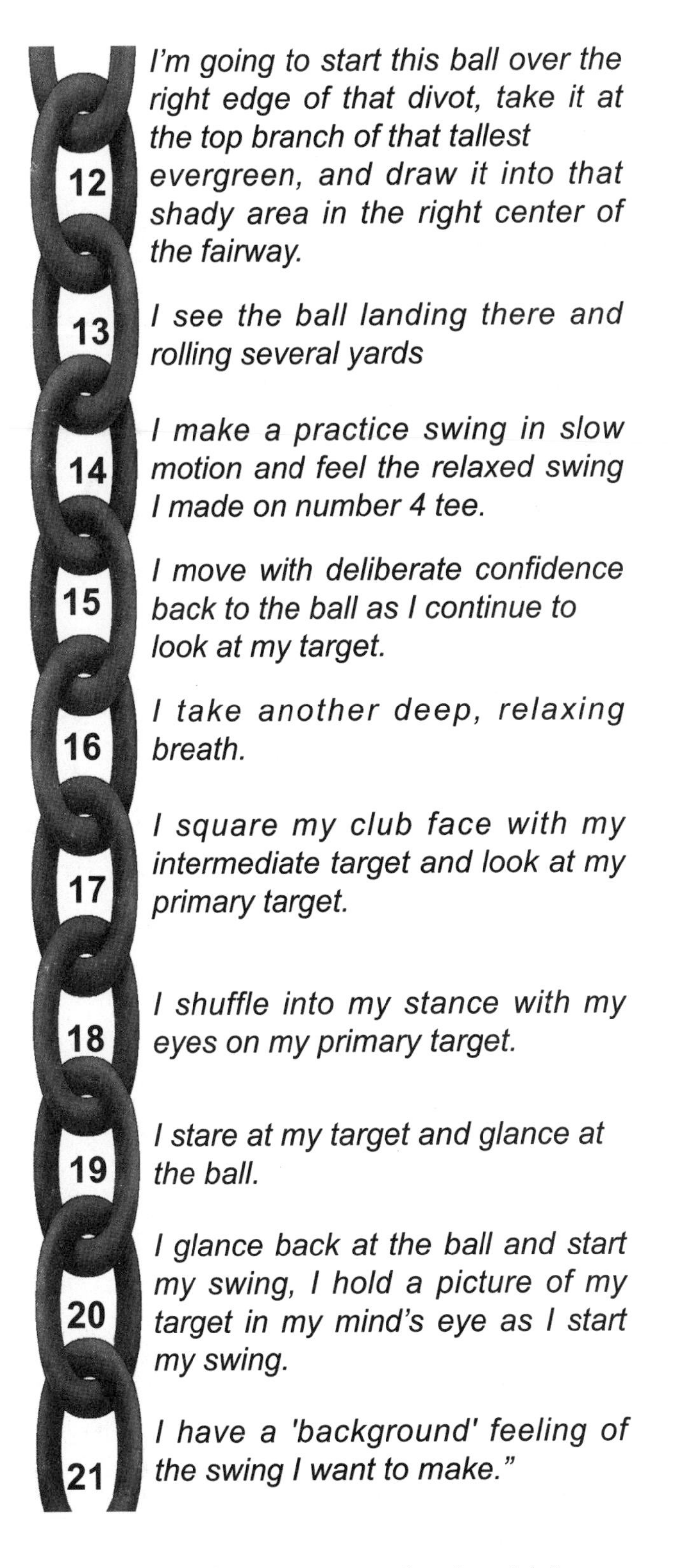

12 *I'm going to start this ball over the right edge of that divot, take it at the top branch of that tallest evergreen, and draw it into that shady area in the right center of the fairway.*

13 *I see the ball landing there and rolling several yards*

14 *I make a practice swing in slow motion and feel the relaxed swing I made on number 4 tee.*

15 *I move with deliberate confidence back to the ball as I continue to look at my target.*

16 *I take another deep, relaxing breath.*

17 *I square my club face with my intermediate target and look at my primary target.*

18 *I shuffle into my stance with my eyes on my primary target.*

19 *I stare at my target and glance at the ball.*

20 *I glance back at the ball and start my swing, I hold a picture of my target in my mind's eye as I start my swing.*

21 *I have a 'background' feeling of the swing I want to make."*

This is one of many examples in which you use *thought stopping* and *rational dialogue* to interrupt an unwanted chain of internal dialogue and substitute a performance enhancing chain. As noted in the chapter titled Routine, these skills must be practiced on the range if you are going to have success on the golf course.

THOUGHT RESTRUCTURING EXERCISE

Take the following situation. You have birdied three of the first four holes at a club you are visiting. You step onto the 5th tee three under par.

Considering your usual level of play, track your thoughts:

1 ____________________________

2 ____________________________

3 ____________________________

4 ____________________________

5 ____________________________

6 ____________________________

Do these thoughts support continued peak performance? Are your thoughts in the present? Are they supportive, relaxing thoughts? Do you need to restructure these thoughts? If so, interrupt the chain of thoughts using *thought stopping* and *rational dialogue*. Write the internal dialogue you would use to break the chain of these negative disruptive thoughts.

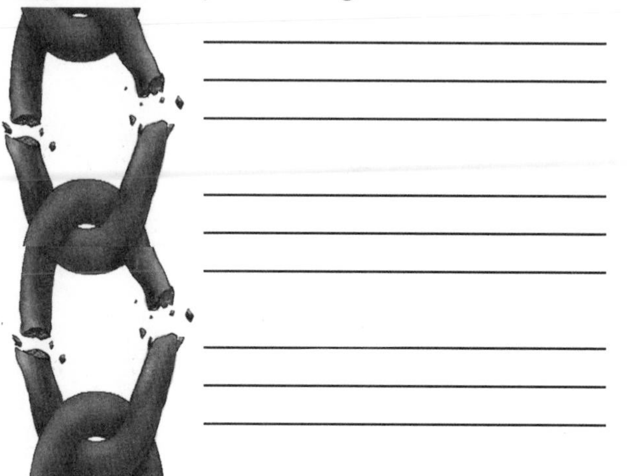

List the thoughts you will use to resume a thought chain that will ensure that you stay focused in the present and in a desired mental routine:

You may have written something like:

"Just breathe deeply and stay focused in the present.

I'm going to play this hole one shot at a time.

I'm just going to keep hitting shots that are eights, nines, and tens, one at a time."

Now you step onto the tee of the 5th hole, a par 4, set up, swing, and pull your shot left into the trees. You find your ball in the trees. You also find a large "window" between the branches of a tree through which you want to hit your shot. You set up, swing, and your recovery shot hits a branch, and your ball settles in the center of the cart path. You have a free drop. However, the shot off the concrete cart path is better than your relief would be with a drop. What are your thoughts?

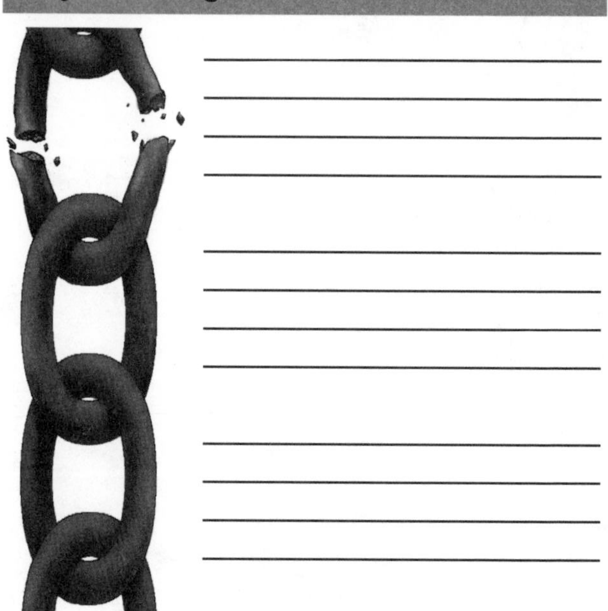

Again, are your thoughts supportive of continued peak performance? How are you doing with the frustration of missing your recovery shot after playing so well to this point? Are your thoughts indicative of patience? Do you need to restructure your thinking?

You just played out three-quarters of a situation that occurred to John Houston in Florida during the 1992 PGA Tour. Let's see how it ends:

John Houston birdied three of the first four holes in the last round of the 1992 Walt Disney World/Oldsmobile Classic. He pulled his tee shot on Number 5 left into the trees, and his recovery shot hit a branch and settled on a concrete cart path. Rather than take a drop in tree roots, Houston played the 160 yard shot off the cart path onto the green. He then made a thirty foot putt for par. He said of this experience: "I thought right then that maybe it was my day." He went on to shoot a final round 62 and win the tournament by three shots.[18]

Do you focus on your good play and turn your focus to what is going well or do you think to yourself: "*That was luck. I wonder when the wheels are going to fall off. I'm playing way over my head.*" Or, "*Okay, I'm still three under. If I can just hold on and and at least bogey that tough par three and not get to greedy on ten and thirteen, I can shoot a really good score*!" Either of these thought styles is self destructive. Both break your mental and physical routine chains. Both are thought chain links that will lead to poor performance.

Let's look at a few other on-course situations that will require calming your thinking to keep you relaxed and focused.

One member of the group you are playing with is painfully slow. You aren't holding up play; however, you find his speed of play is beginning to irritate you. What might you say to yourself in this situation that will keep you focused and in your routine? Please list your thoughts in the following space:

You are playing a tournament and realize your group is being timed. One of the members in your group is playing slowly. Please list what you should say to yourself at this time. Remember, quickened physical movement will likely increase your swing tempo.

Your group is being pushed by the group behind you, and there are one and one-half holes open ahead of you. Again, one of your playing partners is painfully slow. What would you say to your playing partner(s) about delaying play?

____
____
____
____
____
____
____

What should you say to yourself to maintain consistent performance?

____
____
____
____
____
____

Now let's look at day to day life situations and apply the same strategies.

Situation 1

You have an important appointment for which you are late. You encounter one red light after another. The tension builds as you begin to anticipate being late and the potential consequences.

List your mental and physical correction strategies here:

Arousal Reduction:

____
____
____

Thought Stopping and Rational Dialogue:

____
____
____
____
____
____
____

Focused Thinking in the Present:

____
____
____
____
____
____

Your correction should be something like the following:

Arousal Reduction:

"I breathe deeply, inhaling through my nose and exhaling through my mouth. My exhalation is twice as long as my inhalation."

Rational Dialogue, Quiet Movement, and Focused Concentration:

"Getting upset isn't going to do anything positive for me. I'm going to let my arms and shoulders go, and slow down my movement. I'm going to direct this intensity into the rest of my day a moment at a time."

Focused Thinking:

"I'm not going to look at my watch. I feel the sensations of the heaviness in my body and my hands on the steering wheel. I look around me and think about the landscape and cars, and watch the people."

Self-Reinforcement:

"I can feel my nervous system slow down, and I'm getting more and more comfortable. I'm going to continue this."

Situation 2

You have four days of work with a two day deadline. This is in addition to your usual work load. You begin to feel overwhelmed and worry that you will never finish, even if you work the next two evenings.

During the day, your worry increases and you find you can't concentrate on simple tasks; you feel tense, upset, and irritable with your co-workers and family.

List the corrective strategies you would use in this situation:

Arousal Reduction:

____
____
____
____
____
____

Rational Dialogue:

____
____
____
____
____
____

Focused Thinking:

____
____
____
____
____

Self-Reinforcement:

____
____
____
____
____

Your written responses should be something like the following.

Arousal Reduction:

"I breathe deeply, inhaling through my nose and exhaling through my mouth. My exhalation lasts twice as long as my inhalation. I slow down my movement and begin to think about what I am doing."

Thought Stopping and Rational Dialogue:

"I interrupt my undesired thought focus by saying: 'Be Quiet!' I tell myself that worry and negative anticipation will not produce any positive change in the situation. I say: 'If I continue to think like this, I'm going to make myself very anxious, tense, ineffective in my job, and irritable with those around me. I'm going to redirect my thoughts to each job I do and take things one at a time.' "

Quieting Movement and Focused Thinking:

"I start a thought focus on each physical activity, moving slowly and deliberately. I redirect my thoughts and hold my attention on each movement in every job I do. I practice moving slowly from a broad focus to a narrow focus. I hold each focus for

thirty to sixty seconds."

Self-Reinforcement:

"I note that as I practice these corrective strategies I feel more relaxed, in control, and free of distraction."

Note: Success with rational dialogue and thought stopping will last only a brief time when you first begin to use them. With repeated use, however, these strategies will bring relief for longer and longer periods. If you will begin to use these procedures off the course in your day to day life, they will be well-practiced and more effective when you need them on the course.

If you find yourself returning to the same worry repeatedly, consider using thought stopping after completing the steps of rational dialogue.

PROBLEM SOLVING

You use problem solving daily. Each time you choose a club, you weigh a variety of considerations from distance, confidence in shot making ability, wind, lie, and so on. Each time you read a restaurant menu, you review your alternatives and weigh the consequences in costs, calories, money, or taste. Based upon your mental review of the consequences of each alternative, you make a decision. Written problem solving is the identical decision-making strategy on a larger scale.

Written problem solving is obviously something you would not do during play; however, you may bring problems to the course that will affect play. Therefore, I have included a strategy to assist you in unloading the burdens of problems before you get to the course.

This technique is useful when you are facing a problem that requires a decision or some action. When confronted with such a problem, you might be tempted to make an impulsive decision or to ponder the problem for a long time without feeling able to make a decision. In either case, you experience negative consequences. These consequences can include arousal resulting from indecisiveness. These thoughts go everywhere you do and affect internal physiology, mood, concentration, and performance both on and off the golf course.

Problem solving helps structure the process of making a decision and generally helps you feel that you made the best possible decision. Consequently, you can carry on with other day to day activities less mentally burdened.

The 5 steps to problem solving include:

Step 1. Describe the problem as fully as possible.

Step 2. Think of and write down all the possible alternative solutions.

Step 3. Ask yourself if this is a problem on which you need to act immediately.

Step 4. If the answer is "No," then: do the following:

a. Start a list of alternatives. The list doesn't have to be exhaustive, since you will be returning to it to write more. Make an appointment with yourself and others involved to come back to the problem at specific time.

Make an appointment to worry and use that appointment time to redirect your thinking. For example: "I have set aside tomorrow at 4:00 P.M. to meet with my supervisor; worrying about the problem will only ruin the rest of the day and tomorrow. It won't do me any good to worry now."

b. Practice the relaxation procedures and positive predictive imagery as presented in this book.

c. Redirect your thoughts to something positive and productive. Use *thought stopping* and *rational dialogue* if needed.

d. Come back to the problem at the appointed "worry time" and complete **Step 5.**

e. If you find your thoughts return to the problem or you question your decision, practice the relaxation strategies and use *thought stopping* and *rational dialogue.*

Step 5 If the answer is, "Yes, I must act on this problem now,":

a. Identify all the reasonable alternatives.

b. List the pros and cons of each alternative on paper.

c, Make your decision or take action based on the pros and cons.

d. Reinforce yourself for the decision or action and stay with it.

Using the steps outlined here for problem solving will help you feel confident in your decisions and actions and you won't experience the consequences of impulsivity. Use these techniques to help guide your decisions in everything from job changes to relationships to which mini tour you are going to play. You will find it interesting to note how many of your pros and cons are based on emotion versus tangible consequences.

ASSERTION

Players on both the ladies' and men's tours get reputations for things like slow play or doing something distracting as another player starts his routine. Other players have a reputation of verbal negativity about their play, moving around the green or practicing a stroke while another player is preparing to putt or hit. These habits serve as distractions that interfere with another player's concentration. I've heard all of these complaints.

What would you do in this situation? You can be sure you are going to handle it the same way you would any irritating problem off the course. If you say nothing and the irritation is repeated, you will move from a simmer to a boil. This anger will flood your nervous system with irrelevant information that will interfere with your concentration, and your performance suffers.

What should you do? That depends on with whom you are playing. If it is a friend from your usual foursome, it will be easier to communicate your displeasure, that is, if you are able to communicate displeasure off the course. If you are in competition or don't know the person, use the following strategy.

Minimize your distraction from your routine. Take a deep breath, step off the ball, look at the other player, establish eye contact, don't smile, and start your routine over. If that doesn't communicate your displeasure with his behavior, you may need to comment in a calm and relaxed manner: "That's distracting. I would appreciate it if you wouldn't do that." Then, take a deep breath, tell yourself to refocus, and channel your attention back to your target as you start your routine over.

If the behavior is repeated, follow the same strategy with a firmer request to discontinue the action. Remember, if the other player's goal is gamesmanship and to disrupt your concentration, he wins as soon as you boil.

Most nonassertive people become concerned that the "other person" is going to be upset with them if they speak up. Or, once they speak up, they begin to worry that the other person may be upset with them. When this occurs, concentration is lost and performance deteriorates. By using thought restructuring strategies of *thought stopping* and *rational dialogue*, concentration can be returned to the shot being played, and away from what a playing partner is thinking.

Nonassertive people are usually well liked by all. They don't make waves and they agree with most everything, or yield to others' decisions and direction. Their perception is that, if they speak up, they will lose this unconditional positive regard by others, or, at the very least, they will be judged unfavorably, an emotionally intolerable internal state that is mediated by thinking and related perceptions. In reality, when they are assertive and sensitive to others needs, they will be more respected and internally calm. It's difficult to be themselves when they are constantly performing and doing for others in order to safeguard this perception of being the "good guy" by all.

You are going to handle situations on the course that produce frustration and anger the same way you do off the course. What happens when you don't speak up off the course? What happens when you say "Yes," and you really want to say "No?" What happens when you want to tell someone something, but you are concerned he might get upset or become angry with you? You say nothing. Then, you may think about what you should have said or done; or you complain to someone else who isn't involved; or the situation is repeated and you become increasingly upset.

First, your concentration goes, you have intrusive thoughts, and you can't think of much except what is upsetting you. Then you become irritable, and small things you usually tolerate well set you off. You may find yourself raising your voice at your children, or taking out your frustration on another loved one or family pet. The frustration and thinking backs up for so long that you blow up, usually in a "safe" environment.

What should you do? You make eye contact with the person you are addressing. You use "I" statements, for example: "I feel..., I suggest..., I believe..., I would like..," and so on. Then you ask for some change in the situation. For example:

"When you stand in my line while I putt (behind me on the tee, etc.) it's distracting. Please stand to one side," or, "My toast is burned; please ask the chef to prepare some more lightly toasted."

If, after reading this section, you recognize that this pattern of nonassertive behavior fits you, and you feel you are lacking in assertive skills, I suggest you begin with a class at a local college on assertive or social skills training. You will find it in the psychology or communication section of the school catalogue.

Let's return to the golf course. These same irritations build up and have the same effect if you don't address them. As soon as you allow yourself to become distracted and your focus turns to the irritating person or situation, you've lost control and your performance is going to suffer. Again, address the problem as often as necessary. Let your fellow competitor become irritated. Show him you mean what you say in a relaxed, calm, and controlled manner. It is only when you allow these situations to build up inside that they will affect you.

I would suggest that most of the irritations on the course are not meant to be distracting or to interfere with your game. If other players become upset when you calmly point out these things, let it be their problem, not yours.

Sam Snead recalls an incident with "The Mustache," Lloyd Mangrum. Sam says Mangrum would stand in the front corner of his vision on the tee box, and as Sam would start his back swing, Mangrum would cross his legs. After a few times, Sam says he backed off of the ball, walked over to Mangrum, and said: "You've driven your ball. Now get off the damned tee while I have my chance."[19]

Not all irritating habits of other players are purposeful. However, if you don't address them, you are going to boil, and nothing will change except the deterioration in your mood and game.

Nonassertive behavior and its consequences off the course will be taken to the course. If you arrive at the golf course tense, irritable, or upset, your frustration tolerance is lowered. You won't handle bad breaks and missed shots as well as you do when you are relaxed and calm. You also will be quick to anger with other players.

Resolve problems before you get to the course when possible. When it isn't possible to take immediate action, establish a plan to make a phone call, meet with someone, or write a letter after the round. Set it aside mentally. If you are reminded of the situation on the course, mentally recall your plan and redirect your thoughts back to the round.

MINDFULNESS (Flow State, Focused Concentration)

Mindfulness was described in the chapter titled Fine Tuning Your Nervous System as a calming strategy, and in the Concentration chapter as a technique for developing a present, one-shot-at-a-time focus. It is a calming strategy because it incorporates changes in movement, breathing, and thinking. Recall that an aroused nervous system results in faster physical movement and thoughts that are focused in the future. Quieting your movement, and thinking while breathing deeply will quiet your nervous system, and bring your focus to the present.

Mindfulness practice is also called flow state concentration or focused concentration. The "flow state" is described by athletes as being synonymous with the peak performance condition of the "zone."

Let's look at practice strategies for developing this deep state of concentration necessary for peak performance.

1. Develop a plan to practice mindfulness upon awakening in the morning. Keep a writing tablet by your bed. Upon awakening, write all "Things to Do" that come to mind on the tablet. After you complete each entry, turn the tablet face down so you cannot see your list. You will refer to this list once you are dressed and ready to start your day, not before.

Keep the tablet close. When you have an intrusive thought of something you have to do, write it down on the tablet. Instead of continuing to recall and recite to yourself a list of things you have to do, use the written list as your memory and reminder and return to focused concentration.

Most thoughts are future oriented and excitatory. Focusing on the various things you have to do is a part of that process. Use the tablet to assist you in getting out of the future and back to the present. Be sure to turn the tablet face down so you cannot see your list. Looking at your list will likely trigger a future focus.

People whose thoughts focus on past events tend to be angry, sad, or frustrated. Like anxiety, these emotions cause arousal and interfere with a present focus.

2. Upon awakening, begin deep, diaphragmatic breathing. Continue breathing as you make your entries on the tablet and as you follow the concentration exercises

During times of arousal you either hold your breath or begin shallow, rapid breathing. Deep, diaphragmatic breathing will take you out of these states. If you do not change your breathing to diaphragmatic, you will continue to drive your nervous system at a high rate. You will not get adequate oxygenation to your brain or deep muscles, your level of concentration will diminish, and mental and physical fatigue will evolve.

3. Be certain your movement is slow and you continue your deep diaphragmatic breathing. Most dentists have a skill of soft, quiet, gentle touch and movement. This is the type of movement you want to practice.

Slowing or quieting your movement is one of several ways of slowing the activity of your nervous system. Quiet (slow down) your movements in everything you do and be aware of this quieter movement.

4. As you start to get out of bed, notice the sounds of birds singing, see the colors, and experience your sensation of touch. Feel the sheets (texture), the pressure of the bed, and the floor under your feet. Keep your movement slow and relaxed. Note the sensations of your slowed movement, your deep diaphragmatic breathing and the sensations of the sheets, bed, floor, shower, dressing, and so on.

5. Narrate every move you make: "I'm going to slowly extend my arm and turn the hot water valve. Now I'm going to feel the texture of the faucet and sensations as I open the cold water valve. I hear the water running and experience the temperature changes as I balance the water temperature. ...I feel the sensation of the shampoo bottle cap as I open it, and notice the weight of the bottle as I turn it up to pour shampoo into my hand. I feel the texture of the shampoo, hear the water running, and feel the water as it gently hits and runs down my body.

Your goal is to be able to sustain this practice for up to five minutes. Don't get discouraged. When you begin this practice, you will probably have success for five to thirty seconds. You will have the most success if you schedule your concentration practice four times a day by the clock or paired with some activity.

Broad and Narrow Focus

Practice going from a broad (general) focus to a narrow (specific) focus and then return to a broad focus and then again to a narrow attention focus. Spend sixty to ninety seconds in each of these concentration states.

Jack Nicklaus described going from a broad to narrow focus on the golf course with every shot he hit. This is something you unwittingly do off the course at various times. Your goal is to learn to voluntarily move from a broad to narrow focus.

When you read a book in which you are interested, your thoughts are narrowly focused on everything you read. When you read content that is not interesting, you easily lose your focus. The same focus occurs when you watch television. Commercials take you away from a narrow focus on the program content.

Sexual behavior is another example of broad and narrow focus. For women, an inability to focus or a loss of interest causes a deterioration in performance or a less than pleasurable experience. A prolonged narrow focus produces climax. For men, too narrow a focus too soon results in intense arousal, thoughts and images of the sexual experience and "early" or "premature" performance. A broad focus extends performance. Too broad a focus causes a decline in sexual arousal and performance ability.

You have the ability to focus on a specific sensation anytime you choose. Think about the feeling of your big toe on your right foot. That information was always being transmitted through your nervous system to your brain. You simply used a mechanism in your brain stem to focus your attention. This is an example of a narrow focus. The more precise your attention is, the more narrow your focus becomes. Thinking about the sensations of your big toe on your right foot is a narrow focus.

When practicing a broad or narrow focus, be certain your breathing is deep, diaphragmatic and rhythmic and that you make no sudden or abrupt movement. Your movement should be unhurried and deliberate.

INTEGRATING THESE SKILLS INTO DAILY LIVING

When you eat with a narrow focus, concentrate on the color, texture, and taste of your food. Your hand and arm movements are smooth and chewing is slow. You have an awareness of each of these sensations. Your breathing is deep, diaphragmatic and rhythmic. Broad focus during eating is a concentration on the room, colors, people and general sounds. Again, your movement is slow and your breathing deep, diaphragmatic and rhythmic.

Return to a narrow focus and become aware of a distant object in the room.

Direct your narrowed attention to the details of that object. It may be a painting or piece of furniture. Again, your movements are slow and your breathing deep, diaphragmatic and rhythmic.

Another time you can practice a broad to narrow focus is during conversations. When you are talking with someone, be there. Focus all of your attention on every word you hear. Be aware of the content, the color of the speakers' eyes, their hair color, clothing and mannerisms. Your movements should be slow and your breathing deep, diaphragmatic and rhythmic.

As an alternative, if you have children, a good time to practice focused concentration is during your conversations and time with your children. Always be certain your movements are slow and your breathing deep, diaphragmatic and rhythmic.

You will find it helpful to decrease the amount of external stimuli when you practice these concentration strategies such as turning off the television or radio, or closing your eyes momentarily. If you take yourself out of your home or office to less familiar surroundings when you first begin your practice, you will have more success.

A narrow focus while driving is an awareness of the texture and feeling of the steering wheel, the sensation of the seat, a single number or letter on a license plate and so on. Again, be certain your movements are slow and your breathing deep, diaphragmatic and rhythmic.

A broad focus while driving is the traffic, signs, the color and make of cars and the pattern of traffic. A resumption of narrow focus may be a letter on a road sign, a line in the road or the number on a license plate or similar small feature of a car in the distance.

When you listen to music, a broad focus is listening attentively to combined aspects of the song. A narrow focus is listening to one instrument for example, a piano, or a wind or string instrument, or listening to every word of the lyrics with the background sound of the melody.

Be aware of your breathing. With this awareness, practice deep diaphragmatic breathing. Be aware of the sensation of your stomach expansion with deep inhalation. Purse your lips as you exhale and make your exhalation last at least twice as long as your inhalation. Note the sensation of your exhalation through your mouth and over your pursed lips. Count your breaths. Set a goal of practicing focused concentration on your breathing. See how many breaths you can count before you have an intrusive thought.

PRACTICE AT TIMES OF STRESS

The skill of mindfulness or flow state, focused concentration is most useful at times of stress. It must, however, be practiced repeatedly in relatively non-stressful situations in order to be learned and integrated at times of stress. In addition, recognize that you must develop skills of focused concentration at times of stress (internal arousal) off the course if you are going to have success staying mentally focused during stressful times on the course. Stress off the course produces the same aroused and distracted internal state you will experience at times of stress on the course. If you practice these focused concentration strategies off the course, you will have familiar and trusted techniques that will hold up under stress on the course.

Although a broad and narrow focus may be present throughout your day, this does not necessarily mean it is easily accessible any time you choose, especially at times of stress when a flood of intrusive thoughts begins.

It is important that you have the ability to initiate focused concentration during times of stress as well as at set times during the day. When you find yourself in a situation that creates anxiety, a sense of urgency, feeling of conflict, anger or any other condition that takes you out of the present, you will experience arousal of your nervous system. Begin to practice focused concentration, slowed movement and deep diaphragmatic breathing to counter the arousal.

When you have difficulty falling asleep, it is almost always your mind that is too active. You will find you are focused either on the past or future. Write down things you need to do then take your focus to the present. Feel the heaviness of your body as it sinks into the bed and pillow. Note the texture of the sheets. Be certain your movements are slow and your breathing is deep and diaphragmatic. Problems falling asleep are minor forms of stress. Use this focused concentration in other more stressful conditions as well.

Many tournament players describe "being on the clock" as a stressful event. In time, you are going to be "on the clock" if you play competitive golf. This is a good example of a time on the course where slowed movement and focused concentration will help you stay in the present and out of the urgency this situation produces. Have somebody time your routine on the practice range as you quiet your movement and practice your deep breathing and focus. The knowledge that your routine is within a forty-five second period will assure you that you do not need to rush when you are "on the clock."

The other obvious on-course events that produce distraction and arousal are when you let the play, speed of play, or behavior of others intrude on your thoughts. The slightest distraction can interfere with your focused concentration if you allow it to do so. Simply begin deep diaphragmatic breathing, say something to another player or a spectator if the situation calls for it, then return to your mindful, focused concentration. For example: "We need to pick up our pace guys," or "Please don't move until I have played my shot." Once you have made the comment, mentally re-center, for example, think: "Now, leave it and move on: LIMO!"

ON-COURSE CONCENTRATION PRACTICE

What kinds of things can you do on the course to help maintain your concentration?

1. Never add your score until the end of the round. Nothing will take you out of the present faster than becoming score conscious. You have already read what tour players say about a score focus or looking at the leader board. Make a conscious effort to play one shot at a time.

Use your scorecard to rank each shot on a one to ten scale, a "ten" being the best shot you can hit. Set a goal of hitting a "ten" on every shot. The *MIND UNDER PAR* series™ *SCORECARD* provides detailed strategies for using a scorecard to develop focused, one-shot-at-a-time concentration, confidence, a "memory bank" of good and great shots, and an analysis of strengths and weaknesses in your game.

2. **Follow the same routine on every shot.** A consistent preswing, inswing and postswing routine "cues" the same internal and external behaviors on each shot and ensures that you focus only on the shot you are playing. Practice a broad focus as you do yardages, wind, and so on. Narrow your focus from behind the ball as you stare at your target and move into your setup.

3. **Stay target focused.** Pick a target for every shot you are going to play and keep that target integrated through your entire routine. Maintain that target focus during your swing. LPGA Tour player and US Open champion Meg Mallon says: "When I'm playing my best I know I'm focusing right down to the leaf on the tree I'm aiming at."[20]

4. **Never analyze mechanics during a round.** Swing mechanics analysis belongs on the lesson tee. If you don't have "it" during the round, remember what Sam Snead said: "Dance with the one you brought." Return to the lesson tee and ask for drills to work on the changes you need to make after the round.

5. **Practice deep diaphragmatic breathing before, during, and after your round.** Deep breathing will keep your nervous system arousal to a minimum and enhance your ability to purposely focus your thoughts on the shot you are playing.

6. **Practice quiet movement and mindfulness.** Quieting your movement before and during practice and play will help you develop a desired rhythm and tempo that will build a foundation for peak performance. Mindfulness during this quieted movement places you in the present and minimizes distraction. Practice being non-emotional and dispassionate with regard to your performance. Accept the outcome of a shot or situation, and remind yourself to return your thoughts to the present.

7. **Practice supportive, reinforcing internal dialogue.** Supportive dialogue both on and off the course will teach you to be patient and to manage emotional and physical decay that produces mental distraction and physical arousal.

8. **Feel the swing you want to make, then repeat that feeling.** Focus your thinking on a feeling of the swing you want to make as you take your practice swings. Focus your thinking on repeating that feeling as you swing. I once heard it stated that you can't think of two things at the same time. I disagree. You can feel the swing you want to make and still hold an image of the target. It takes practice, but you can do it. You are accessing two separate sensory systems, feeling and vision, simultaneously. Imagery takes place in the same part of the brain as vision.

Remember, none of these things turn on and off like a light switch. The more you practice them off the course, the more accessible and successful you will be during play. Develop a plan for on and off the course use of these concentration strategies

Practice focused concentration on the range and putting green. Follow your full routine with each practice shot or putt you hit. Practice going from a broad focus to a narrow focus within each shot. Change clubs with every shot you hit on the range.

Select a club you are going to use and consider the shot you want to hit (beginning of a broad focus). Stand behind the ball and describe each shot (focus begins to narrow). For example, describe where you are going to start the ball ("...over that divot..."), the line of the shot ("...at the shingle on the top right side of that chimney..."), and where the ball will land ("...on that brown spot about six feet from the flag...").

Direct all of your attention to a small target, for example, the brown spot on the green or the shingle on the top right side of the chimney (narrow focus). As you approach the shot, stay focused on that narrow target through setup and swing. Stare at the target and glance at the ball. As you make your practice swing, feel the swing you want to make and retain that feeling through the shot. As you make your swing you should have a feeling of the swing you want to make (background) and an image of the target in your mind's eye (foreground). Both are a narrow focus. Practice working the ball left to right then right to left to a specific target. Describe to yourself a specific line the ball will take. Hit only one shot with a club, then change clubs.

Remember, the average player sees the fairway and decides to hit the shot "somewhere out there." His practice swing is a meaningless ritual that is usually occupied with mechanical thoughts. The focus may be narrow on mechanical thoughts but not on a feeling of the swing or consideration of a specific target or line of ball flight.

If you are going to learn broad and narrow focus, practice first off the course, then on the range, and then take it to the golf course. As I already noted you will enhance both your performance and enjoyment on and off the golf course.

How do you know when you have achieved flow state, focused concentration off the golf course? You will feel a peacefulness. You will experience a relaxed calm that is mentally uncluttered. Your sense of time will be altered and your movements and thoughts will flow effortlessly in the present.

Flow state concentration practice will help you enhance both the quality of your life and your performance on and off the golf course. Be sure to plan times and situations where you will practice. Enjoy the sense of control and present focus this state brings.

This quiet movement and focus will produce a sense of total calm and control with repeated practice. Establish times throughout the day you will practice being mindful. It is an excellent way to start the day upon awakening, while grooming, dressing, driving, and so on. Finally, take this practice to the range and onto the course. It will help you stay focused in the present, and keep you relaxed and calm.

Mindfulness is a strategy you can use to build your concentration skills, quiet your nervous system, and block nonproductive thinking. The following are three additional strategies of mindfulness that, with practice, you can apply on and off the golf course. This is particularly true when behavior from others promotes some momentary distraction, an emotional response, or similar interference in concentration.

Dispassionate or Nonemotional Reaction

When an event on or off the course creates a disruption in concentration or an emotional response, remind yourself to be objective and nonemotional. For example, you may hit a bad shot or start to become irritated with the speed of play of another player. Off the course, you may find yourself becoming upset when cut off by another car or when interrupted while working on something. Tell yourself to accept the intrusion without an emotional response or intellectual judgment. Remind yourself to be dispassionate or nonemotional. Practice deep diaphragmatic breathing. Assume the emotional posture of an uninvolved observer. Leave it and move on: LIMO!

You can practice this style of thinking upon awakening in the morning, driving to the golf course, on the range, during play, or at home or work. Listen to your thoughts. Recognize recurrent themes that drive your nervous system, and produce arousal and irritability. Listen for thought themes that produce relaxation and comfort. Be detached as you listen in. Then, remind yourself to return to a one hundred percent present focus. LIMO!

One Hundred Percent Present Focus

On the course, direct your thoughts to the feeling of the grip, weight of the club, and the ground as you walk. Direct your attention to the color of the target and only on the shot you are playing. Remain completely void of any thoughts of swing mechanics. Incorporate all five senses in this attention focus.

If you are awakening, experience the sensation of the bed sheets in your hand and on your feet as you roll over to get out of bed. In the shower, experience the sensation of the feeling and sound of the water. Be in the present. Recognize the impulse to rush as you shower. Acknowledge the impulse; accept it; treat the impulse "as if" you are a detached observer, and return your thoughts to the present. LIMO! Note your intention to shampoo, use soap, or rinse. Turn your thoughts to your breathing.

When you eat, experience the texture of the food. Again, recognize the impulse to rush from one bite to the next. Quiet your thinking, and return to one bite at a time. Be aware of your movement, swallowing, and intention to eat. Be aware of intrusive thoughts during eating that may result in a mood which drives your eating behavior. Is it hunger, anxiety, depression, anger, or time of day?

When you dress, experience the sensation of the feeling and color of each item of clothing. Become aware of your intention to raise your arms to put on a shirt, or to raise your leg as you dress. Be aware of your thoughts that create the intention of your clothing selection, for example, where you are going, whom you will see, and color match. Experience the sensation of each article of clothing as you dress.

Breathing Awareness

Be aware of your breathing as you go about your day. Experience the sensation of breathing as you inhale and exhale. Note the expansion of your chest and stomach as you breathe. Note that with deep breathing your stomach protrudes more than your chest, as your diaphragm pushes downward on the contents of your stomach.

Remember that the common denominator for behavior change is keeping positive daily diaries. You will find that writing your restructured thoughts in a diary will be useful and facilitate continued change. What you feed attention grows. Be certain your entries are all positive. If you have a habit of negativity, your entries will tend to be negative. Negative entries will only fuel frustration, anger, sadness or depression.

You will also find it helpful to create "reminders" to practice the various thought restructuring strategies. For example, make notes to yourself that remind you to self-reinforce or focus on what is right with your life. Remind yourself to be mindful. Schedule times to be mindful. Start with awakening in the morning and getting out of bed. Continue mindfulness until you finish dressing. As you become more proficient with mindfulness, you will begin to feel more relaxed, happier, and in control. You won't mentally be residing in the future or the past. You will be experiencing the only part of life over which you have control, the present. Extend your practice into the day. Continue to remind yourself through written notes or other cues to bring yourself back to the present.

This chapter has covered many different mental strategies for improving performance. Most of these are procedures to be applied in forming your reaction to disruptive, nonproductive thinking which interferes in some way with your performance. The following chapter presents examples of how to behave differently in particular situations. These examples are a comprehensive integration of the thinking, relaxation, and concentration strategies presented in the prior chapters.

ENDNOTES

1. Golf Digest Staff, "David Feherty," *Golf Digest* (November, 1992): p. 108.

2. Chris Millard, "Congressional Landslide," *Golf World* (July 7, 1995): p. 14.

3. Harvey Penick and Bud Shrake, *And If You Play Golf, You're My Friend* (New York: Simon and Schuster, 1993), p. 107.

4. Jack Nicklaus and Ken Bowden, "How to Beat Tension," *Golf Magazine* (July, 1993): p. 90.

5. Jack Nicklaus and Ken Bowden, "My Strongest Weapon," *Golf Magazine* (December, 1993): p. 45.

6. Johnny Miller, "One Day Wonders," *Golf Illustrated* (October, 1990): p. 20.

7. Golf Digest Staff, "Tom Watson," *Golf Digest* (May, 1993): p. 186.

8. Charles Price, "Bobby Jones Reveals His Inner Psychology," *Golf Digest* (August, 1989): p. 40.

9. Sandra Ackerman, *Discovering the Brain* (Washington, D.C.: National Academy Press, 1992), p. 41.

10. Ackerman, *Discovering the Brain* p. 40.

11. Price, "Bobby Jones Reveals His Inner Psychology," p. 40.

12 . Jim Moriarty, "Remember Me," *Golf World* (July 9, 1993): pp. 30-32.

13. Gary Van Sickle, "Sob Story," *Golf World* (July 24, 1992): p. 26.

14. James Loehr, Ed.D., *Mental Toughness in Sport* (Lexington, Massachusetts: The Stephen Press, 1982), pp. 28-35.

15. Gary Player, *Positive Golf* (New York: McGraw Hill, 1967), p. 15 and p. 82.

16. Golf World Staff, "Tour Talk: The Dawn is Everlasting," *Golf World* (March 27, 1992): p. 54.

17. Anne Marie Palli, Personal Communication (July, 1993).

18. Golf World Staff, "Houston Had the Magic Touch," *Golf World* (November 6, 1992): p. 36.

19. Sam Snead and Al Stump, *The Education of a Golfer* (New York: Simon and Schuster, 1961), p. 235.

20. Andy Brumer, "Be A Thinking Golfer," *Golf Tips* (May, 1994): p. 38.

Mike Shelton

8

LIFT, CLEAN AND PLACE

Applying What You've Learned

PROCESS VERSUS OUTCOME

This chapter will show you how to combine thought restructuring, arousal management, and focus strategies to move you closer to your peak performance state.

Do you have calm, reassuring thoughts, or do you engage in outcome thinking that creates an undesired arousal of your nervous system? A focus on outcome is a major contributor to arousal and disrupted performance. Positive process behaviors reduce undesired arousal, produce a flow state, and enhance performance.

Consider the following on-course outcome thoughts:

- Do you find your thoughts going to score or hazards as you prepare to set up to a shot?
- Do you ever "call up" similar missed shots as you address the ball?
- Do you ever stand on the first tee hoping you will get your first shot in the fairway?
- Do you think about the value of a putt (birdie, bogey, double) as you read, set up, or stroke a putt?
- Do you find yourself embarrassed by your performance on the course or worry that others will judge you unfavorably?
- Do you find that attention for your performance or approval from others is important to you?
- Prior to competition do you go to the range and compare yourself to your fellow competitors?

What about off the golf course. Does your thought focus tend to be on outcome?

- Do you ever awaken in the morning and begin to think of all the things you must do for the day or upcoming week?
- Do you begin to feel overwhelmed?
- Do you start to toss and turn, or complain aloud to yourself?
- Do you recite to yourself the things you need to do for the day as you shower and dress?
- Do you find yourself going about your day with a sense of urgency?
- Do you wonder what people think about something you have said or done?
- Does your mind jump from one thing to another?
- Do you find that your thoughts are routinely on the events of the future?

These thought patterns, both on and off the course, carry images of negative anticipation, take you out of the moment, create acceleration of your nervous system, increase irritability, lower frustration tolerance, and disrupt performance. These behaviors are all outcome in nature. That is to say, these behaviors are all related to some future event. Albeit that event may be five seconds or five weeks away. The focus is not in the present.

Let's look at examples of process behaviors. All process behaviors are ongoing in the present or serve to return your focus to the present. These are the same behaviors you have been learning in the preceding chapters.

The ideal process behaviors in golf are following a set routine, images of successful performance, and a concentrated focus only on the shot you are playing. Other process behaviors include positive, supportive, confidence building conversations with yourself, and practicing movement, breathing, thinking and postural strategies that promote relaxation, and a sense of peacefulness and calm. Ideal life process behaviors are identical to those for golf.

I teach positive process behaviors. I tell players I don't care what score they shoot. If they can tell me their behavior was ninety to one hundred percent in a positive process, I am happy with their performance. If a player practices positive process behaviors, exercises, and sets performance goals for every aspect of their golf game and life, they will perform their best. When players become consumed by score, future, and mechanics, (outcome and negative process) they are lost.

The following two pages are matrices that show a break down of both process and outcome behaviors on and off the golf course. Note that each matrix presents both positive and negative process and outcome behaviors.

Don't let the word positive fool you. It is true that you are going to play your best golf with positive process behaviors (shaded area). However, positive outcome behaviors take you out of the present and your performance will deteriorate.

The sections titled negative process and negative outcome are obviously not conducive to peak performance either.

ON THE GOLF COURSE

	PROCESS	OUTCOME
POSITIVE	*• Broad to Narrow focus in routine* *• Repeating positive, automatic, simple routine* *• Pos i t i ve (inner calm)* *• Complete confidence* *• Positive image of ball flight/roll* *• Image of target thru swing and/or* *• Feeling of swing* *• Movement and posture is relaxed* *• Diaphragmatic breathing* *• 100% a shot at a time* *• 100% present focus* *• Focus on past success in shots* *• Positive course management* *• Self supporting internal dialogue* *• Effortless* *• Strong resistance to decay (Patience)* *• Determined*	• "This is for eagle/birdie..." • In clubhouse e.g., on 16th tee • Score: " I could shoot ..." (SOS)* • Image of holding the trophy • "Hearing" congratulations from peers/family / media, etc. * • "I could win!" (SOS)* • "If I can hang on and par the tough par 3 and birdie that easy par 5, I could..." * • Too excited about good play *
NEGATIVE	• Tension (SOS)* • Mechanics focus • Breath holding or shallow breathing* • Hazard focus* • Image=0 • Intrusive thoughts* • Second guess club/shot • Movement/Tempo faster* • Fear (SOS)* • Negative focus on bad shots* • Guarding/Steering • "I don't care" • No confidence • Rushing and feeling of urgency* • "I hate this club/shot/hole/course." • Doubt ability to perform • Excitement (SOS)* • Negative attitude • Inconsistent routine • "I give up..."	• "Ok, it's going well, don't screw it up" • Fear of bogeys, doubles, triples (SOS)* • Score: "Don't... just finish!" * • "Do I have a future in this game?" • Hazard focus: "What if..." (SOS)* • "I don't know where this is going!" * • Live and die with each shot (SOS)* • "What are people going to think?" (SOS)* • "You think that was bad, watch this!"(SOS)* • Self punishing: "You stupid $&*!?*" * • "I can't get a break!"* • "These greens/fairways are awful!" * • "I quit!" (SOS)* • Anger (SOS)* • Negative focus on situation: e.g., losing PGA/LPGA card and playing mini tours, missing card at tour school and playing mini tours, missing cut, losing to lesser player, ball striking, putting, bunker play and/or wedge play is off, finances are bad, not the best practice or playing facility, etc.

***Signs Of Stress**

OFF THE GOLF COURSE

	PROCESS	OUTCOME
POSITIVE	***• Established long term goals in all aspects of life (work, play, physical, social, educational, and financial) • Broad to Narrow focus in daily activities (inner calm) • Repeating positive, automatic, simple routines • Pos i t i ve • Relaxed posture and movement • Diaphragmatic breathing • Complete confidence • Positive image of activity • 100% present focus • Focus on past success • Self supporting internal dialogue • Strong resistance to decay (Patience) • Determined***	• "This could be...!" (SOS)* • Too excited about performance (SOS)* • "If I can do this...people will think..."
NEGATIVE	• Tension (SOS)* • Breath holding or shallow breathing* • Negative Images* • Intrusive thoughts* • Second guess decisions • Movement fast* • Fear (SOS)* • Negative focus on performance* • "I don't care" • No confidence • Rushing and feeling of urgency* • "I hate my... job...life...situation... " • Doubt ability to perform • Excitement (SOS)* • Negative attitude • "I give up..."	• "Ok, it's going well, don't screw it up" * • Fear of (SOS)* • "Don't... just finish!" • "Do I have a future in this life?" • "What if..." * • Live and die with every outcome* • "What are people going to think?" (SOS)* • "You think that was bad, watch this!"(SOS)* • Self punishing: "You stupid $&*!?*" * • "I can't get a break in life!" * • "These people are awful!" * • "I quit!" (SOS)* • Anger that fuels anger (SOS)* • Negative focus on situation: e.g., health, job, family, friends, appearance, etc.*

***Signs Of Stress**

THOUGHTS FROM THE TOP

One of the greatest teachers of all time, Harvey Penick, said the following regarding thinking: "A simple thing to remember, but a hard thing to grasp and do, is this-if you want to change yourself, you must change how you think."[1]

Jack Nicklaus says that a lifelong basic of his mental approach has been to learn his capabilities in his warm-up and first few holes, and then to play within those capabilities. He says that his capabilities allow him to fly the ball right at the flag stick one day, and the next day might dictate that he hit at the fattest part of the green. Nicklaus allows his performance during his warm-up and first few holes to determine his preswing thinking regarding strategy and expectancy.[2]

As a golf professional, I know there is no substitute for a good setup and good swing mechanics. As a psychologist, I know that bad mental habits will only make good or bad mechanics worse.

PGA Tour player Mark Wiebe says: "The guys who are champions are guys who are really good at clearing their minds and just playing the shots."[3]

One of the greatest players of all time, Walter Hagen, reportedly wrote in an unpublished instruction book that one of his most important mental strategies was his ability to forget about the bad shot.

Gary Player describes the comments and outcome of negative thinking. He refers to the effects of negativity in comments like: "Gee, I'm unlucky; I never get a good bounce; I know I'm going to land in the water; I work hard and don't get anywhere. These golfers are beaten before they begin. To win, first, you must want to win; second, believe you will win; and third, think only positive thoughts. We create our success or failure on the course primarily by our thoughts."[4] [In follow-up correspondence I had with Gary Player in 1995 regarding permission to use this quote, he added a statement: "The harder I practice, the luckier I get."[5]]

Gary Player is probably one of the most positive golfers who ever played the game, perhaps right up there with Chip Beck. He wasn't just positive with everything he did; he worked hard to correct negative thinking in order to stay positive. He relates the following story as an example: "At Indianapolis one year I said: 'There's no way I could win on a golf course like this! The fairway grass is too long-all I'm doing during practice is hitting fliers. There's no way you can control the ball!' I made the double mistake of saying this to newspaper reporters. The next morning I read my words-and so did everyone else.

"Lying in bed that night before the tournament, however, I realized I'd been doing my best all day to talk myself out of winning, so I decided to change my thinking. 'I'm going to win this tournament!' I told myself. 'I love to play from these kinds of lies.' I did win the tournament."[6]

You have read quotes from the top players in the world from over a ninety year period. They described how they think and behave when they play their best and when they play poorly. Remember that these same great players shared many things in common. One common characteristic was that they had a model they observed and emulated. These players copied their mentor's swing, how they thought and behaved, how they played under pressure, or how they hit particular shots. This is an opportunity for you to take the thinking and behaving strategies of the world's greatest players, combined with an understanding of human behavior, and to incorporate these changes in your life both on and off the golf course.

MOVING FROM OUTCOME TO POSITIVE PROCESS BEHAVIORS

If you are going to decrease the frequency of negative thoughts, you must pay close attention to what you think and say to yourself, and to the associated images which emerge. Selectively applying the content from the following material can help you change some of these habits.

Review the following examples and apply the correction techniques you have learned to your undesired thought and behavior patterns. Notice that these examples contain either an outcome focus or negative process behaviors. The corrections are all positive process behaviors.

I frequently hear about the player who has all the talent in the world but they just can't put it together during tournaments or at tour school. Most players agree that the only thing that separates good players from great players is their mental approach.

The majority of the corrections shown draw upon quotes from some of the world's greatest players and their thoughts in the same or similar situations. These statements are from some of the greatest golf psychologists who ever lived. I would encourage you to begin to model their thought styles if you want to improve your game.

ON COURSE SITUATIONS

"I plan to go to the course early; however, I routinely find myself rushing at the last minute. I often don't have the time or take the time to warm up. I go to the first tee with this feeling of quickened movement and urgency. It often takes me a few holes to calm down and relax."

"As If" Personality

I recall what Jack Nicklaus said about the "hurry up" mode: "You can overcome the 'get-it-over-with, can't-stand-the-suspense' syndrome by consciously slowing down. Step back and take a deep breath or two or three while focusing your mind exclusively on the various practical factors-distance, lie, ground conditions, wind, hazards, etc.- that you must evaluate to decide your best course of action. Don't even take a club from your bag until you've done this clearly and conclusively."[7]

I also recall what Byron Nelson did for Tom Watson. "To help him slow down his swing, Byron Nelson taught Tom Watson to move more deliberately as he set up to his shots. By shuffling his feet into his stance at a slower speed, and feeling the slow waggle of the club before his take away, he ingrained a more fluid feeling into his swing."[8]

Deliberate Movement, Breathing, Body Scans, Focused Concentration, and Mindfulness

"As I drive to the club to play, I purposely slow down my movement and breathing. I can feel the steering wheel in my hands. I am very aware of every sensation around me. I feel very much in control. I do a body scan with each exhalation. My body is free of all tension. I continue this movement and relaxation strategy as I pull into the parking lot."

Focused Concentration

"I get out of my car slowly, feeling every movement and sensation. I feel the door handle, the heaviness in my arms and shoulders, and the ground under my feet."

"As I put my shoes on, I feel the sensation of the slow, deliberate movement of putting my foot into my shoes. I feel the laces. I deliberately tie my shoes."

"I continue this style of moment to moment focus as I enter the pro shop. My speech is calm and deliberate, and I feel very much in control."

"As If" Posture

"My shoulders are back and my head is erect. My eyes never drop below the horizon. I move 'as if' I have all the time I need."

Quiet, Deliberate Movement, and Focused Concentration

"If I have time to warm up, I maintain this quiet, relaxed movement as I go to the practice green and range. If there isn't time to warm up, I make my way slowly and calmly to the first tee where I meet my group, aware of every sensation as I do."

"I feel the head of my driver as I slowly remove it from my bag. I feel the sensations of my deliberate movement as I remove a tee from my pocket and a ball from my bag.

"As If" Posture

I assume a posture 'as if' I am totally relaxed, confident and calm. I walk with my shoulders back and relaxed, my eyes are above the horizon and my head is erect."

Mindfulness, Movement and Focused Concentration

"If I have intrusive thoughts during these focused thought and relaxation procedures, I remain dispassionate, detached, and non-emotional. I remove myself emotionally and do not react to the thought. I continue deep diaphragmatic breathing, and return my thought and movement to a deliberate focused concentration."

"As I approach the tee, my thoughts and mental images go to the trees to the right, a frequent placement of my first shot. When I find myself thinking like this, I am going to:"

Thought Stopping and Rational Dialogue

"Stop - Be quiet - Relax. I tell myself: 'Step back from the ball and start your routine over from behind the ball.' "

"As if" Personality

I recall what Nick Price said after he won the 1993 Western open: "My concentration was unbelievable this week. For the ten seconds leading into every shot, all I focused on was the target."[9]

Or I will think about what Meg Mallon said: "When I'm playing my best I know I'm focusing right down to the leaf on the tree I'm aiming at."[10]

Relaxation, Breathing, Body Scans, and Mindfulness

"I take a deep breath and do a body scan. I

focus my attention back to the moment and upon my movement."

Rational Dialogue

"I tell myself: 'If I focus on the trees, the trees will become my target. I'm going to focus my thoughts on that brown discoloration in the center of the fairway.' "

Positive Predictive Images, Rational Dialogue, Breathing and "As If" Posture

"I begin to think about similar shots I have hit well in the past. I experience the feeling and image of that shot. I tell myself: 'I'm going to hit my tee shot to that spot in the fairway.' As I breathe deeply and exhale, I notice the images of the shot become clearer. I see my ball landing and rolling through the brown spot I have picked as a target."

"My shoulders are back and my head is erect. I have an 'as if' posture of confidence and calm and my movement reflects this attitude."

Deliberate Movement, Narrow Focused Concentration, Mindfulness, and Balanced Posture

"As I move back to the ball slowly and deliberately, I continue to see my target. I assume my grip, align my club face with an intermediate target, and slowly and deliberately shuffle my feet into my stance. My posture feels balanced as I feel an athletic position in my setup. "

"My thoughts and images return to my target. I stare at the target and glance at the ball. I slowly and deliberately waggle as I look to and from my target to the ball and back again. I maintain an image of the target in my mind's eye as I make my swing."

Self-Reinforcement

"I positively evaluate my performance. I tell myself what was good about my swing. For example, 'The tempo felt good, I felt balanced, I made solid contact, I liked my finish position, I hit my target,' and so on."

"When I miss a shot or I don't like a swing I have made, and I find myself getting upset or self-critical, I say:"

Thought Stopping, Rational Dialogue, Body Scans, and Deliberate Focus

"Stop! Be quiet! Getting upset isn't going to do anything but make me tense. I'm going to stand right here and make the swing I wanted to make. I'm going to set up, go through my preswing routine slowly and deliberately, and maintain a comfortable tempo with a balanced finish position. I'm going to hold a visual image of my target as I feel my practice swing."

"As If" Personality

I'm going to recall that Jack Nicklaus said that when he and Hogan were playing their best game, they expected to hit only a handful of shots in a round exactly the way they wanted to. He further says that even at the highest levels of golf, perfect shots are mostly accidental and extremely rare.[11]

I am going to work toward being like Walter Hagen and expect to hit bad shots during my round.[12] I will recall that when he hit a bad shot, he just "chalked it up" to one of the seven bad shots he was going to hit that day.

Mindfulness and "As If" Posture

"I resume a mindful, detached, nonemotional internal state. I accept the consequences of my action as a passive observer, and go find my ball and next target with an even temperament. My eyes are always above the horizon. I move and carry myself 'as if' I just hit the greatest shot of my life."

"I find myself thinking of score on the eighth hole and say to myself:"

"As If" Personality

I recall what Gary Player said about concentration and score: "... A golfer has to discipline his mind to keep absolute attention on what's happening that very moment- not on the bogey he made on the last hole or on the tough par 5 coming up next, but on the particular shot at hand to the exclusion of everything else. ...during every major championship I've won I concentrated so hard that I played rounds without knowing my score! I've often been in a don't-know-who-I-am sort of daze - total relaxation with complete control."[13]

Rational Dialogue and Focus

"A score focus takes me out of the moment, creates pressure, and disrupts my concentration. I'm going to focus all of my attention on this shot. I'm not going to add my score until the end of the round. When I begin to think about my score, I'm going to bring my thoughts and images back to the shot I'm about to make. All I am going to do is play each shot, one at a time, 'as if' it is the only shot I'm going to hit today. My goal is to hit a ten on every shot I play."

"I find myself thinking about score again as I address the ball on the tenth tee and I say:"

"As If" Personality

Again I think about what Gary Player said and I recall what Greg Norman says about his best rounds of Golf: "Doral and Turnberry stand out. The 62 at Bay Hill and the 62 at the 1986 Canadian Open come to mind. All it is, you get so focused on what you're doing that you don't even know what score you're shooting."[14]

Thought Stopping and Rational Dialogue

"Stop! Be quiet! Shut up! Move off of the ball and start your routine over! Be mindful. Hit a ten on every shot. That's the only score I'm going to focus on, one-shot-at-a-time."

Breathing, Body Scans, Deliberate Focused Movement and Mindfulness

"I step back from the ball slowly and deliberately. I walk behind the ball as I become very aware of the heaviness of the club in my hand and the ground under my feet. I breathe deeply, doing a body scan and releasing all of the tension from my shoulders and arms. I feel the heaviness in my shoulders."

Positive Predictions and Images, Deliberate Movement and Focus, Breathing, Body Scans, Mindfulness, Set Up and Balanced Posture

"I find my target in the fairway, a dark green patch that shines in the sun. I describe to myself the shot I'm going to hit, as I breathe deeply doing a body scan. I think about that same shot I have hit well in the past. I experience the feeling of the shot and recall an image of the ball flight. As I breathe deeply a second time, describing the shot, the image begins to become clearer."

"I move slowly and deliberately back to my ball, feeling the ground under my feet and the heaviness of my club, as I maintain a visual focus on my target."

"I assume my grip and align my club face with an intermediate target. I stare at my primary target as I slowly and deliberately shuffle my feet into my stance. My Posture feels balanced. I look from my target to my ball and back again, continuing to deliberately shuffle and waggle; I stare again at my target. I feel grounded as I settle in and start the club back, maintaining a visual picture in my mind's eye of the target."

Self-Reinforcement

"I tell myself how good it was that I stepped back from the ball when I lost my concentration. I positively evaluate my shot and the feeling of my swing."

Note: This same strategy is very effective in putting as well. How many times have you stroked a putt with your thoughts on score or your last shot and not on rolling the ball into the hole or your target?

"I have a habit of feeling as if people are watching me and judging my performance when I play golf." Or, "I need acknowledgment, attention, and approval from others. When I feel this way in the future, I'm going to do and say the folowing:"

Body Scans

"I breathe deeply, filling my lungs completely, and I make my exhalation last twice as long as my inhalation. I do a body scan as I focus on relaxing each muscle group from forehead to feet."

Rational Dialogue

"As I relax like this, I tell myself that I'm here for me, not to please or behave for others. I'm going to think and act in ways that are comfortable for me. I am a good internal coach. What I think and feel is most important in this situation."

"As If" Personality

I recall what Greg Norman said about the importance of self reinforcement: Everybody "...likes to hear words of encouragement as he faces a tough shot, and congratulations after he pulls it off. Unfortunately, unless you play golf with your mother you can't depend on hearing these things. That's why I talk to myself. Not aloud, but inside my head. The tougher the shot I'm facing, the more I talk. If I'm on the last hole of a tournament, facing a long iron shot to the green and needing a birdie to win, I'll say to myself, 'You know this shot cold, you've knocked it stiff a thousand times, and now you're going to do it again. I also talk after I hit shots. After a particularly long, straight drive I'll often say, 'Damn, Greg, I'm pretty impressed with that one.' These inner words can be more encouraging than the cheers of the gallery. You don't want to linger too long on your shots-good or bad-but you do want to stamp the good ones on your mind for future reference in pressure situations. Silent self-congratulations is one way to do that."[15]

Positive Predictions and Images, and Deliberate, Focused Movement, and Mindfulness

"As I stand behind the ball, I describe the shot I want to hit. I think about all the great drives I've ever hit. I move deliberately and slowly back to the ball as I stare at my target. I am one hundred percent focused in the moment. I maintain this positive focus through my swing. My tempo matches my movement around the ball."

Body Scans and Deliberate Movement

"I notice my breathing is faster than normal, so I'm going to continue my deep breathing and body scans, and slow down my movement."

Rational Dialogue

"I'm going to continue to ask myself, 'For whom am I behaving?' I will practice saying and doing things for me, and I will not behave for others."

"As If" Posture

"I assume a posture 'as if' I possess all the confidence in the world; 'as if' I need only to perform for me, nobody else."

Self-Reinforcement

"My postswing routine is a focus on what went well. I am self-supporting in my internal dialogue. I enjoy my game."

Rational Dialogue

"If I become concerned about what others are thinking or saying about me, I remind myself that I'm here for me, not for them. Then I refocus my attention and play one-shot-at-a-time."

Mindfulness, Focused Concentration

"I focus only on the moment, slow down my movement, and relax and enjoy myself."

You have had trouble getting out of sand bunkers your last few rounds. You find yourself in a greenside sand bunker for the third time in a round. You begin to think about the difficulty you had from the prior two bunkers. Vivid images of the first two missed bunker shots flood your mind as you survey your lie in the sand, slope of the green and position of the flag. Your confidence in this shot is low. Your posture is slumped and you look puzzled and uncertain about your ability to execute the shot.

Thought Stopping

"I tell myself to be quiet and I step away from the ball."

Rational Dialogue

"I remind myself: 'This focus will only lead to poor performance.' "

Relaxation

"I take a deep breath and relax my shoulders, arms, and open my hands as I exhale; I become 'mindful' and quiet my movement."

"As If" Personality

I tell myself that PGA Tour player Fred Couples never hits a shot without "calling up" a similar shot he hit well in the past.[16]

Visualization

"I recall a similar shot I have hit well in another round. I experience the feeling of that shot as I replay it in my mind. I see the shot trajectory and feel the swing I need to make. I picture the swing I want to make in my mind's eye."

Feel and Visualization

"I make a practice swing outside the

bunker, and feel and see the swing I want to make."

Confidence and Visualization

"As I recall the shot out of the past, I describe that same shot I'm going to reproduce. I describe the ball flight, landing, and roll to my target, and I see each phase of my description: I'm going to land my ball on that dark green spot. The ball will bounce twice, move about two inches left to right, hit the flag stick, and drop into the hole."

"As If" Posture

"This internal dialogue eases me into a confident posture. I behave and look 'as if' I've knocked this same shot stiff a thousand times."

Movement

"My movement is quiet and confident, and reflects the tempo of my swing as I step into the bunker."

Focused Concentration One Hundred Percent in the Present

"As I move around the ball to my setup position, my eyes are constantly on my target. I only have thoughts and images of the shot I am going to play."

Feel the Swing and Target Focus

"As I set up to the ball, my focus is two fold: The target and the feeling of my practice swing I want to put on the ball. I stare at my target and glance at the ball."

These procedures will apply to any shot you play.

"I notice when I play well and begin to think about what a great round I might have, I add my score or find myself calculating my score in my head, and my performance begins to deteriorate. I lose my concentration, my swing tempo increases, and I begin to try to create shots rather than let the shot happen. My concentration level diminishes. This style results in poor play. In the future when I find myself thinking like this, I am going to say:"

Thought Stopping

"Be Quiet! Knock it off!"

"As If" Personality

I recall what Tom Kite said when he holed a pitch shot in the last round on hole number 7 at the 1992 US Open: "I wanted to jump up and down, but the reality was I still had most of the golf course to play."[17]

I also recall what late teaching great Harvey Penick said about focus: "Are you thinking ahead to future holes? Perhaps you are thinking: 'I'll knock this wedge stiff for a birdie, then par that long hard hole, reach the 17th in two for a cinch birdie-and par on the final hole will pay me a great big fat check.' Not only are you living too far in the future to be playing a sharp game of golf, you have let the thought of gold enter your mind... You reach your reward stroke by stroke. You must be mindful of each stroke as it is played. Golf is played in the present. If you can wash your mind clean each time while walking to your next shot, you have the makings of a champion."[18]

Rational Dialogue and Mindfulness

"When I think like this, I get out of the present and begin to play poorly. I'm going to refocus my thoughts and think only about what I am doing. I'll stay in the process I treat intrusive thoughts with detached indifference."

Relaxation

"I breathe deeply and do a body scan feeling the muscles relax throughout my entire body as I purposely scan for any tension and relax."

Focused Recall, Visualization, and Broad to Narrow Focused Concentration

"OK. The ball is slightly below my feet. That means the ball is going to move a little bit right out of this lie. I see a shady area on the left side of the green. That's my target. Let's see that's 152 yards. I'll just set up and make my normal swing with my 7 iron. I feel the swing I want to make.

"I had a similar 7 iron shot two weeks ago on the 4th hole. I made a great swing there. I can feel that swing and see that shot as I think about it. I see this ball start at my target, fade, bounce on the green, and roll into the hole."

"As If" Posture

"My shoulders are back and my head is erect. My eyes never drop below the horizon. I move 'as if' I have all the time I need."

Focused Movement and Mindfulness

"I feel the ground under my feet and breathe deeply again as I move deliberately to my bag to pull my 7 iron. I feel the temperature of first the club head and then the shaft, as I remove my 7 iron from my bag and move quietly behind my ball."

Set My Tempo

"My movement around the ball is the same tempo as my golf swing."

Focused Concentration

"My thoughts are only on the shot I'm hitting. My goal is to hit a ten."

Feel Swing

"I can feel the shot as I make my practice swing. I stay focused on the feeling of a slower tempo. I'm going to repeat that feeling in my swing."

Target Focus

"My eyes are focused only on my target as I move back to the ball."

"As If" Posture

"I move with confidence. I assume a posture 'as if' I successfully hit this same shot a thousand times."

Setup, Relaxation and Target Focus

"As I move deliberately into my setup position, I take another deep breath and relax. I glance at the ball and stare at my target as I set up. My focus narrows to the shady spot on the left side of the green. I hold an image of that spot and the feeling of the swing I want to make through my shot."

"I tend to start thinking about swing mechanics when I hit a couple of bad shots. When I catch myself doing this in the future, I'm going to say:"

Thought Stopping

"OK, knock it off!"

Rational Dialogue

"As Sam Snead said, dance with the one you brought. The only place for me to work on mechanics is the range. When I start thinking mechanics, my tempo increases and I start to steer. I'm going to quiet my tempo, focus on my target, and play the fade (hook, slice, and so on) I'm hitting. I can always work it out on the range. I'm going to dance with the one I brought."

"As If" Personality

I am also going to recall what Jack Nicklaus said about focusing only on preswing setup during times of struggle. I remember that Nicklaus described his thought focus when he sets up to a shot during play as being directed by "...plain willpower...you just have to force other thoughts aside. ...make yourself think exclusively about your aim and alignment and your ball position and your posture; make yourself do what you know is right in those areas, and make yourself keep on doing it time and time again, even though it doesn't seem to be working. ..if you have enough resolution-they will ultimately begin to work."[19]

Movement

"I know my movement around the ball is going to match my swing tempo, so I'm going to slow down. I've been too fast."

Focused Concentration, Rational Dialogue and Nonmechanical

"I'm going to play the fade, focus on my targets, stay in my routine, and forget about mechanics until after the round."

"When my playing partners offer advice about my swing when they see me struggling, I am going to say:"

Assertion

"Thanks, but I'm just going to play this fade. I've learned that if I start working on my mechanics when I'm playing, I have a swing hemorrhage and my scores go up."

"When I'm not putting well, I find myself pressing to hit the ball close. Then I start to steer my shots as I press to hit it closer to the flag. When this happens in the future, I'm going to say:"

Rational Dialogue

"I'm going to stop pressing to hit it close. I hit the ball consistently until I start to press. I can hit the green a reasonable percentage of the time when I don't press. My goal is to hit a ten. I'm going to stay in my putting routine, and really work on breathing and relaxation as I approach every green."

Routine

"I'm going to relax and stay in my mental and physical routine over every shot, and make my normal swing."

Rational Dialogue and Focused Concentration

"I'm also out of my mental routine during putting. I'm thinking about getting it close or not missing, rather than getting the ball on line and feeling the distance with my eyes and practice stroke. I'm going to make sure I stay in my mental routine during putting as well."

"As If" Posture

"I move with a focused determination. I

assume a posture of confidence 'as if' I never miss a putt."

"When I have a shot over a hazard, my thoughts go to the hazard. When I have a tee or fairway shot where hazards can come into play, I tend to think about the hazard. When I find myself thinking about hazards from the tee or fairway, I'm going to say and do the following:"

Thought Stopping

"Be quiet! Stop thinking like that."

As If Personality

I recall how Greg Norman talks to himself when he has a tough shot: The tougher the shot I'm facing, the more I talk. If I'm on the last hole of a tournament, facing a long iron shot to the green and needing a birdie to win, I'll say to myself, 'You know this shot cold, you've knocked it stiff a thousand times, and now you're going to do it again.'"[20]

I also recall what Meg Mallon said about her thinking when she was playing her best golf: "When I'm playing my best I know I'm focusing right down to the leaf on the tree I'm aiming at."[21]

Rational Dialogue

"When I think about trouble, the images of hazards those thoughts produce become my target. I'm going to stay with my mental routine and pick only targets that are landing areas."

Narrowing My Focus

"Once I choose a club, recall a similar shot and feel the swing I want to make, I'm going to pick a target and not take my eyes or thoughts off that target during my entire routine. I am going to glance at the ball and stare at my target."

Visualization

"When I set up to the ball, I'm going to keep a visual image of the target, and feel the swing I want to make. I'm going to hold an image of that target and feel the swing I want to make through my entire swing, just like I practiced on the range."

"When I'm not hitting my woods (irons, wedges, and so on) well, I try to create the shot. When this happens, my confidence diminishes, my tempo quickens, and I hit poor shots. In summary, I have low confidence and faster tempo when hitting a club with which I recently have not had good success."

Routine

"I find my ball, check the lie, and note the natural trajectory that lie will produce."

"As If" Personality

I think about what Fred Couples says about hitting any shot. He says he never hits a shot without "calling up" that same shot from the past. He says if he has an 8 iron to the green at the Masters, he recalls that same shot, for example, from the LA Open. He sees it, feels it, and then puts that same swing on the ball.[22]

Recall Visualization, Feel

"I hit the same shot well a month ago on hole Number 7. I can see the ball flight and feel the swing I made as I recall the shot."

Movement Tempo

"I'm going to breathe deeply and quiet my

movement around the course and the ball. I'm going to focus on carrying that same tempo and relaxation into my swing."

Routine

"In particular, I'm going to quiet my movement in my routine as I approach the ball."

"As If" Posture

"I assume a posture 'as if' I have total confidence in my ability. Anyone can see my confidence and determination in every move I make."

Focused Concentration

"As I pull a club from my bag, I feel the temperature of first the club head and then the shaft. I quiet my movement as I set up to make my practice swing."

Feeling the Shot

"My practice swing is so relaxed and fluid it almost feels as if it's in slow motion. I feel the shot I hit on hole Number 7 last month, and experience the swing I want to put on the ball."

Narrowly Focused Concentration, Routine

"My target is precise. It is a mower track or sprinkler head in the fairway or roof tile or chimney corner on a house in the distance. My eyes never leave my target as I move into my routine confidently, quietly, and deliberately."

Postswing

"I accept the outcome of the shot, and focus on how well I used the corrective strategies to get my mind off of my difficulties with a particular club."

"When I have to wait on groups in front of me, I get irritated. My tempo quickens, my concentration level diminishes, and my score rises. In the future when this happens, I am going to use the following strategies."

Thought Stopping

"Be Quiet! Knock it off!"

Relaxation, Deep Breathing, Movement, and Mindfulness

"I take a few deep breaths and relax my shoulders and arms with each exhalation. I quiet my movement and begin to focus on the feeling of each movement, hearing the sounds and seeing the colors in the landscape, my golf bag, and the clothing of my playing partners."

"As If" Posture and Focused, Deliberate Movement

"I assume a posture 'as if' I have all the time I need. My quiet, deliberate movement conveys an attitude of patience and a relaxed calm."

Broad to Narrow Focus

"Once I have my yardage and make my club selection, I picture the shape of the shot and feel the swing I want to make. My focus narrows to a very small, precise target in the fairway or on the horizon."

Rational Dialogue

"I'm going to be patient. This is a great time for me to practice my mental toughness. I can't be responsible for the speed of play of other groups. I'll let the marshal do that. I'm not going to allow this wait to affect my performance."

"Another player in my group is playing slowly. I find myself rushing through my shots to pick up the speed of play. As a result, I am not mentally focused, my tempo quickens, and I hit poor shots. When this happens in the future, I am going to do the following:"

Relaxation

"I breathe deeply and relax all the muscles in my body as I exhale."

Assertion

"I say to my group: 'We need to pick it up; we're a hole behind. Let's play 'ready golf.' "

Rational Dialogue

"All I can do is tell them. When I am ready to play, I'll hit and let them take care of themselves. I'm not going to be responsible for their speed of play or let their play affect me."

"As If" Personality

I recall what Jack Nicklaus says about rushing: "You can overcome the 'get-it-over-with, can't-stand-the-suspense' syndrome by consciously slowing down. Step back and take a deep breath or two or three while focusing your mind exclusively on the various practical factors-distance, lie, ground conditions, wind, hazards, etc.-that you must evaluate to decide your best course of action. Don't even take a club from your bag until you've done this clearly and conclusively."[23]

"As If" Posture and Broad to Narrow Focus

"I assume a posture 'as if' I am relaxed and calm. I drop my shoulders and open my hands. My head is erect and my movement is slowed and deliberate. My Concentration moves from a broad focus on lie, shot and club selection to a narrow focus on the feeling of the swing I want to make, ball flight and specific chimney corner at which I want to start my ball. I know the more precise my target is, the better my performance will be."

Relaxation and Focused Concentration

"I take another deep breath and quiet my movement. I direct all of my thoughts to the shot I am playing. My goal is to hit a ten."

"When someone makes a comment about my swing on the range or on the course and suggests a change, I tend to listen, even if he isn't my instructor. I attempt to incorporate his suggestion and become mechanically focused. I almost always regret trying to make the suggested changes; however, I seem to continue to listen to everything I hear."

Rational Dialogue

"In the future, I am going to remind myself that a consistent swing is most important. Chi Chi Rodriguez, Arnold Palmer, Lee Trevino, Ray Floyd, Jim Furyk and many more tour players don't have technically perfect swings. These players simply repeat the same swing on every shot with a focus on targets and getting the ball in the hole."

Assertion

"Then, I will thank the person for his suggestion and tell him I only take lessons from my instructor."

Note: *PGA teaching professional Hank Haney was an instructor at a PGA Business School I was attending a few years ago. I'll never forget what he told us about instructors: They tend to teach what they are working on in their swings. I knew immediately what he meant. I was guilty of the same thing in some of my lessons. If someone who isn't an instructor is giving you advice, their suggestions are likely something they have stumbled onto that works for them, at least for the moment.*

I see the "wanna be" instructors on the practice range daily-passing out unsolicited advice-or even worse, bringing their unsuspecting friends out for a lesson.

My advice to you is to find one PGA or LPGA teaching professional in whom you have confidence and stay with that one instructor. That instructor will learn your swing and be able to put you back on track quickly when you are having problems. Having multiple instructors, no matter how good they may be, is a sure formula for disaster.

"I am short tempered at times. I become irritable in traffic, at home, or at work. I don't like being this way. I seem to get caught up in anger and it takes on a life of its own. I find myself getting upset and angry when I hit a series of bad shots or when I have a few bad breaks during a round. I am going to develop a plan to deal with this anger, write down the plan, and read it before each round of golf I play and each morning when I start my day."

"When I find myself getting angry, I am going to allow myself ten seconds to be upset. After ten seconds I'm going to say:"

Thought Stopping

"Knock it off! Stop it!"

"As If" Personality

I am going to recall what Sam Snead said about anger: "At some point in every outburst of anger, if it lasts long enough, you throw yourself into reverse gear. The minute you blow, a charge seems to go through your opponent and he begins to play better golf. ... by blowing, you bleed off your own energy from the job of making shots. Getting sore and staying that way is hard work."[24]

I also recall that Snead advised not to hold anger in. He said: "Show me the fellow who walks along calmly after topping a drive or missing a kick-in putt, showing the world he is in perfect control, yet burning up inside, and I'll show you one who is going to lose. This boy is a fake. His nervous system won't take what he's handing it. If you bottle up anger entirely, it poisons your control centers. But if you go all the way in the other direction, the practice of kicking tee markers, abusing shrubbery, and wrecking equipment can become such a habit that it spoils your muscular reflexes.

"Good golfing temperament falls in between taking it with a grin or shrug and throwing a fit. I believe you should blow up at times, if it helps, but only if you can keep your wits about you. I couldn't beat any pro if I couldn't get my temper outbreak over with fast, then start thinking out the next shot. It's like opening a steam valve for a moment, then shutting it."[25]

Rational Dialogue

"If I stay angry, my play is only going to deteriorate. You let it out; now get your head back in play and leave that behind you! Getting upset and staying upset is only going to result in poor play. I'm going to break this pattern. I'm going to work on being mindful and treat situations that routinely make me angry with detached indifference. I'm going to remain unemotional as I accept the consequences of my performance. If I feel anger starting to build, I'll 'open the steam valve' and vent a little. However, I will keep it under control."

"As If" Posture

"I assume a posture 'as if' I am happy. I smile both outwardly and inwardly. My shoulders are down and relaxed and my hands are open. My movement is quiet and deliberate."

Relaxation

"I breathe deeply. With each exhalation I drop my shoulders, open my hands, and allow the feeling of relaxation to travel from my forehead to my feet. I mentally search for the tension produced by my anger and relax those areas."

Rational Dialogue, Movement and Broad to Narrow Focused Concentration

"Now the tension won't spill into my golf swing. I'm just going to quiet my movement and go from a broad to narrow focus as I move to my ball and next shot. My entire focus of attention is on my next shot. I go through my broad focus of course management, decide the shot and club I am going to hit.

"I narrow my focus and pick a small, precise target on the horizon, the 'V' formed by the branches of that tall tree top in the left center of the fairway. I stay focused on that target as I feel the swing I want to make. I pick an intermediate target in line with the 'V' formed by the branches, my primary target. As I move slowly into my setup, I square my clubface with my intermediate target. Then my eyes return to the 'V' formed by the branches as I assume my stance. I stare at that 'V' and glance at my ball as I waggle in preparation to swing. I hold a foreground image of the target and experience a background feeling of the swing I want to make through my entire swing."

Two Shots Later:

Self-Reinforcement

"This is working. I'm feeling more relaxed and in control. My mood is so much better. I'm going to stay focused and continue working on my anger management and stay in my routine and targets one shot at a time. Moving from a broad to narrow focus really helps."

"I find myself looking at others to see if they have noticed me, or I look for praise from others for something I have done. I seem to thrive on the approval of others, both on and off the course. When I hit a good shot, I look at my playing partners right away to see if they noticed how good it was. It seems that what they say and think is more important than what I say to myself.

"I recognize that I give control of my behavior to others with these habits. In order to change these habits, I am going to review the following each morning

when I awaken. This is a plan for how I am going to think and behave around others both on and off the golf course."

Rational Dialogue

"What I think and believe about my appearance, behavior, and performance on and off the course is more important than what others say and think. When others compliment me on my appearance or performance, I say, 'Thank You.' I don't dwell on their comment. I praise myself for my appearance and performance daily. When I find myself looking to others for approval or acknowledgment, I say the following:"

Thought Stopping

"Knock it off."

Relaxation, Focused Concentration and Mindfulness

"I take a deep breath and as I exhale I drop my shoulders, open my hands, and let go of all the muscle tension in my body. As I continue to breathe deeply and rhythmically, I begin to return my focus to my senses and become very aware of everything in the present. As I relax, I practice going from a broad to narrow focus and back."

Rational Dialogue

"What I think and feel in these situations is most important. If I begin to think about what others think about me and my performance, I will start to behave for them, become tense, lose control, and my performance will deteriorate. It's nice to hear the positive comments from others; however, these comments should only reinforce my thoughts and beliefs, not be the reason for my existence. When I am able to reinforce my performance, and behave for the enjoyment and satisfaction of my accomplishments, I remain in control."

"I find that how I play the first few holes determines how my round will go. I tend to 'give up' if I play the first six or seven holes poorly. When I hear myself start an internal dialogue of letting poor play the first few holes dictate the rest of my round, I am going to do and say the following:"

"As If" Personality

I recall what Jack Nicklaus said in 1974 about his week to week performance twelve years after joining the tour: "No matter how much work I did, one week I would have it and the next I couldn't hit my hat. This is still true today. I am a far better golfer than when I started out on the tour twelve years ago and I feel that I have improved to some degree each year. But that is more the result of maturity and competitive experience than of improvement in the mechanics game."[26]

I also recall what Sam Snead said about giving up: "In tossing in your cards after a bad beginning you also undermine your whole game, because to quit between tee and green is more habit forming than drinking a highball before breakfast."[27]

I am going to adopt the attitude of Jack Nicklaus when determining how I will play my round. If he was flying the ball at the flag his first few holes, he played aggressively. If his ball striking was off, he played for the center of the green.

"As If" Posture

"I assume a posture 'as if' I am confident in myself and my abilities. My shoulders are back and my head is erect. My eyes never drop below the horizon. I move 'as if' I have all the time I need. I act 'as if' I am internally confident and independent."

Relaxation

"I breathe deeply and do a body scan feeling the muscles relax throughout my entire body as I purposely scan for any tension and relax."

Focused Movement and Mindfulness

"I feel the ground under my feet and breathe deeply again as I move deliberately to my bag to pull my driver. I feel the temperature of first the club head and then the shaft, as I remove my driver from my bag and move quietly onto the tee."

Set My Tempo

"My movement around the ball is the same tempo as my golf swing."

Focused Concentration

"My thoughts are only on the shot I'm hitting. My goal is to hit a ten."

Feel Swing

"I can feel the shot as I make my practice swing. I stay focused on the feeling of a slower tempo. I'm going to repeat that feeling in my swing."

Target Focus

"My eyes are focused only on my target as I move back to the ball."

Setup, Relaxation and Target Focus

"As I move deliberately into my setup position, I take another deep breath and relax. I glance at the ball and stare at my target. I hold an image of my target through my swing and I repeat the feeling of my practice swing.

"My goal is to stay in this process on every shot. If I can stay in this process on every shot, regardless of what the outcome of the shot is, I will feel I have had a successful day. My evaluations of my play are going to change from score to how well I stay mentally focused on my targets and in my routine. I am going to score a 10 on the process and forget about shot outcome."

"When I am playing in competition, I arrive at the practice range the first day and begin to size up my fellow competitors. I compare myself to others. By the time I am finished comparing myself, I either am convinced I am going to win the tournament or I have no chance. When I arrive at a tournament site and begin to make these comparisons, I am going to say and do the following:"

"As If" Personality

I recall Ben Hogan's approach to tournaments: He never concerned himself with competitors or leader boards. His focus was the course. The contest was between his playing ability and the course. He would walk the course during a practice round, assess the conditions, and decide what score he had to shoot to win. As part of his tournament preparation, Hogan walked the course backwards starting on the 18th green. He determined the best landing areas for approaches to the greens. He would place his skills in a contest with the course, not his competitors.[28]

Rational Dialogue

"As I relax like this, I tell myself that I'm

here for me and to test my skills on this course: that's the true competition. If I become occupied with thoughts of how good someone is or isn't, I won't be in my game. I've decided where I am going to finish before I tee it up on the first hole. I am going to think and act in ways that are totally in the process of preparing for each phase of the tournament without consideration of who is playing.

"I am a good internal coach. I am going to play this tournament one hole at a time and one shot at a time. Staying in the process of my game is my primary goal, not score or whom else is competing. When I notice any variation from my routine or focus I will bring myself back to the present."

When I am playing in multiple day tournaments, I tend to focus on making the cut rather than staying in a present focus one shot at a time. I notice that I frequently finish on the bubble. When I find myself thinking about making the cut in the future I am going to do and say the following:"

Thought Stopping

"Be Quiet! Knock this thinking style off!"

Rational Dialogue and Mindfulness

"When I think like this, I get out of the present and begin to play poorly. I'm going to refocus my thoughts and think only about what I am doing. I'll stay in the process. I treat intrusive thoughts with detached indifference."

"As If" Personality

I recall what Gary Player said about thought focus: "...A golfer has to discipline his mind to keep absolute attention on what's happening that very moment-not on the bogey he made on the last hole or on the tough par 5 coming up next, but on the particular shot at hand to the exclusion of everything else. ...during every major championship I've won I concentrated so hard that I played rounds without knowing my score! I've often been in a don't-know-who-I-am sort of daze - total relaxation with complete control."[29]

Relaxation

"I breathe deeply and do a body scan feeling the muscles relax throughout my entire body as I purposely scan for any tension and relax."

Course Management

"OK. The ball is slightly above my feet. That means the ball is going to move a little bit left out of this lie. I see a dark area on the right side of the green. That's my target. Let's see that's 180 yards. I'll just set up and make my normal swing with my 5 iron.

Focused Recall and Visualization

"I had a similar 5 iron shot Saturday on the 14th hole. I made a great swing there. I can feel that swing and see that shot as I think about it. I see this ball start at my target, draw, bounce on the green, and roll to the hole."

"As If" Posture

"My shoulders are back and my head is erect. My eyes never drop below the horizon. I move 'as if' I have all the time I need."

Focused Movement and Mindfulness

"I feel the ground under my feet and breathe deeply again as I move deliberately to my bag to pull my 5 iron. I feel the temperature of first the club head and then the shaft, as I remove my 5 iron from my bag and move quietly behind my ball."

Set My Tempo

"My movement around the ball is the same tempo as my golf swing."

Focused Concentration

"My thoughts are only on the shot I'm hitting. My goal is to hit a ten."

Feel Swing

"I can feel the shot as I make my practice swing. I stay focused on the feeling of a slower tempo. I'm going to repeat that feeling in my swing."

Target Focus

"My eyes are focused only on my target as I move back to the ball."

"As If" Posture

"I move with confidence. I assume a posture 'as if' I successfully hit this same shot a thousand times."

Setup, Relaxation and Target Focus

"As I move deliberately into my setup position, I take another deep breath and relax. I glance at the ball and stare at my target as I set up."

Broad to Narrow Focused Concentration

I feel the swing I want to make. My focus narrows to my target as I setup behind the ball. I see the shady spot on the right side of the green. I hold an image of that spot and the feeling of the swing through my shot."

"When I am playing well, I think something awful is going to happen. This can't continue to go well. When I catch myself thinking like this in the future I am going to say the following:"

Thought Stopping

"Be Quiet! Knock this thinking style off!"

Rational Dialogue and Mindfulness

"When I think like this, I get out of the present and begin to play poorly. I'm going to refocus my thoughts and think only about what I am doing. I'll stay in the process. I treat intrusive thoughts with detached indifference."

Relaxation

"I breathe deeply and do a body scan feeling the muscles relax throughout my entire body as I purposely scan for any tension and relax."

"As If" Personality

I recall what late teaching great Harvey Penick said: "...You reach your reward stroke by stroke. You must be mindful of each stroke as it is played. Golf is played in the present. If you can wash your mind clean each time while walking to your next shot, you have the makings of a champion."[30]

I also recall what PGA Tour player Mark Wiebe says: "The guys who are champions are guys who are really good at clearing their minds and just playing the shots."[31]

Rational Dialogue

"Okay, I'm playing well. So what! I got here playing one shot at a time. That's what I'm going to keep doing. Now be quiet and continue the process of going from a broad to narrow focus.

Course Management

"OK. The ball is slightly below my feet. That means the ball is going to move a little bit right out of this lie. I see a light area on the left side of the green. That's my line. Let's see that's 140 yards. I'll just set up and make my normal swing with my 8 iron right down my target line.

"When my fellow competitor is playing well, I find myself pressing to knock my approach shot inside his. If he birdies a hole, I begin to think as much about his game as mine."

Thought Stopping and Rational Dialogue

"Stop! Be quiet! Shut up! Move off of the ball and start your routine over! Be mindful. Hit a ten on every shot. That's the only thing I'm going to focus on, one-shot-at-a-time."

"As If" Personality

I begin to recall what Ben Hogan's focus was during play: He never concerned himself with competitors or leader boards. His focus was the course. The contest was between his playing ability and the course, not his competitors.[32]

Breathing, Body Scans, Deliberate Focused Movement and Mindfulness

"I step back from the ball slowly and deliberately. I walk behind the ball as I become very aware of the heaviness of the club in my hand and the ground under my feet. I breathe deeply, doing a body scan and releasing all of the tension from my shoulders and arms. I feel the heaviness in my shoulders."

Positive Predictions and Images, Deliberate Movement and Focus, Breathing, Body Scans, Mindfulness, Set Up and Balanced Posture

"I find my target in the fairway, a dark green patch that shines in the sun. I describe to myself the shot I'm going to hit, as I breathe deeply doing a body scan. I think about that same shot I have hit well in the past. I experience the feeling of the shot and recall an image of the ball flight. As I breathe deeply a second time, describing the shot, the image begins to become clearer."

"I move slowly and deliberately back to my ball, feeling the ground under my feet and the heaviness of my club, as I maintain a visual focus on my target."

"I assume my grip and align my club face with an intermediate target. I stare at my primary target as I slowly and deliberately shuffle my feet into my stance. My posture feels balanced. I look from my target to my ball and back again, continuing to deliberately shuffle and waggle; I stare again at my target. I feel grounded as I settle in and start the club back, maintaining a visual picture in my mind's eye of the target and a feeling of the swing I want to make. I make my swing with that focus."

Self-Reinforcement

"I tell myself how good it was that I stepped back from the ball when I lost my concentration. I positively evaluate my shot and the feeling of my swing."

Rational Dialogue and "As if" Personality

I am going to continue to play every shot like this. No matter what my score or shot outcome, I am going to stay in a positive process. I am going to remember that the only competitor Ben Hogan focused on was the golf course. The course is my competitor.

"I never get a break. If my shot has a chance to kick into the fairway or rough, it will. If there is a bad break out there waiting, you can be sure I'll get it."

Thought Stopping, Rational Dialogue

"Be Quiet! Knock it off! This is an old habit. You're not so special that all the bad breaks are bestowed upon you. That's magical thinking! Dream on! This focus on bad breaks is an old habit that you have to stop if you are ever going to get anywhere in golf. Everybody plays from the same tees and fairways and putts on the same greens. Now, knock it off! You are not special! Stop whining!"

"As if" Personality

When I begin to think like this I am going to remember what Sam Snead used to say about breaks: "Whenever I've been able to pull myself out of a slump, it's because I didn't forget that breaks always even out, over the long pull, and that the bane of golf-and life in general-is to remember your mistakes and not your right moves. In clubhouses, you'll see men sitting around complaining going over their bad shots. They should think back to their good shots, then try to repeat them.

"This is the only way to build that feeling called confidence. You can build it-or tear yourself down. The choice is up to every individual. If you know yourself to be a whiner, you'll never play up to your full ability. It takes guts to be an optimist in golf. He who thinks like a winner will win."[33]

When I am playing with another player I admire who doesn't know me, I find myself telling them about my abilities, scores I have shot or tournaments I have won.

Rational Dialogue

"I want to perform for me, not for them. The only reason I am saying these things is that I want them to know how good I am. I want them to like me. As soon as I start worrying about what they think, I lose control.

I'm going to perform for me. No matter how I play, I'm accountable to me, not to them. I am going to continue to ask myself: 'For Whom am I Behaving?' If the answer isn't: 'for myself,' I am going to restructure my thinking and get back to performing for me. My game speaks for itself."

"As If" Personality

I recall what Greg Norman said about how important it is to praise yourself. He said everybody: "...likes to hear words of encouragement as he faces a tough shot, and congratulations after he pulls it off.

Unfortunately, unless you play golf with your mother you can't depend on hearing these things. That's why I talk to myself. Not aloud, but inside my head. ...After a particularly long, straight drive I'll often say, 'Damn, Greg, I'm pretty impressed with that one.' These inner words can be more encouraging than the cheers of the gallery. You don't want to linger too long on your shots-good or bad-but you do want to stamp the good ones on your mind for future reference in pressure situations. Silent self-congratulations is one way to do that."[34]

"When I am playing in a tournament and I'm not playing well, I begin to think about staying out of the way of a 'known' player in my group. I get more concerned about not being in their way than playing my game."

Rational Dialogue

"I'm out here to play golf, not collect autographs! I'm as entitled to be here as anyone else. I am going to allow myself to be comfortable with that entitlement. I really don't care what these people think. As soon as I do care, I lose control.

"As If" Posture and Broad to Narrow Focus

"I assume a posture 'as if' I am relaxed, calm, confident and as if this is the only place I belong. I drop my shoulders and open my hands. My head is erect and my movement is slow and deliberate. My concentration moves from a broad focus on lie, shot and club selection to a narrow focus on the feeling of the swing I want to make, ball flight and specific chimney corner at which I want to start my ball. I know the more precise my target is, the better my performance will be. This is my only concern and focus for the rest of my round."

OFF-COURSE SITUATIONS

"I often awaken in the morning and negatively anticipate the day. In the future, when I wake up I am going to:"

Body Scans, Mindfulness

"I tell myself: 'Breathe deeply, inhaling through my nose and exhaling through my mouth. My exhalation lasts twice as long as my inhalation, and I note the relaxation progressing from my forehead to my feet as I feel my body sink deeper and deeper into the bed.' "

Thought Stopping and Rational Dialogue

"As I breathe and relax, I tell myself to 'Stop-Relax-Stop,' and continue breathing and doing body scans. I am responsible and competent. I do all I am capable of doing, and I am satisfied with my efforts."

Rational Dialogue

"I'm only going to make myself tense if I continue to think negatively. I am going to start my day one minute at a time and take things one at a time. I have a full day ahead."

Mindfulness, Focused Concentration

"I remind myself to remain mindful and listen to my thoughts as a detached observer. I focus on my inhalation and exhalation. I return my thought focus to all my senses and become one hundred percent present focused."

Deliberate Activity and Mindfulness

"I am going to continue my body scans and slow down my movement. I can feel the pillow beneath my head as I sink deeper into the bed; now my shoulders and back are relaxing. My speech is slow and deliberate."

Self-Reinforcement and Deliberate Activity

"This is working; I'm feeling so relaxed and in control! I'm going to continue this focus and relaxation. I can feel my legs as I very slowly move my left leg and then my right as I get out of bed. Now, I'm really feeling in control."

Five minutes later, negative thoughts about the day resume.

Rational Dialogue and Thought Stopping

"I can feel myself getting anxious and tense as I think about my day and all of the things I need to do. Stop-Relax-Stop!"

Body Scans

"I'm going to continue my breathing and let go of the tension."

Deliberate Focus

"Now I am going to slowly get dressed. I feel every move."

Self-Reinforcement

"This is great! I really am feeling much more in control."

Rational Dialogue

"I'm going to follow my planned schedule and take one thing at a time. If I have negative thoughts or feel overwhelmed, I'll simply return to these strategies."

Prevention, Deliberate Focus and Body Scans

"I'm going to practice prevention throughout the day, continuing a here and now, present focus and doing body scans every time I walk through a doorway or hear a phone ring.

"When I stand in lines or wait in traffic, I find myself becoming impatient and irritable with the situation as I look repeatedly at my watch."

Relaxation and Mindfulness

"I breathe deeply, inhaling through my nose and exhaling through my mouth. My exhalation lasts twice as long as my inhalation. As I exhale, I drop my shoulders and arms, and open my hands. I become mindful and quiet my movement."

Rational Dialogue

"I let these situations control me, and I become aroused and impatient and irritable. Patience is something I need to work on. I'm going to put my watch in my pocket and not look at any clocks. I'm going to be mentally tough, relax, and wait patiently."

"As If" Posture, Diaphragmatic Breathing, and Deliberate Movement

"I assume a posture 'as if' I am relaxed and calm. I drop my shoulders with each deep breath and open my hands. My movement is slow, relaxed and deliberate."

Mindfulness

"I'm going to treat all intrusive thoughts with quiet, detached indifference and then return my focus to the present moment. I can feel the heaviness in my arms and shoulders. I see the colors and hear the sounds around me. I'm going to stay focused in the present."

Self-Reinforcement

"I'm doing well. I feel more relaxed. I can see how this is going to help me on the golf course."

"I find myself wondering what others are thinking about what I am saying or doing. When I think like this, I tend to think and behave for others."

Thought Stopping

"Be quiet - Knock it off!"

Relaxation

"I breathe deeply several times, relieving my arms and shoulders of all tension, and opening my hands. I become 'mindful' and quiet my movement."

Rational Dialogue

"If I focus on what others are thinking, I'll behave for them rather than for me. I'm going to be myself. I'm going to continue to redirect any thoughts of what others are thinking back to this theme. People will either accept me for me or not at all. I don't do things that offend or upset people. If they don't like me or my behavior, it's their problem."

"As If" Posture

"I assume a posture 'as if' I am totally independent and void of any concerns of what others might be saying or thinking. I never look at others for their approval."

Self-Reinforcement and Rational Dialogue

"This isn't easy, but it's a good first step toward making an important change. The more I practice this, the more comfortable I'm going to be on the first tee, in tournaments, and off the course around other people. Life is too short to worry about other people. I am going to please myself. It actually feels pretty good. I feel more in control."

"I find my thoughts focused on anticipated events of the future during routine daily activities. I find myself impatient, short-tempered, and difficult to please."

Thought Stopping

"Be Quiet!. Knock it off!"

"As If" Posture, Diaphragmatic Breathing, and Deliberate Movement

"I assume a posture 'as if' I am totally relaxed. I breathe deeply, drop my shoulders and arms, and open my hands. I become 'mindful' and quiet my movement."

Rational Dialogue

"When I think like this, my nervous system accelerates, and I become internally and externally agitated. This is physically and emotionally unhealthy, and interferes with my day to day performance and relationships with the people I care about most. I am going to change this state. I'm going to write down the things I need to remember, so I can set them aside and return mentally to the present."

Mindfulness, Quieted Movement and Posture

"I'm going to think about only what I'm doing, and quiet my movement and my mood as I do. I'll treat intrusive thoughts with quiet indifference. My eyes are always above the horizon."

Relaxation

"I breathe deeply as I begin to quiet my movement and focus only on the activity in which I am involved."

Your thoughts return to future events and you feel the tension begin to build.

Thought Stopping

"Stop! Knock it off!"

Rational Dialogue

"I'll make an appointment to think about those things tomorrow morning at 9:00 A.M. when I can call somebody and resolve the situation. Thinking about it now is only going to put me in a bad mood and give me a miserable evening. I have a choice here. I choose to have a pleasant evening. I am going to think only of what I am doing now.

"I am going to slow my movement and practice going from a broad to narrow focus."

Relaxation, Mindfulness and Focused Concentration

"I quiet my movement, take a deep breath, drop my shoulders and open my hands. I continue breathing deeply as I begin to flood my thoughts with all the input from my senses as I become increasingly more mindful."

"I frequently feel a sense of urgency throughout the day. My movement accelerates and I find myself getting ahead in my thinking. These are the times my frustration tolerance lowers and I am easily irritated."

Thought Stopping

"Stop! Wait a minute! Slow down your thoughts and your movement."

Relaxation

"I quiet my movement and breathe deeply as I drop my shoulders and open my hands. The relaxation increases with each exhalation. Quieting my movement enhances the relaxation."

Concentrated Focus, Quiet Movement and Mindfulness

"My thoughts are on every sensation I experience as I focus on each quiet, relaxed movement I make. My thoughts are one hundred percent in the present. I begin to treat intrusive thoughts 'as if' I were a casual observer with detached indifference. I note the theme of these thoughts and direct my focus to one hundred percent in the present."

"I am short-tempered at times. I become irritable in traffic, at home, or at work. I don't like being this way. I seem to get caught up in anger and it takes on a life of its own."

Relaxation

"I breathe deeply and quiet my movement. I drop my shoulders and open my hands with each exhalation."

Rational Dialogue

"I know this agitated feeling is a result of an acceleration of my nervous system and future focus. I am going to stay focused only on what I am doing (mindfulness), and quiet my movement and focus my thinking."

"As If" Posture, Diaphragmatic Breathing, Deliberate Movement and Mindfulness

"I assume a posture 'as if' I am totally relaxed. I breathe deeply, drop my shoulders and arms, and open my hands. I become mindful and quiet my movement."

Self-Reinforcement

"I can feel myself begin to calm down already and I feel much more in control. I am going to continue to stay focused in the moment, breathe deeply, and quiet my movement."

Mindfulness, Quieted Movement, and Relaxation

"When I awaken in the morning, I am going to stay in bed and take deep diaphragmatic breaths. I'm going to listen to my thoughts and related themes with detached indifference. I will note the themes that drive my nervous system, and those that create calm and relaxation. I allow these thoughts to pass without emotionally responding to them.

"Next, I focus my attention on the feeling of the bed, the sheets, my pillow. and the sensations on my body as I slowly get out of bed. My thoughts are one hundred percent in the present as I feel the sensations of every step I take across the bedroom floor. I continue deep diaphragmatic breathing. With each exhalation, I drop my shoulders and relax all the muscles in my body. My movement is quiet, fluid, and relaxed. I feel in control. I continue this present focus as I shower, groom, and dress. I feel the faucet as I adjust the water temperature. My movements continue to be quiet, relaxed, and fluid in everything I do.

"I experience all of the sensations of touch, sound, taste, hearing, and smell in everything I do. I feel the sensation of the toothpaste tube as I unscrew the cap. I taste the toothpaste and experience the sensations of the bristles of my toothbrush as I brush my teeth with quiet movement. I note the intention of my movements. I continue deep, rhythmic diaphragmatic breathing as I go about my morning routine. My movements remain relaxed and fluid. I notice the sensation of control that comes with this quiet, relaxed style.

"When I find my thinking drifting to the future or past, I resume listening to my thoughts in a detached, nonemotional style. Then, I remind myself to return to a one hundred percent present focus.

"I feel the texture of every article of clothing I remove from my dresser and closet as I continue the same relaxed, fluid movement. I experience these sensations on my body as I dress.

"I maintain this relaxed, fluid movement and one-hundred percent present focus every morning upon awakening. I return to these same strategies at predetermined times throughout the day while driving, working, and playing. In particular, I am present focused with my family and those I care about most.

"I continue to remind myself that if I want to

improve my concentration on the course, I must develop these skills off the course."

"There are times when I find it difficult to either get to sleep or return to sleep upon awakening. I find myself looking at the clock and mentally calculating how many hours of sleep I can get 'if I can go to sleep right now!'

When I have difficulty falling asleep, I am going to recognize that it is my thinking that is keeping me awake.

When this happens in the future, I am going to use the following strategy:"

Relaxation and, Mindfulness

"I'm going to begin breathing deeply. With each exhalation, I allow my body to sink deeper and deeper into the bed. I feel the weight of my body as it sinks into a state of relaxation. I focus my thinking on my breathing and begin to count each breath. I turn all of my thinking to the present. As I count my breathing, I continue to focus my thoughts on the sensation of the heaviness of my body."

Rational Dialogue and Thought Stopping

"When I find my thoughts returning to the future or past, I use the strategies of thought stopping and rational dialogue to bring my thinking back to the present, the sensations of the bed, and my breathing. I make an appointment with myself for a time to think about the things that are keeping me from sleep. For example, I might say, 'Thinking about these things now is only going to keep me awake, I'll be tired tomorrow and less alert than normal. I'll think about these things tomorrow at 10:00 A.M. at the office when I can do something about them.' "

"If these thoughts return, I will resume the strategy of being a detached listener to my thinking."

"When I awaken in the middle of the night, look at the clock, and begin to calculate how many hours of sleep I'll get if I can just get back to sleep now, I will do the following:"

"I'll get out of bed, turn the clock around so I can't see it, and begin to follow the same procedures I used to fall asleep."

Note: One of the primary sleep disturbers for people is worrying about how much sleep they need when trying to go to sleep. Mental calculation of time is part of this process. If this pattern fits you, it's a good idea to set your alarm, and turn your clock around before you go to sleep. If you are worried that your alarm won't work, set two alarms and place both clocks out of your sight.

"I set my watch ahead: I have a sense of urgency in most things I do; I worry about being late; my thoughts tend to be on things in the future; I always seem to be rushing."

"To Do" List and Relaxation

"Upon awakening, I begin breathing deeply. Before I get out of bed, I make a list of all the things I need to accomplish or pending problems. I prioritize my list and decide what can be accomplished for the day. I schedule a time to think about things that don't require my immediate attention."

Focused Concentration, Movement, Relaxation and Stretching

"I feel the sensation of first the bed, and then the floor as I quietly get out of bed. My breathing is deep and my focus is on every step I take. I move to a comfortable area and begin a gentle stretching program. I feel every muscle stretch as I continue breathing deeply."

Focused Concentration, Movement and Breathing

"I am completely aware of every sensation of each movement I make. I feel the water of the shower, the sensation of the shampoo, and the soap lather. I continue to breathe deeply as I go about my morning routine, experiencing the present. I experience the present in everything I do, from putting my arm through my shirt sleeve to feeling the sensation of the steering wheel of my car as I drive. I focus on colors and sounds that I have not noticed in the past."

Rational Dialogue and Relaxation

"When I find myself rushing, I take a deep breath and begin an internal dialogue that is calming. I remind myself that hurrying will only increase muscular tension and create an internal irritability which interferes with my mood and performance. As I quiet my movement, I return my focus to every move I make. If I have intrusive thoughts about things to be done, I write down those things I need to do and schedule a time to do each one; then I return my focus to the present."

DEVELOP A PLAN

European and PGA Tour player David Feherty made an interesting observation about the importance of how you handle adversity. He said: "...It's not what happens to you that matters in the long run. It's your attitude. That's what determines how you cope with the next experience that comes along...Quite often it's how you deal with failure that determines how you achieve success...The mental process is like building a muscle. It's not letting your whole framework of thinking fall down around you. It's having the resolve and mental toughness to take it on the chin, keep your head up, and feel good about yourself for having done that. You can either feel bad because you failed or good because of your positive reactions to it. That will give you the armor to cope with it the next time."[35]

Our behavior off the course dictates the way we will behave on the course. Therefore, if you're going to change the way you mentally approach golf, you will need to change the way you mentally approach your day to day life. Practicing the mental strategies presented in this book both on and off the course will provide you with well-rehearsed skills for play. Keeping a daily diary of your goals and successful completion of these goals will help you stay on track.

As noted in an earlier chapter, a common denominator to successful behavior change programs is a daily journal or diary. This diary should include specific monthly, weekly and daily goals. Your daily entries should be in reference to your success in accomplishing your daily goals. Keep the process positive. Remember, what you feed attention grows.

I'm sure you have found examples both on and off the golf course that apply to you. If you want to change your mental behavior in these situations, you must develop a plan of action. Make a copy of the situations and the recommended change strategies from this chapter. Review each of these at least daily and preferably multiple times a day as part of your morning routine and prior to and following each round of golf.

Make an audio tape recording of your planned change and listen to it on the way to work, driving to the golf course and at as many other times during your day as possible. Every player I work with has an audio tape of changes they are working on. This tape is updated as necessary.

Change will occur most rapidly through repetition and "overlearning." This is most easily accomplished by reading your plans for change and listening to your "new ideal behavior" on audio tape upon awakening and as frequently as possible throughout the day. Put your audio tape in your car and listen to it as often as possible.

You have an opportunity to experience changes both on and off the course. It's going to require setting goals, structuring change, and following the plan daily over several straight weeks. You will find that change will follow and, as you experience success, your tendency will be to think "I am fixed." Subsequently, you will notice regression. All you need to do is get back on the program and success will follow again.

The change you will experience will be like climbing a ladder. When you discontinue setting goals and practicing the change strategies, you will plateau at times and regress at others. Once you get back on the program, setting goals and following a daily plan, you will find yourself doing well again. Remember, an important part of this process is a daily recording of your goals and successes in a diary.

The key to changing your "mental mechanics", as in your swing mechanics, is repetition. The more you saturate yourself visually, auditorily and through practice with your planned mental mechanics change, the more automatic these new behaviors will become.

When our military has a mission, they rehearse their actions in writing, in classroom discussions, by teaching each other, and by practicing mock exercises of their drills. When it is time to execute these behaviors in the real situation, they are automatic. In fact, soldiers who are interviewed after a military action describe their behavior as "automatic" and "without having to think."

Improvement on and off the course is a lifetime pursuit. Set goals, establish a structured plan, follow your plan, and your changes will soon become automatic. Then, set new goals and new structure. You can take these changes as far as you choose.

I'm sure you have realized that this book was not written just to impart information. It was written as a manual offered for continued reference, review, study, and planning of further personal changes both on and off the golf course.

May your drives be long and your putts be short.

ENDNOTES

1. Harvey Penick and Bud Shrake, *And If You Play Golf, You're My Friend* (New York: Simon and Schuster, 1993), p. 144.

2. Jack Nicklaus and Ken Bowden, "My Lessons of a Lifetime," *Golf Magazine* (March, 1993): pp. 58-59.

3. Mark Wiebe, "When Want Gets in the Way," *Golf World* (August 20, 1993): p. 30.

4. Gary Player, *Positive Golf* (New York: McGraw Hill, 1967), p. 17.

5. Gary Player, Personal Correspondence (February 9, 1995).

6. Player, *Positive Golf*, p. 21.

7. Jack Nicklaus and Ken Bowden, "How to Beat Tension," *Golf Magazine* (July, 1993): p. 90.

8. Peter McCleery, "How Nelson Helped Watson Become a Champion," *Golf Digest* (January, 1991): pp. 66-67.

9. Geoff Russell, "The Dominator," *Golf World* (July 9, 1993): p. 43 and p. 46.

10. Andy Brumer, "Be A Thinking Golfer," *Golf Tips* (May, 1994): p. 38.

11. Jack Nicklaus and Ken Bowden, "My Strongest Weapon," *Golf Magazine* (December, 1993): p.45.

12. Charles Price, "Bobby Jones Reveals His Inner Psychology," *Golf Digest* (August, 1989): p. 40.

13. Player, *Positive Golf*, pp. 16-17.

14. Golf Digest Staff. "Greg Norman," *Golf Digest* (December, 1992): p. 164.

15. Greg Norman and George Peper, "Greg Norman's Instant Lessons," *Golf Magazine* (April, 1993): p. 52.

16. Golf Digest Staff, "Fred Couples," *Golf Digest* (July, 1992): p. 114.

17. David Barrett, "Major Accomplishment," *Golf Magazine* (August, 1992): p. 92.

18. Harvey Penick and Bud Shrake, *And If You Play Golf, You're My Friend* (New York: Simon and Schuster, 1993), p. 107.

19. Jack Nicklaus and Ken Bowden, *Golf My Way* (New York:Simon and Schuster, 1974), pp. 98-99.

20. Norman and Peper, "Greg Norman's Instant Lessons," p. 52.

21. Brumer, "Be A Thinking Golfer," p. 38.

22. Golf Digest Staff, "Fred Couples," *Golf Digest* (July, 1992): p. 114.

23. Jack Nicklaus and Ken Bowden, "How to Beat Tension," *Golf Magazine* (July, 1993): p. 90.

24. Sam Snead and Al Stump, *The Education of a Golfer* (New York: Simon and Schuster, 1961), p. 84.

25. Snead and Stump, *The Education of a Golfer*, pp. 82-83.

26. Nicklaus and Bowden, *Golf My Way*, p. 22.

27. Snead and Stump, *The Education of a Golfer*, p. 34.

28. Michael McDonnell, Golf: The Great Ones (New York: Drake Publishers, 1971), p. 69

29. Player, *Positive Golf*, pp. 16-17.

30. Penick and Shrake, *And If You Play Golf, You're My Friend,* p. 107.

31. Mark Wiebe, "When Want Gets in the Way," *Golf World* (August 20, 1993): p. 30.

32. McDonnell, Golf: The Great Ones, p. 69.

33. Snead and Stump, *The Education of a Golfer*, pp. 243-244.

34. Norman and George, "Greg Norman's Instant Lessons," p. 52.

35. Golf Digest Staff, "David Feherty," *Golf Digest* (November, 1992): p. 111.

Week of ___/___/___ ON / OFF COURSE PROCESS DIARY

BEHAVIORS ON COURSE	goal	Sun	Mon	Tues	Wed	Thur	Fri	Sat
Broad to narrow focus								
Repeating positive routine								
Positive images of ball flight behind ball								
Image of target/flight thru swing								
Feeling of swing								
Movement and posture relaxed								
Diaphragmatic breathing								
100% one shot at a time								
100% present focus								
"Call up" past success in similar shots								
Hit high probability low risks shots								
Self supporting internal dialogue								
Relaxed effortless swings								
What was right with the shot								
Strong resistance to decay -- Patient								
Determined -- stay in the process								
Positive course management								
Reinforce self for staying in the process-on and off the course. What's going right?: Patience, focused, breathing, good internal caddie, staying calm, positive response to bad breaks and bad shots-- see them as a challenge-- No matter what: one shot at a time, Hit a 10 on every shot, "As if" posture and internal dialogue.								
BEHAVIORS OFF COURSE								
Broad to narrow focus in daily activities								
Stay positive and redirect negativity								
Relaxed posture and movement								
Diaphragmatic Breathing								
Focus on and "call up" past success Self supporting/encouraging internal dialogue Strong resistance to decay--Be patient--Be mentally tough--See problems as a challenge--Stay determined to be successful in everything I do								
100% present focus in all activities								
Predict and expect success, even in the face of difficulty--stay positive								
Nonjudgemental of self and others								
Be passionate and compassionate								

Epilogue

Jennifer Wyatt, LPGA TOUR February, 1996

MIND UNDER PAR is an eye-opener. So many of us waste precious time being scattered in our thinking and unorganized in our planning. David does all the planning and thinking for us in his brilliantly packaged *MIND UNDER PAR series™*. This ingenious compilation applies to everybody, not just golfers.

When I first began reading *MIND UNDER PAR* I said, "This book was written for me!" Actually it is a book for anyone who wants to enhance and improve his or her performance, concentration, focus, awareness and enjoyment in life. It is an "everyday" book, a reference book. I take it everywhere with me.

I have learned that it is my responsibility to use the information. It takes effort and willingness to change. I have learned that negativity is both an emotional and physical feeling and I have learned how to stop the downward spiral. I have also learned how to re-phrase those self-defeating thoughts into useful, advantageous positive ones.

I have experienced success using the methods of the *MIND UNDER PAR* series™. Some significant elements have been present tense focus, deep breathing and realistic goal-setting. Even something as seemingly unimportant as good posture has had a strong impact on me. I made audio tapes of influential content. When I listen to the tapes regularly, I get positive results.

It is difficult to condense what I have learned because I have learned so much. The *MIND UNDER PAR* series™ is definitely a package deal. It is part of my daily regime because it works!

Laurie Rinker-Graham, LPGA TOUR February, 1996

I had the opportunity to read each draft of *MIND UNDER PAR* and to personally work with David on many occasions over the last two years. I am very excited with the results I have experienced.

The most important thing I can tell you is you must do more than read *MIND UNDER PAR*. You need to apply the content from this book to both your golf game and your everyday life. Without some hard work, patience and practice, it is difficult to change old ways.

I would like to share a few of the many things *MIND UNDER PAR* and David have helped me with. I have learned how important my routine is. When I am playing in tournaments, I have much more confidence because I have practiced my routine. I plan my shot; I take a deep breath and relax my body and I execute my shot. Repeating my same routine gives me the best chance of playing well.

I am in control of my thoughts and how I react to situations. I have realized I can calm myself when I am anxious, mad or frustrated. This helps me save many shots. I slow my movement, take some deep breaths, and bring my focus back to the moment. What I tell myself results directly in how I feel. One of David's best lines is "What you feed attention grows." So, if you want to be confident , you must continuously tell yourself you can do it. Thoughts like,

"I can hit this shot" and "I am a great player" are part of this process. Then, at the end of each round, I focus only on the good shots I have hit.

I would encourage you to read *MIND UNDER PAR* and apply it to your life and your golf game. Remember, what you feed attention grows! My goal is to continue to focus on the positive aspects of my life and my golf game. As a result, I am a better player and a happier person.

About the Author

David F. Wright, Ph.D. is a PGA Tour Instructor, a Class "A" PGA Member teaching professional and a clinical and Sport Psychologist. He holds two doctorates, both in psychology. His specialties are psychophysiology, learning and performance enhancement. Dr. Wright has been a member of the clinical faculty of the University of Southern California School of Medicine since 1974 and he is a licensed Clinical Psychologist..

Dr. Wright has written many publications on the integration of the mental and mechanical sides of golf. Additionally he has worked with numerous PGA, Nike and LPGA tour players. He has participated in hundreds of golf schools in the United States and Japan and playing and teaching workshops for the PGA of America.

Dr Wright is also a research and development consultant to Callaway Golf, Carlsbad, CA. He was elected by his peers as 1996 Teacher of the Year in the Southern Californa PGA Metro Chapter. Currently, he resides in Coto de Caza, California with his family. He is a full time teaching professional at Pelican Hill Golf Club and Resort in Newport Coast, California.